D1596185

THE WATER'S EDGE AND BEYOND

THE WATER'S EDGE AND BEYOND

Defining the Limits to Domestic Influence on United States Middle East Policy

Mitchell Geoffrey Bard

Transaction Publishers
New Brunswick (U.S.A.) and London (U.K.)

Copyright © 1991 by Transaction Publishers.
New Brunswick, New Jersey 08903

Library of Congress Catalog Number: 90-42375
ISBN: 0-88738-346-7
Printed in the United States of America

Library of Congress Cataloging-in-Publication Data
Bard, Mitchell Geoffrey, 1959–
    The water's edge and beyond: defining the limits to domestic
influence on United States Middle East policy/Mitchell Geoffrey
        Bard. p. cm.
    Includes bibliographical references and index.
    ISBN 0-88738-346-7
    1. United States—Foreign relations—Israel. 2. Israel—
Foreign relations—United States. 3. Jews—United States—
Politics and government. 4. United States—Foreign relations—
Middle East. 5. Middle East—Foreign relations—
United States. 6. Israel-Arab conflicts. I. Title.
E183.8.I7B37   1990
327.7305694—dc20   90-42375
                                                              CIP

This book is dedicated
to my mother and father
who continue to have faith
when all others doubt

Contents

List of Tables

Table

Acknowledgments

I would like to thank the Lyndon Baines Johnson Foundation for providing me with a Moody Grant to conduct research at the LBJ Library. This grant allowed me to use primary source material for the case study on President Johnson's decision to sell Phantom jets to Israel. I would also like to thank Nancy Green, Linda Hanson, and all the other archivists at the LBJ Library for their assistance.

I would also like to thank the Anti-Defamation League (ADL), the YIVO Institute for Jewish Research, and the American Jewish Committee for allowing me access to their records.

This book could not have been done without the guidance of Professors Steven Spiegel and John Petrocik at UCLA, whose contrasting styles and areas of expertise are reflected in the qualitative and quantitative parts of the analysis. To the extent that this project has any academic merit, it is because of their high standards.

This study covers the period from 1945 to 1984. The research and writing was done at UCLA without any inside information or assistance from the American Israel Public Affairs Committee.

1

Introduction

One of the most commonly held notions in American politics is that American Jews have a great deal of influence on U.S. foreign policy. In the view of some people, Jewish-Americans control American policy in the Middle East to the detriment of the national interest. General George Brown, former chairman of the Joint Chiefs of Staff, asserted during his tenure that Israel had too much influence in the United States and that Jews owned the banks and newspapers here.[1] The day after the October 1973 War began, Senator J. William Fulbright, chairman of the Senate Foreign Relations Committee, told a national television audience: "Israelis control the policy in the Congress. The emotional and political ties are too strong. On every test, on everything the Israelis are interested in, in the Senate the Israelis have 75 to 80 votes."[2] Another Senator, James Abourezk, told a Democratic audience in 1977:

> The Israeli lobby is the most powerful and pervasive foreign influence in American politics today . . . its enormous influence in the U.S. Congress is dangerous.

> It is dangerous because the U.S. and its Mideast foreign policy is likely to become, if it has not already, a captive of its client state. This happened to a lesser extent in Vietnam, and we must surely be aware that it can happen to us in the Middle East.[3]

More recently, former Congressman Pete McCloskey told *Time* magazine: "We've got to overcome the tendency of the Jewish community in America to control the actions of Congress and for them to force the President and Congress not to be evenhanded.

. . . We have to respect the views of our Jewish citizens, but not be controlled by them."[4] A year later, McCloskey told the *San Francisco Examiner* that "the Jewish community in America is so powerful that it distorts American foreign policy."[5]

These views are readily accepted by the leaders of the Arab world, who are anxious to find a scapegoat for their own failure to persuade American officials that U.S. and Israeli interests are inconsistent. At the same time, the belief that the Israeli lobby is omnipotent has led Arab officials to sometimes cultivate the support of American Jewish leaders. For example, Egyptian diplomats in the United States engaged in discussions for two years prior to Anwar Sadat's dramatic trip to Jerusalem to help build the foundation for the support he would need to bring America into the peace process.[6]

All of the critics cited above were ardent supporters of the Arab cause; nevertheless, their bias neither explains nor refutes their claims. The purpose of this study, then, is to determine the forces that affect whether the Israeli lobby is in fact able to exert influence over American Middle East policy and the conditions under which they operate.

Competing Models

The United States Constitution leaves the authority for the making of foreign policy ambiguous, creating "an invitation to struggle."[7] Nevertheless, the Supreme Court has interpreted the Constitution to mean that "the President alone has the power to speak or listen as a representative of the nation" (*Curtiss Wright* 299 U.S. 304, 1936); consequently, foreign policy in the United States has come to be seen as whatever the president says it is.

This legal interpretation, combined with the conviction that governmental unity strengthens U.S. credibility abroad, has led the legislative branch to accept the notion that "politics stops at the water's edge." Empirical evidence for this distinction between domestic and foreign policy was first presented by Wildavsky and led him to postulate the "two presidencies thesis."[8] The study of foreign policy decision-making has, for the most part, acquiesced in this belief and offered models that minimize the role of domestic politics in policy outcomes. The predominant pe₁ₒᵣ is probably that of the realists.

According to the realists, the policy-making process consists of a rational, unitary decision-maker. The decision-maker has a single goal, the pursuit of the national interest, and calculates the most efficient way to reach the goal. The calculation requires a consideration of alternative courses of action available to attain the goal, and the consequences of each of those alternatives. The rational actor will choose the alternative that offers the greatest benefits; that is, the fulfillment of the objective, at the lowest cost. According to Morgenthau, the national interest is "to keep power, increase power, or to demonstrate power."[9]

There may be an irreducible interest in survival, but beyond that there is no consensus on *a* national interest. In the case of the Middle East, the United States has pursued at least five interests: (1) protection of oil supplies, (2) containment of the Soviet Union, (3) maintenance of regional stability (for the purpose of 1 and 2), (4) expansion of economic and diplomatic relations with the Arab world, and (5) assurance of Israel's security. These interests often conflict (or are at least thought to), but the realist perspective provides no clue as to the resolution. In addition, contrary to the realist belief that foreign policy may be conducted unencumbered by domestic or partisan political influence, every president has included domestic political aides in national security policy debates.[10]

A second model of foreign policy decision-making is the bureaucratic politics model which is frequently summarized by the statement: "Where you stand depends on where you sit."[11] According to this model, the natural concern civil servants have with the enhancement of their own prestige and power colors their images of the national interest. Since these officials believe that they are in a superior position to objectively determine that interest, they tend to eschew outside influence. These officials place a high priority on controlling their own resources to insure their independence. Although the bureaucracy may not always be able to make the final decision, it often is able to sabotage or affect the implementation of decisions made elsewhere. The bureaucratic politics model ignores the role and power of the president, however, and, as we will see, it is the president, and not the bureaucracy, who plays the major role in the outcomes of Middle East policy decisions. This model most accurately describes policy implementation, rather than formulation, and it is the latter that is of interest here.

A third model of decision-making emphasizes the role of the president and his closest advisers. According to the variants of this model, the personality, ideology, experience, and perceptions of leaders determine U.S. foreign policy. In other words, "the more the players change the more policies change."[12]

There are also difficulties with this model because typologies that attempt to categorize individuals' personalities, beliefs, and ideologies are inevitably controversial. Moreover, there is a tendency to make ex post facto estimations of individual perceptions. In addition, it may be possible to attribute policy changes to differences among leaders, but how then can policy consistency be explained? In the case of Middle East policy, for example, how can this model explain the fact that U.S. policy has generally been pro-Israel and solicitous of the Arabs? Or to give a more specific example, why did Presidents Ford, Carter, and Reagan sell sophisticated weapons to Saudi Arabia, despite having very different ideologies, personalities, and advisers?

This model also fails to provide any guidance as to how a decision is reached when there is no consensus among advisers. For example, in chapters 5 and 6 we will see that Harry Truman's key foreign policy advisers were George Marshall and James Forrestal, and yet he sided with two aides, David Niles and Clark Clifford, on several key issues relating to Palestine. This model cannot explain these outcomes, nor those where the views of Marshall and Forrestal were accepted (trusteeship and the arms embargo) over the opposition of the two aides. Finally, this model does not take into account decisions that require congressional approval; that is, leaders can indeed determine outcomes when the president has the authority to make the final decision, but there are also decisions made or ratified by Congress that are beyond the leader's direct and exclusive control.

The pluralist model might be summarized as: "which way you lean depends on who's pushing you."[13] Pluralism, as defined by its leading exponent, Robert Dahl, refers "to the existence of a plurality of relatively autonomous (independent) organizations (subsystems) within the domain of the state." By "relatively autonomous," Dahl means that an organization engages in actions that "(a) are considered harmful by another organization and that (b) no other organization, including the government of the state, can prevent, or could prevent except by incurring costs so high as to exceed the gains to the other actor from doing so."[14] Although many people have misinterpreted pluralism to mean that public policy can best be understood as the product of the free play of group pressures, and that an "invisible hand" working through competing interests yields an outcome that is beneficial to society,[15] pluralism does not assume that all interests are equal. In fact, most interests are unequal and it is the most powerful, that is, the one that enjoys the balance of lobbying power, which should dominate the market of political ideas.

Each of the models provide valuable insight into the decision-making process, and help the analyst understand how the alternatives were formulated and presented, which actors played a role, and some of the factors that influenced the decision. The most glaring deficiency is that each model does little more than provide us with *descriptions* of the process, but none of them offer any guidance for *predicting* outcomes. In other words, each model would allow us to say, for example, that the decision to sell Airborne Warning and Control Systems (AWACS) to Saudi Arabia would entail a particular decision-making process, but none of them can tell us whether or not the sale would be expected to be approved by the Congress. Moreover, none of the models give any indication of the relative weights of the different variables they examine. They fail to explain for what issues and under what conditions they apply.[16]

Foreign policy-making is actually a far more complex process than the models imply. Geostrategic factors do come into play, but so do domestic political ones. In the end, it is usually the president who must make the final decision. The individual models each describe important components of the decision-making process, but need to be integrated to provide an accurate picture of how U.S. Middle East policy is made.

The remainder of this book will demonstrate that pluralist forces, specifically, the Israeli lobby, shape U.S. Middle East policy. The lobby's influence is not unlimited as its critics suggest; however, it is constrained by the power of the president and the extent to which he can frame issues in terms of the security interests of the United States. The realist and leadership models provide the means to understand those cases where the pluralist model seems to break down. By examining a series of case studies, it is possible to see, in historical context, how these models interact and then, by using aggregate data collected on U.S. Middle East policy decisions for the 1945–1984 period, it will be possible to define the limits of Israeli lobby influence. First, it is necessary to examine the Israeli lobby to see what it is and why it would be expected to have any influence on U.S. policy.

Middle East Policy-Making

One of the reasons there has been so much confusion about the role of interest groups is that they have been imprecisely defined. For example, reference is often made to the "Jewish lobby" in an effort to describe Jewish influence, but the term is both vague and inadequate. American Jews are sometimes represented by lobbyists, but such direct efforts to influence policymakers are but a small part of the lobby's ability to influence policy. There are also organized groups that attempt to directly influence legislation. One of these, the American Israel Public Affairs Committee (AIPAC), is a registered domestic lobby. These groups comprise the *formal lobby*. There are also organizations that do not engage in direct lobbying (e.g., B'nai B'rith and Hadassah), but do disseminate information and encourage their members to become involved in the political process. There is also a large component of political influence that is unorganized—Jewish voting behavior and American public opinion. These indirect means of influence may be designated as the *informal lobby*.

The formal and informal components tend to intersect at several points so the distinction is not always clear-cut. Together, however, they form the Israeli lobby. This is a more accurate label than Jewish lobby, because a large proportion of the lobby is made up of non-Jews. This term also reflects the lobby's objective. The Israeli lobby can then be defined as *those formal and informal actors that directly and indirectly influence American policy to support Israel.*

The Israeli lobby does not have the field to itself; there is a competing interest group—the Arab lobby. The National Association of Arab-Americans (NAAA), like AIPAC, is a registered domestic lobby that forms the core of the formal lobby. There is also an informal lobby that exerts indirect influence. Just as the Israeli lobby is not exclusively comprised of Jews, the Arab lobby is not composed entirely of Arabs; nevertheless, the label is appropriate in this case because it, like Israeli lobby, reflects the lobby's objective. Specifically, the Arab lobby refers to *those formal and informal actors that attempt to influence U.S. foreign policy to support the interests of the Arab states in the Middle East.*

Given these competing lobbies, there appears to be fertile ground for competition in the pluralistic tradition where "the legislature referees the group struggle" and the legislative vote tends to reflect the balance of lobbying power among contending groups.[17] To see why we would expect the Israeli lobby to have influence, an examination of the balance of lobbying power is required to round out the analysis. It will then be necessary to consider the role played by the president in the legislative struggle, as well as in those cases unaccounted for by Latham; that is, cases where decisions are made in the executive branch independent of congressional input.

The Informal Lobby

American Jews recognize the importance of support for Israel because of the dire consequences that could follow from the alternative. The perceived threat to Israel is not military defeat, it is annihilation. At the same time, American Jews are frightened of what might happen in this country if they do not have political power. As a result, Jews have devoted themselves to politics with almost religious fervor. This is reflected by the fact that Jews have the highest percentage voter turnout of any ethnic group. The Jewish population in the United States is under six million, roughly three percent of the total population, but 89 percent live in twelve key electoral college states. These states alone are worth enough electoral votes to elect the president. If you add the *non-Jews* shown by opinion polls to be as pro-Israel as Jews, it is clear Israel has the support of one of the largest veto groups in the country.[18]

The disproportionate influence of the American Jewish population is in direct contrast with the electoral involvement of Arab-Americans. There are approximately three million Arabs in the United States, and roughly 80 percent of them are Lebanese Christians who tend to be unsympathetic to the Arab lobby's goals. This reflects another major problem for the Arab lobby—inter-Arab disunity. This disunity is reinforced by the general discord of the Arab world, which has twenty-one states with competing interests. The Arab lobby is thus precluded from representing "the Arabs."

The political activism of Jews forces congressmen with presidential ambitions to consider what a mixed voting record on Israel-related issues may mean in the political future. There are no benefits to candidates taking an openly anti-Israel stance and considerable costs in both loss of campaign contributions and votes from Jews and non-Jews alike. Potential candidates therefore have an incentive to be pro-Israel; this reinforces support for Israel in Congress. Actual candidates must be particularly sensitive to the concerns of Jewish voters; it follows that the successful candidate's foreign policy will be influenced, although not bound, by the promises that had to be made during the campaign.

There is a natural assumption that Jewish congressmen will be supportive of Israel and, with the exception of occasional odd votes, this is true. Historically, however, few Jews have held elective office or primary positions of power, even though they have always been politically active. In the past decade, this has gradually begun to change however, and there were more Jewish members of the Ninety-eighth Congress than any previous Congress; coincidentally, that Congress was called the most pro-Israel ever.[19]

Political campaign contributions are also considered an important means of influence; typically, Jews have been major benefactors. It is difficult to assess the influence of campaign contributions on legislative outcomes, particularly with regard to Israel-related issues, where support or opposition may be a consequence of non-monetary factors. In addition, one does not know if a candidate is pro-Israel because of receiving a contribution, or receives a donation as a result of taking a position in support of

Israel. In the past, Jewish contributions were less structured and targeted than other interest groups,[20] but this has changed dramatically as Israel-related political action committees (PACs) have proliferated.

Initially, the Jewish community feared that post-Watergate election campaign financing reforms would reduce their influence, but the evidence so far suggests the opposite. According to the American Jewish Committee's Milton Himmelfarb: "Financial participation in campaigns has declined but the anticipated decrease in Jewish influence has not come about."[21] This view was seconded by Morris Amitay, a former AIPAC executive director: "The reforms have helped primarily by stimulating more political activism in the Jewish community."[22]

The first pro-Israel PAC was formed in 1978, but there was little activity until 1982 when thirty-three pro-Israel PACs contributed $1.87 million to congressional candidates.[23] Like other PACs, most of this money was given to incumbents and, because of the long association of Jews with the Democratic party, nearly 80 percent went to Democrats. The number of PACs more than doubled in 1984 as did their contributions. It was estimated that over seventy pro-Israel PACs spent a little over $4 million in 1984. By 1988, the figure was nearly $5 million.[24]

The PACs' contributions became increasingly focused in 1984 and, apparently, they had a high degree of success in choosing winning candidates. In the two most expensive and publicized Senate campaigns, Percy-Simon in Illinois and Helms-Hunt in North Carolina, however, the Israeli lobby had to settle for a split decision with its preferred candidate winning only in Illinois.[25]

On the Arab lobby side, only three PACs spent a trivial sum through 1988. The lobby did take a more active and visible role than ever before, however, in the 1984 election. The most obvious manifestation of this came in the congressional race involving seventy-six-year-old Maryland Democrat Clarence Long. Long, chairman of the House Appropriations subcommittee on Foreign Operations and a driving force behind increasing aid to Israel, was targeted by the Arab lobby: "to serve notice to members of Congress that the Arab lobby is ready and able to make life uncomfortable for Israel's friends on Capitol Hill."[26]

Like the visible campaign undertaken in 1982 by the Israeli

lobby to defeat pro-Arab Congressman Paul Findley of Illinois, the Arab lobby claimed victory when Long was defeated. As was the case in the Findley campaign, where the Congressman's district suffered from a high unemployment rate, and had been gerrymandered to his disadvantage, the reasons for Long's defeat were rooted in politics unrelated to the Middle East. In Long's case, redistricting took away a large percentage of his constituency and, after a narrow victory in 1982, he became a high priority target of the Republican National Committee.[27]

In Jesse Jackson the Arab lobby found, for the first time, a presidential candidate receptive to their interests. Jackson had a long record of support for the Arab cause and was particularly outspoken in support of Palestinian rights, having met with Palestine Liberation Organization (PLO) chairman Yasir Arafat. As a result of his stands, Jackson received substantial financial support from members of the Arab lobby.[28] The divisions of the lobby were again apparent, however, when the president of the American Lebanese League said Jackson turns his constituents off: "He seems interested in the welfare of Arab countries but not Lebanon or the United States."[29]

Overall, the comparative impact of the two lobbies on elections was probably best summed up by Harry Truman in his frequently repeated statement to Paul Porter, a Washington attorney appointed as the ambassador to the Arab-Israeli peace talks in Geneva in 1948: "I won't tell you what to do or how to vote, but I will only say this. In all of my political experience I don't ever recall the Arab vote swinging a close election."[30]

Public Opinion

The absence of a large voting bloc requires the Arab lobby to develop sympathies among the general public if it is to use public opinion or the electoral process as a means of influencing U.S. policy. The lobby has tried to support sympathetic American groups, such as Third World organizations, and cultivate friendships in the academic and business realms, but, as opinion polls have consistently shown, there is relatively little popular support for the Arab cause. Since 1967, polls have found that sympathy for Israel varied between 35 and 56 percent, while sympathy for the Arabs has oscillated between 1 and 14 percent. On average, support for Israel has exceeded that of the Arab nations by about four to one.[31] In the last five years there has been a slight increase in support for the Arabs, but this has not affected sympathies toward Israel.

Not only has the Arab lobby been unable to increase its standing significantly with the public, it has also failed to convince the American people that the Israeli lobby controls U.S. Middle East policy. In fact, polls indicate the public sees the Arab lobby as more of a threat than the Israeli lobby. For example, in a poll conducted several weeks after the Senate vote on the sale of AWACS to Saudi Arabia, 53 percent of the public agreed Israel has "too much influence" on American foreign policy, but only 11 percent felt the same way about American Jews. By contrast, 64 percent said Saudi Arabia had too much influence, and 70 percent believed oil companies were too influential. A March 1983 poll asking which groups have "too much" political influence found that only 10 percent of those asked said "Jews." Business corporations and unions were considered too powerful by over 40 percent of the respondents, with Arab interests next at 24 percent.[32]

Thus, the Arab lobby's problem is two-fold; it suffers from a very negative image and Israel enjoys a very positive image. This has gradually begun to change. To combat negative Arab stereotypes, former Senator James Abourezk founded the American Arab Anti-Discrimination Committee (ADC) in 1980. The ADC is modelled after the Anti-Defamation League, but is considerably smaller and weaker.

The Arab lobby is also working to undermine Israel's image. Fredelle Spiegel has illustrated how the Arab lobby uses classic propaganda techniques for this purpose:

> Historically, it was the Jews of Palestine who were ready to accept less than "half the loaf" for their homeland and the Arabs who rejected the notion of compromise. The necessity of changing this historical fact is obvious. This has been done in several ways—both by attempting to rewrite history and also by trying to recreate it.[33]

As an example, she cites an American Educational Trust (AET) editorial which condemned Israel's "predatory behavior" in southern Lebanon. "The record would suggest," according to the AET, "that Israel is still secretly scheming for more, even though it already has the whole loaf that was being argued over in 1947. . . . To the Israelis, one-and-a-half loaves look a lot better than one." It may be too early to tell how effective the Arab lobby's efforts have been, but they seem to have had little impact on public opinion so far.

The Formal Israeli Lobby

The organization which directly lobbies Congress on behalf of the "Israeli lobby" is AIPAC. The lobby was founded in 1951 by I.L. (Sy) Kenen, when Israel's supporters decided to appeal directly to Congress for legislation to provide aid to Israel, in order to circumvent State Department opposition. Up until 1973, Kenen was AIPAC's only lobbyist. In 1989, there were six lobbyists, a staff of more than 100, and a budget of nearly $11 million. The current executive director is Thomas A. Dine, a former legislative aide to Senators Church and Muskie. The executive director of AIPAC is generally considered one of the most influential men in Washington, and Dine is no exception.

AIPAC was not the first domestic lobby to concern itself with foreign affairs, but it is regarded as the most powerful. The lobby strives to remain non-partisan and thereby keeps friends in both parties. By framing the issues in terms of the national interest, AIPAC is able to attract broader support than could ever be possible if it was perceived to represent only the interests of Israel. This does not mean AIPAC does not have a close relationship with Israeli officials, it does, albeit unofficially. Even so, there are times when the lobby comes into conflict with the Israeli government. One of the most blatant examples occurred when Thomas Dine was quoted on the front page of the *New York Times* as saying the 1982 Reagan peace plan had some good points (and many bad ones) after the Israeli government had rejected the plan in toto. Despite such disagreements, the Israeli lobby tends to reflect Israeli government policy fairly closely.

Lobbyists usually roam the halls of Congress trying to get the attention of legislators so they can explain their positions. AIPAC has the luxury of being able to call its allies in Congress to pass along information, and then leaves much of the work of writing bills and gathering co-sponsors to the legislative staffs. The lobbyists themselves are mostly Capitol Hill veterans who know how to operate the levers of power.

Since it does not use stereotypical lobbying tactics, the Israeli lobby depends on the network it has developed to galvanize the Jewish community to take some form of political action. The network is comprised of at least seventy-five different organizations, which in one way or another support Israel. Most cannot legally engage in lobbing, but are represented on the Board of Directors of AIPAC, so they are able to provide input into the lobby's decision-making process. Equally important is the bureaucratic machinery of these organizations, which enables them to disseminate information to their members and facilitate a rapid response to legislative activity.

A second coordinating body is the Conference of Presidents of Major American Jewish Organizations. It is composed of leaders of thirty-eight different organizations and is responsible for formulating and articulating the "Jewish position" on most foreign policy matters. The conference allows the lobby to speak with one voice in a way its opponents cannot. The conference is the main contact between the Jewish community and the executive branch, while AIPAC tends to be the conduit with the legislative branch.

Even with the Jewish population concentrated in key states, there are still only a total of about six million Jews; therefore, the Israeli lobby is dependent on the support of non-Jewish groups and actively works to form coalitions with broad segments of American society. The lobby has successfully built coalitions comprised of unions, entertainers, clergymen, scholars, and black leaders. The coalitions allow the lobby to demonstrate a broad public consensus for a pro-Israel policy.

The Formal Arab Lobby

There has always been an Arab lobby in the United States composed of what I.L. Kenen has called the petro-diplomatic complex consisting of the oil industry, missionaries, and diplomats. According to Kenen, there was no need for an Arab lobby because the petro-diplomatic complex did the Arabs' work for them.[34]

One of the earliest activities of the petro-diplomatic complex began in 1951 when King Saud of Saudi Arabia asked U.S. diplomats to finance a pro-Arab lobby to counter the American Zionist Committee for Public Affairs (later the American *Israel* Public Affairs Committee—AIPAC).[35] The Arab lobby became an official, active, and visible spokesman for the Arab cause in the wake of the oil embargo. "The day of the Arab-American is here," boasted Richard Shadyac, "the reason is oil."[36]

From the beginning, the Arab lobby has faced not only a disadvantage in electoral politics but also in organization. There are several politically oriented groups, but many of these are one man operations with little financial or popular support. Dr. M.T. Mehdi's Action Committee on American Arab Relations is one such organization. Mehdi is an ardent PLO supporter who has said Robert Kennedy's support for the sale of Phantom jets to Israel justified his murder by Sirhan Sirhan. Americans for Justice in the Middle East was formed by a group of Americans at the American University in Beirut after the 1967 war to combat "Zionism's virulent thirty-year campaign of hate and vindictiveness." Two anti-Zionist Jews are also active supporters of the Arab lobby. Elmer Berger runs American Jewish Alternatives to Zionism and Alfred Lilienthal publishes his own newsletter— *Middle East Perspectives*.

There are a number of larger and more representative groups, including the aforementioned NAAA and ADC; the Middle East Research and Information Project; the Middle East Affairs Council; Americans for Near East Refugee Aid; the Arab American Institute; and the American Palestine Committee. Typically, these organizations have boards of directors composed of prominent retired state officials. For example, the executive director and president of the American Arab Affairs Council are both former State Department officials. Board members have included former Ambassador to Jordan, L. Dean Brown; Herman Eilts, former Ambassador to Syria and Egypt; Parker T. Hart, former Ambassador to Saudi Arabia, and several others.

The Arab lobby is the National Association of Arab-Americans (NAAA), a registered domestic lobby founded in 1972 by Richard

Shadyac. The NAAA was consciously patterned after its counterpart, the American Israel Public Affairs Committee (AIPAC). Shadyac believed the power and wealth of the Arab countries stemming from their oil reserves, would allow the Arab lobby to take advantage of the political process in the same way the Jews have been thought to.

The NAAA has remained relatively small and has had difficulty raising money. About 70 percent of the budget, *Congressional Quarterly* reported in 1981, came from U.S. corporations, and a high percentage indirectly from Arab governments and the PLO advertising in its *"Middle East Business Survey* (MEBUS).[37] Like AIPAC, the NAAA makes its case on the basis of U.S. national interests, arguing a pro-Israel policy harms those interests. Aid to Israel is criticized as a waste of taxpayers' money, and the potential benefits of a closer relationship with the Arab states is emphasized.

The highlight of the NAAA's early efforts was a meeting between President Ford and twelve NAAA officials in 1975. Since then, the NAAA has participated in meetings with each president and obtained access to top government officials. In 1977, for example, after Sadat's historic visit to Jerusalem, the Arab lobby made its displeasure over United States support for the initiative known to President Carter, who wrote in his diary: "They [Arab-Americans] have given all the staff, Brzezinski, Warren Christopher, and others, a hard time."[38] Although the lobby's concerns began to reach the highest levels of government, there were no perceptible changes in United States policy.

It is not only Arab-Americans who have made the lobby's case; the Arab lobby, like the Israeli lobby, has successfully built coalitions with other interest groups. As noted earlier, the petro-diplomatic complex was *the* lobby until 1972, when the NAAA was formed. Even today, arguably, it is the most influential component of the lobby. Nevertheless, most of the nation's major corporations have not supported the Arab lobby. In fact, prior to the AWACS sale, oil companies were about the only corporations willing to openly identify with Arab interests. The reason is that most corporations prefer to stay out of foreign policy debates; moreover, corporations may feel constrained by the implicit threat of some form of retaliation by the Israeli lobby.

The major oil companies feel no such constraints. According to Steven Emerson, four companies, Exxon, Standard Oil of California (SoCal), Mobil, and Texaco, have "conducted a surreptitious multimillion-dollar campaign to manipulate public opinion and foreign policy on the Middle East" for more than a decade.[39] These companies as a group comprise the Arabian American Oil Company (ARAMCO). Participation in the public relations campaign amounted to the price of doing business in the oil-producing nations.

The campaign began after the 1967 War when ARAMCO established a fund to help present the Arab side of the conflict. In May 1970, ARAMCO representatives met with Assistant Secretary of State Joseph Sisco and warned him American military sales to Israel would hurt U.S-Arab relations and jeopardize U.S. oil supplies. The former chairman of ARAMCO testified before Congress that the United States' pro-Israel policies were harming U.S. business interests. In 1972, at Kuwait's urging, Gulf Oil joined the campaign, providing $50,000 to create a public relations firm to promote the Arab side.[40]

The campaign took on greater urgency in 1973 after Frank Jungers, then Chairman of the Board of ARAMCO, met with Saudi King Faisal, and was pressured to take a more active role in creating a sympathetic attitude toward the Arab nations. In June, a month after the Jungers meeting, Mobil published its first advertisement/editorial in the *New York Times*. In July, SoCal's chairman sent out a letter to the company's 40,000 employees and 262,000 stockholders asking them to pressure Washington to support "the aspirations of the Arab people." The chairman of Texaco called for a reassessment of U.S. Middle East policy.[41] When the October War broke out, the chairmen of the ARAMCO partners sent a memorandum to the White House warning against increasing military aid to Israel.[42] Since 1973, ARAMCO has maintained its public relations campaign and become involved in occasional legislative fights, such as the AWACS sale, but, on the whole, the campaign has had no observable impact on U.S. policy.

There are other non-oil companies that are involved in the Arab lobby, the most well-known being Bechtel, and we can expect an increasing number to be willing to participate as Arab investment in the United States grows. Estimates of Arab investment range from $50 billion to $200 billion, and Arab investors (nations and individuals) have bought shares and, in some cases, controlling interests in a wide range of American corporations, creating the potential for expanding Arab political influence.[43]

A relatively ignored component of the "Arab lobby" is found among the Christian community, most notably, the National Council of Churches (NCC). The NCC is composed of thirty-two Protestant denominations, including virtually all major church bodies. The Council has taken consistently anti-Israel stands, and its 1980 policy statement on the Middle East called for the creation of a PLO state. Besides passing anti-Israel resolutions, the NCC puts on seminars, radio shows, and conferences. From 1972 to 1977, it published the ARAMCO financed *SWASIA* (*Southwest Asia*) newsletter. When *SWASIA* ceased publication, the NCC established an Islamic desk to "enable American Christians to understand Arab Christian and Muslim attitudes."[44] The relationship between the NCC and other Arab lobby organizations is primarily informal, with NCC leaders serving on many of their boards.

Contrasts

There are at least two major differences between the Arab and Israeli lobbies. First, the Arab lobby almost always lobbies negatively; i.e., *against* pro-Israel legislation rather than for pro-Arab legislation. In her study of the Arab lobby, Spiegel found only three legislative initiatives by the NAAA relating to the Arab world. They involved Lebanon, promoting Arab trade, and countering negative Arab stereotypes. The rest of their efforts related to Israel: (1) opposition to "Israel's occupation and annexation of the West Bank, Golan Heights, and Gaza Strip and the attendant violations of human rights of their inhabitants"; (2) attempts to cut U.S. aid to Israel to prevent the "establishment of illegal settlements and annexation of occupied territories, including Jerusalem"; (3) a call for enforcement of the Arms Control Act "with reference to Israel's misuse of United States supplied military equipment for attacks on Lebanon"; and (4) a call for a Palestinian state and recognition of the PLO.[45] This agenda contrasts with that of the Israeli lobby, which, with the exception of arms sales to Arab states hostile toward Israel, directs its activities toward promoting a pro-Israel, rather than anti-Arab foreign policy.

The other major difference between the two lobbies is the use of paid foreign agents by the Arab lobby. Pro-Arab U.S. government officials can look forward to lucrative positions as lobbyists, spokesmen, and consultants for the Arab cause. For example, the outspoken critic of the Israeli lobby, former Senate Foreign Relations Committee Chairman J. William Fulbright, was hired by the Saudis and the United Arab Emirates. It was the Saudis' agent, Fred Dutton, a former Assistant Secretary for Legislative Affairs and special assistant to President Kennedy, who spearheaded the AWACS campaign and reputedly conceived the "Reagan vs. Begin" angle. Other top officials who have provided their services to the Arab lobby include: Clark Clifford, President Johnson's Defense Secretary; Richard Kleindienst, President Nixon's Attorney General; and William Rogers, Nixon's Secretary of State.[46]

Overall, the Israeli lobby is effective because it enjoys advantages in every area considered relevant to interest group influence. It has (a) a large and vocal membership; (b) members who enjoy high status and legitimacy; (c) a high degree of electoral participation (voting and financing); (d) effective leadership; (e) a high degree of access to decision-makers; and (f) public support. Moreover, for reasons at least partly attributable to the lobby's efforts, the lobby's primary objective—a U.S. commitment to Israel— has been accepted as *a* national interest. Thus, the Israeli lobby is expected to exert an observable degree of influence on Middle East policy, and it remains to be shown how much influence and under what conditions.

Policy Types

U.S. foreign policy may be classified in many different ways, but the most useful for the purpose of studying interest group influence is probably the policy type. Different policy types are then associated with distinctive political processes. Many scholars have developed typologies for distinguishing foreign policies, but they all share a common shortcoming; that is, they predict that different policy types will lead to different policy processes, but then do no more than *describe the process.*[47] They do not provide a means of predicting policy outcomes. Thus, we may know, for example, that distributive policies will involve a process of "logrolling," but we have no way of predicting who the winners and losers of the bargaining process will be. What these models lack is an estimation of the degree of influence each domestic variable exerts on any given policy.

The typology described here enables us to examine how the Israeli lobby's influence is limited by the president and realist concerns. First, policies are defined by the decision arena. The locus of decision is important because access is required for political influence, and the degree of access varies depending on the location where a decision is ultimately reached. There are two loci of decision: the executive and legislative branches.

The president of the United States is generally acknowledged to be the single most influential lobbyist in foreign affairs; consequently, if the president supports the position of an interest group, ceteris paribus, the decision will be favorable to that group. This is true because the president will always assert that his position reflects the national interest, and because of traditions of deference, presidential power, and superior information, his position will usually prevail. In fact, his position should always prevail when decisions are reached in the executive branch, since the president has the final say.

On the whole, the president is expected to support the Israeli lobby because he seeks re-election. As noted earlier, the informal lobby encourages candidates for president to support the lobby's objectives and this motivation remains potent for incumbents. The Jackson-Vanik case is illustrative as Richard Nixon, a Republican with no hope of winning a majority of the Jewish vote in 1972, made a concerted and ultimately successful effort to double the percentage of the Jewish vote he had received in 1968. It may be argued that a second term president is released from this constraint, but the desire not to harm the party's election hopes may inhibit a president from making any drastic changes in policy.

In general, the Israeli lobby has less influence over decisions made in the executive branch because of the president's relative isolation; that is, both his inaccessibility and remoteness from the voters. Crisis decisions, in particular, are usually beyond the influence of interest groups; nevertheless, presidents still must be concerned with the potential electoral repercussions of their actions.[48]

Typically, the executive branch is the setting for new proposals to solve a particular noncrisis problem, incremental changes in existing policy, or an entirely new policy toward a nation or region. Examples of presidential decisions include the recognition of governments and choices regarding United Nations (UN) votes. Presidential decisions are expected to result from bargaining within the executive branch, although it may also be necessary to confer and bargain with Congress to some extent. Unlike crisis decisions, the public and interest groups will have some opportunity to express their views on the contemplated decision, and while the country will usually rally around the president in a crisis, there will be more careful scrutiny of policy changes in a noncrisis atmosphere. The exception to this generalization are those decisions that are made secretly; in which case, the decision-making process should resemble that of crisis decisions. Even in such cases of national security, however, domestic political advisers are included in the deliberations.[49]

The Israeli lobby has enjoyed access to every president, enabling it to at least obtain a hearing for its position. Prior to 1967, access to the White House was primarily through personal friends of the president. People like Eddie Jacobson, Abe Feinberg, Arthur Krim, Max Fisher, Jacob Stein, and Philip Klutznick enjoyed personal friendships with presidents that gave them, and hence the Israeli lobby, entreé to the Oval Office. After 1967, the formal lobby became more important, but personal relationships have remained a means of access. Access is not synonymous with influence, however, as one Israeli lobby leader explained to the author:

> Those who claim a high level of influence at the executive level for the pro-Israel lobby are wrong. . . . Each and every one of the meetings that I have had with past Presidents Nixon, Carter, Ford, and my White House service with the current President indicates to me that, while there is access and there is input, there is very little influence on the executive decision-making process.

The pressure of the Israeli lobby has frequently been the object of presidential frustration in the course of complex deliberations. Paradoxically, almost every president has established a staff person to act as a liaison with the Jewish community. The explanation for the paradox of setting up a mechanism, by which interest groups can have access the White House prefers to avoid, may be that influence works in both directions; that is, *interest groups may be the target of administration pressure*. This can again be seen in the Jackson-Vanik case, where Richard Nixon arranged meetings to lobby Jewish leaders to withdraw their support for the legislation.

The relative isolation of the president is not the only reason the Israeli lobby's influence on executive decisions is limited; there are also countervailing pressures from advisers and bureaucrats within the executive branch who do not have to face re-election and can claim objectivity. Although the Israeli lobby has some access to the State Department, it has very little influence over policy originating there. There are few Jews in the department, there is little or no accountability to voters, contributors, or public opinion, and the department has a predominantly pro-Arab orientation, all of which operate against the Israeli lobby's interests. The department's support for the Arabs is not irrational; it is largely a product of the perception that the interests of twenty-one states with more than 150 million people, *and* most of the world's oil reserves, is more important to the national interest than one country the size of New Jersey with less than five million people. In addition, since the majority of Arabs are Muslims, many bureaucrats believe the Arab world has a natural antipathy to communism that can be exploited by the United States.

Given conflicting pressures and the need to consider all the five United States interests in the Middle East mentioned above, it is not immediately clear what the president's position will be on any particular issue. The most important consideration, I believe, is the compatibility of the choices with the president's ideology. It is extremely difficult, however, to collect data on the positions of advisers and bureaucrats, and even more difficult to classify the individual characteristics of presidents. This hypothesis is therefore difficult to test; nevertheless, there is support for such an understanding provided by the case studies. For example, chapters 5 and 6 suggest that Truman was influenced by the Israeli lobby on issues where he was neutral, and had to choose between competing pressures as long as the lobby's position was consistent with his own ideology.

Unlike most of the other analysts of individual characteristics, I would argue that presidential decisions, like congressional ones, are partially derived from an estimate of the benefits and costs in domestic political terms. The results of this Downsian calculation of the benefit/cost ratio will vary, but will usually favor the Israeli lobby because there is so little to gain from opposing its interests. For example, the Defense Department maintained that Israel did not need Phantom jets, but President Johnson knew that there would be no political cost to supplying the planes, and that a favorable decision would help his vice president's chances for becoming president.

The predominant models of foreign policy decision-making are particularly deficient when it comes to explaining decisions reached within the legislative branch. In the House, for example, the environment in which members consider floor amendments is not conducive to rational decision-making. Congressmen spend little time studying the amendments, few attend the debates, and votes are often cast without any appreciable knowledge of the issues or consequences of the proposed action.[50] The Senate operates in a similar manner. In legislative cases, such as those presented in part I, interest groups have far greater access to decision-makers; thus, the pluralist model should provide a better explanation of past decisions than the other models.

Israeli lobby influence is best explained by Mayhew's simple dictum that congressmen are single-minded seekers of reelection.[51] As such, they respond to interest groups with the most political resources. In this case, there is little countervailing pressure to inhibit the congressional response to the Israeli lobby. As Jacob Stein, a leading member of the lobby, explains: "The influence of Jewish community thinking is felt primarily by Congressmen who are up for election every two years and are continuously fund-raising for their next election campaign."

Generally, Congress will not initiate foreign policy legislation unless stimulated by interest group activity. "Most committees," according to Rep. Les Aspin, "wait for the Administration to send over its proposals and then they consider them from what might be described as a board-of-trustees' perspective."[52] In contrast to this traditional view that the president proposes and Congress disposes, the truth is that the legislature not only debates executive proposals but also offers proposals of its own. Cases where the Congress does initiate legislation, especially of a type unlikely to be introduced in the absence of a lobby, are particularly good examples of pluralist influence. The discussion of the Jackson-Vanik amendment and antiboycott bill in chapters 3 and 4 provide two such examples.

In addition, Congress may not simply "dispose" of an executive initiative. In fact, proposals originating in Congress, as well as those initiated by the executive branch, which require congressional approval, are frequently the subjects of heated debates. The president is often forced to act as a lobbyist and engage in "logrolling" to have his position supported by the Congress. Even then, he does not always succeed. The AWACS case described in chapter 2 is a particularly good example of the extent to which a president may be forced to lobby in order to overcome the opposition of the Israeli lobby.

Content

If the leadership was correct, then the president's position should prevail over that of the interest group in every case. Conversely, the pluralist model suggests the Israeli lobby should achieve its objectives so long as it holds the balance of lobbying power. In fact, as we shall see in chapters 9 and 10, the Israeli lobby does reach its objective in a majority of cases, but that success is largely dependent on the president's position. If the president supports the lobby, it wins virtually every time. This would seem to support the leadership model; however, the lobby also is able to reach its objective, despite the opposition of the president, 27 percent of the time. This raises the questions, how and when does this happen?

Part of the answer to these questions was given above; that is, lobby influence varies according to the locus of decision. As a coequal branch of government, the legislature does not always go along with the wishes of the president; moreover, congressmen have no political incentive to oppose the Israeli lobby, and significant electoral and financial incentives for supporting its interests. Like the president, congressmen recognize that the United States has several interests in the Middle East, but the only one with a significant domestic constituency is the interest in maintaining the security of Israel. Thus, it is not surprising that the Congress would sometimes act against the wishes of the president when he opposes the lobby, as it did in the Jackson-Vanik and antiboycott cases.

The Israeli lobby does overcome presidential opposition in Congress more than half the time, but we are still left without an explanation for why the lobby wins those particular cases. This is where the realist model provides some guidance. The president will always assert that his position represents the national interest, but there may be competing perceptions of the national interest. If Congress does not believe the president's argument or sees another interest as preeminent in a particular case, it will oppose the president. This is more likely to happen when the issue involves economic rather than security interests. This is true because economic issues tend to have strong domestic constituencies; consequently, economic issues are the one area of foreign affairs where interest groups have been said to exert influence. The Israeli lobby is extremely successful on economic issues such as the antiboycott bill and, in fact, passage of the foreign aid bill has become largely dependent on the lobby's support for aid to Israel.

On the other hand, by virtue of superior information and the tradition of deference in foreign affairs, the president is usually supported on security issues. Knowing this, presidents will try to present issues in terms of national security. This was the case, for example, during the debate on the Jackson-Vanik amendment. The Nixon administration argued in apocalyptic terms that the amendment would undermine detente and thereby threaten world peace, but the amendment was seen by Congress as an economic and political issue and, therefore, was more willing to challenge the president's position. In the Saudi arms sales cases, however, security was clearly an issue and Congress was more reluctant to overrule Presidents Carter and Reagan. There was substantial opposition to the sales because many congressmen did not believe they represented the grave security issues the presidents made them out to be, and because the maintenance of Israel's security, which was seen as being threatened by the sales, was also considered a U.S. security interest. In the majority of security-related cases, however, the president's position prevails.

In the case of decisions made in the executive branch, the Israeli lobby must persuade the president that its position represents the national interest. In security-related cases, the president will be more likely to accept the recommendations of his advisers than the pleadings of the lobby, because most presidents would be expected to put national security above domestic politics. On nonsecurity related issues; however, the president will be more receptive to the lobby's concerns.

The succeeding chapters will examine a series of case studies that illustrate how the Israeli lobby influences Middle East policy and the constraints on that influence. The cases will be followed by an analysis of an aggregation of U.S. Middle East policies for the postwar period, which will document the statistical relationship between a series of domestic political variables and the Israeli lobby's success in achieving its objectives.

Notes

1. Will Maslow, "Jewish Political Power: An Assessment," *American Jewish Historical Quarterly* (December 1976), 350.
2. I.L. Kenen, *Israel's Defense Line* (NY: Prometheus, 1981), 301.
3. Peggy Strain, "Abourezk Rips Israel-Lobby Power As 'Dangerous,'" *Palestine Digest*, (April 1977), 9.
4. "Questioning the Israeli Lobby," *Time* 27 July 1981, 23.
5. "McCloskey Said to Claim Anti-Arab Media Bias," *San Francisco Examiner* 11 October 1982.
6. Wolf Blitzer, *Between Washington and Jerusalem* (NY: Oxford University Press, 1985), 235.
7. Cecil V. Crabb, Jr. and Pat Holt, *Invitation to Struggle: Congress, the President and Foreign Policy* (DC: Congressional Quarterly, 1980).
8. Aaron Wildavsky, "The Two Presidencies," in Wildavsky, ed., *Perspectives on the Presidency* (MA: Little, Brown, and Co., 1975), 449.
9. Hans Morgenthau, *Politics Among the Nations* (NY: Knopf, 1978), 36.

10. Joseph Bock and Duncan Clarke, "The National Security Assistant and the White House Staff: National Security Policy Decision-Making and Domestic Political Considerations, 1947–1984," *Presidential Studies Quarterly* (Spring 1986), 273.
11. Graham Allison, *Essence of Decision* (Boston: Little, Brown and Co., 1971); Werner Feld, *American Foreign Policy: Aspirations and Reality* (NY: John Wiley and Sons, 1984), 23; Morton H. Halperin, *Bureaucratic Politics and Foreign Policy* (DC: Brookings, 1974), 115; Steven L. Spiegel, *The Other Arab-Israeli Conflict* (IL: University of Chicago Press, 1985), 384–5.
12. See, for example, Spiegel, "*Other Arab-Israeli Conflict*," 392; Robert Axelrod, "Schema Theory: An Information Processing Model of Perception and Cognition," *American Political Science Review* (December 1973); James D. Barber, *The Presidential Character* (NJ: Prentice-Hall, 1977); Lloyd Etheridge, "Personality Effects on American Foreign Policy, 1896–1968," *American Political Science Review* (June 1978); Bruce Buchanan, *The Presidential Experience* (NJ: Prentice-Hall, 1978); Robert Jervis, *Perception and Misperception in International Politics* (NJ: Princeton University Press, 1976); Ole Holsti, "Cognitive Dynamics and Images of the Enemy," *Journal of International Affairs* (1967); Erwin Hargrove, "Presidential Personality and Revisionist Views of the Presidency," *American Journal of Political Science* (November 1973); Fred Greenstein, *Personality and Politics* (NY: W.W. Norton and Co., 1975); John Steinbruner, *The Cybernetic Theory of Decision* (NJ: Princeton University Press, 1974); Thomas Mongar, "Personality and Decision-Making: John F. Kennedy in "Four Crisis Decisions," *Canadian Journal of Political Science* (June 1969).
13. Robert Pastor, *Congress and the Politics of U.S. Foreign Economic Policy* (CA: U.C. Press, 1980), 49.
14. Robert Dahl, *Dilemmas of Pluralist Democracy* (CT: Yale University Press, 1982), 5, 26.
15. David L. Sills, ed., *International Encyclopedia of the Social Sciences* (NY: Crowell, Collier and Macmillan, 1968), 12:168; Theodore J. Lowi, *The End of Liberalism* (NY: W.W. Norton & Co., 1979), 58; Anthony Downs, *An Economic Theory of Democracy* (NY: Harper and Row, 1957) 34; S.J. Makielski, Jr, *Pressure Group Politics in America* (DC: University Press, 1980), 319–25.
16. Robert Art, "Bureaucratic Politics and American Foreign Policy: A Critique," *Policy Sciences* (December 1973).
17. Earl Latham, *The Group Basis of Politics* (NY: Ithaca, 1952), 35–6.
18. S.M. Lipset and William Schneider, "Carter vs. Israel," *Commentary* (November 1977), 29.
19. Thomas A. Dine, Executive Director, American Israel Public Af-

fairs Committee, Speech to AIPAC Policy Conference (DC: 19 April 1984).
20. Congressional Quarterly, *The Washington Lobby* (DC: Congressional Quarterly, October 1979), 14.
21. Interview with Milton Himmelfarb.
22. Interview with Morris Amitay.
23. Cheryl Rubenberg, "The Middle East Lobbies," *The Link* (January–March 1984), 8; Herbert A. Alexander, "Pro-Israel PACs: A Small Part of a Large Movement," (Unpublished Paper, 1985), 2.
24. John Fialka and Brooks Johnson, "Jewish PACs Emerge As A Powerful Force in U.S. Election Races," *Wall Street Journal* (26 February 1985); *PACs And Lobbies* (1 March 1989) and unpublished data from the editor, 1; Alexander, 1.
25. Fialka and Johnson, "Jewish PACs Emerge," 26; Rubenberg, "The Middle East Lobbies," 6.
26. Ira Mehlman, "Arab American Lobby Takes on Rep. Long, Other Israel Allies," *Jewish World* (20–26 January 1984), 37.
27. Ibid., 3.
28. *Washington Times* (22 June 1984) cited in *Boycott Report* (July–August 1984), 9.
29. Matt Moffett, "Arab-Americans Seek to Fight Stereotyping and Get Political Voice," *Wall Street Journal* (30 August 1984), 10.
30. Francis O. Wilcox, *Congress, the Executive, and Foreign Policy* (NY: Harper and Row, 1971), 138.
31. Gallup Poll Index, 1967–1989; Eytan Gilboa, *American Public Opinion Toward Israel and the Arab-Israeli Conflict* (MA: DC, Heath and Co., 1987), 91, 127–128.
32. Murray Friedman, "AWACS and the Jewish Community," *Commentary* (April 1982), 31; *Near East Report* (28 May 1982).
33. Fredelle Z. Spiegel, "The Emperor's Clothes: The New Look in Arab Public Relations," *Middle East Review* (Spring/Summer 1983), 28.
34. I.L. Kenen, *Israel's Defense Line* (NY: Prometheus, 1981), 114.
35. Kenen, *Israel's Defense Line*, 115.
36. Congressional Quarterly, *The Washington Lobby* (DC: Congressional Quarterly, 1974), 117.
37. Congressional Quarterly, "Supporters of Israel, Arabs Vie for Friends and Influence in Congress, at White House," *Weekly Reports* (22 August 1981), 1527–8.
38. Jimmy Carter, *Keeping Faith* (NY: Bantam Books, 1982), 299.
39. Steven Emerson, "The ARAMCO Connection," *The New Republic* (19 May 1982, reprint), 3.
40. Russell W. Howe and Sarah H. Trott, *The Power Peddlers* (NY: Doubleday, 1977), 342–3.
41. Anti-Defamation League, *The U.S.-Saudi Relationship* (NY: ADL, Spring 1980), 6.

42. Ibid, 7.
43. Ibid, 9–10; Fredelle Z. Spiegel, "The Arab Lobby," Background Paper of the Academic Association for Peace in the Middle East, (November 1981), 9; Hoag Levins, *Arab Reach* (NY: Doubleday, 1983), 224–84.
44. Rael Jean Isaac, "Liberal Protestants Versus Israel," *Midstream* (October 1981 reprint), 4.
45. Spiegel 1981, "The Arab Lobby," 6.
46. Congressional Quarterly, "Arab Lobby: Opening Previously Closed Doors," *Weekly Report* (6 September 1975), 1916.
47. Theodore J. Lowi, "American Business, Public Policy, Case Studies, and Political Theory," *World Politics* (July 1964); James Rosenau, *The Scientific Study of Foreign Policy* (NY: Free Press, 1971), 120; Rosenau, *Domestic Sources of Foreign Policy* (NY: Free Press, 1967); Rosenau, ed., *Comparing Foreign Policies* (NY: John Wiley and Sons, 1974); Michael Brecher, et al., "A Framework for Research in Foreign Policy Behavior," *Journal of Conflict Resolution* (March 1969); William Zimmerman, "Issue Area and Foreign Policy Process: A Research Note in Search of a General Theory," *American Political Science Review* (December 1973); John Spanier and E.M. Uslaner, *Foreign Policy and the Democratic Dilemmas* (1985); Barry Hughes, *The Domestic Context of American Foreign Policy* (CA: W.H. Freeman and Co., 1978); Pastor, *Congress and the Politics*, 1980.
48. Allison, *Essence of Decision*, 1971; John Rourke, *Congress and the Presidency in U.S. Foreign Policymaking* (CO: Westview Press, 1983); Morton Berkowitz, et al, *The Politics of American Foreign Policy* (NJ: Prentice-Hall, 1977); Allan Dowty, *Middle East Crisis* (CA: U.C. Press, 1984); Theodore Lowi, "Making Democracy Safe for the World," Rosenau, ed., 1967.
49. Bock and Clark, "The National Security Assistant," 273.
50. Charles W. Whalen, *The House and Foreign Policy* (NC: University of North Carolina Press, 1982), 127.
51. David R. Mayhew, *Congress—The Electoral Connection* (CT: Yale University Press, 1974).
52. John Roehm, "Congressional Participation in Foreign Policy: A Study of Congress' Role in U.S. Middle East Policy Vis-A-Vis the Confrontation States in the Arab-Israeli Conflict From the Yom Kippur War to the End of the Ford Administration," (Unpublished Ph.D. Dissertation, University of Pittsburgh, 1980), 283.

Part I

LOBBY INFLUENCE AND THE LOCUS OF DECISION 1: THE LEGISLATIVE BRANCH

Introduction to Part I

One of the most crucial prerequisites to exerting political influence is to gain access to the people and institutions that are responsible for making and implementing policy decisions. The ability of an interest group to obtain access depends on three factors: (1) the group's strategic position in society, (2) the internal characteristics of the group, and (3) the characteristics of the governmental institutions to which access is sought. Truman explains:

> In the first category are: the group's status or prestige in society, affecting the ease with which it commands deference from those outside its bounds; the standing it and its activities have when measured against the widely held but largely unorganized interests or "rules of the game," the extent to which government officials are formally or informally "members" of the group; and the usefulness of the group as a source of technical and political knowledge. The second category includes: the degree and appropriateness of the group's organization; the degree of cohesion it can achieve in a given situation, especially in the light of competing group demands upon its membership; the skills of the leadership; and the group's resources in members and money. In the third category are: the operating structure of the government institutions, since such established features involve relatively fixed advantages and handicaps; and the effects of the group life of particular branches of the government.[1]

In chapter 1, I suggested that the Israeli lobby does enjoy substantial prestige, since its members are highly educated and disproportionately represented in higher income groups and high status professions. There are many members of the lobby within the government, and even those who are not members consider the lobby a useful and legitimate source of information. The lobby also is very cohesive, with a reputation for competent leadership.

This section will take up the third category described by Truman—the structure of the government.

Since World War II, Congress has taken an increasingly active role in foreign policy, as is evident from the proliferation of committees that deal with international policy issues, from a handful before the war, to seventeen of twenty-two committees in the House, and sixteen of nineteen in the Senate today. The increasing interest of Congress in foreign policy has been accompanied by a growth in the number of lobbies vying for the members' attention. In 1945, there were two thousand registered lobbies; by 1980, the number had grown to fifteen thousand. The increase in the number of committees gave the lobbyists a larger number of access points. In general, lobbyists are wise to focus their attention on Capitol Hill, rather than the White House, for the simple reason that there are 535 points of access in Congress and only one in the White House. As a Johnson aide told Light: "You can get an hour to present your case before each representative; you get fifteen minutes once a year with the President. Where would you put your effort?"[2]

In the case of foreign policy, congressmen play at least three roles. One role is to express personal opinions on foreign affairs as informed members of the public. Another role is to represent the opinions of their constituents and voice them to decision-makers. Chairmen and members of foreign affairs related committees, such as Foreign Relations, Armed Services, and Government Operations, also have the additional obligation to represent the institutional interests of Congress in the foreign policy area.[3]

Since 1967, Congress has been particularly active and effective in translating the interests of the Israeli lobby into foreign policy outputs. For example, arms sales credits were appropriated before each of the decisions to sell Israel Phantom planes were announced; economic and military aid was increased over the levels requested by the administration; and Israel's policies were publicly endorsed. In fact, just as the Israeli government sometimes has to give the Israeli lobby the "red light" to prevent it from going too far, the lobby sometimes has to try to hold back its supporters in Congress, who occasionally attempt to do things that would be counterproductive. Thus, the Middle East Policy

Data Set contains a number of legislative proposals that expressed ideas supported by the lobby, but were initiated with little or no stimulation from the lobby. Offering a resolution, after all, is a very low cost means of currying favor with the lobby. As a consequence, as noted in chapter 11, the lobby's batting average is lower than it would be if it were not for the overzealousness of its supporters on Capitol Hill.

Congressional support for Israel is by no means a recent phenomenon. In fact one can look back to the congressional resolutions of 1922 and 1944 endorsing the Balfour Declaration, and to the pro-Zionist American Palestine Committee, founded by a group of congressmen in 1932 and revived in 1941 with a membership of sixty-eight senators and more than two hundred congressmen, to find its early manifestations.[4]

The congressional affinity toward Israel was explained earlier in terms of electoral politics and public opinion, but there are a number of other reasons that can be cited to explain the pro-Israel bias of Congress. One is that the United States and Israel share the same social, cultural, religious, and political values. In addition, Israel is perceived as a democratic outpost in a region marked by autocratic regimes. Americans also tend to sympathize with underdogs, and for at least the first two decades of Israel's existence, Israel was seen as David in the fight with the Arab Goliath. In more recent years, conservatives have been especially supportive of Israel because they believe that Israel is a strategic asset that can counter Arab radicalism and Soviet expansionism. Support for Israel also has roots in American feelings of guilt arising from the Holocaust. Critics of U.S. Middle East policy frequently attribute congressional support for Israel to the fear of being labeled an anti-Semite. There is no question that this is also a factor, but it is far less significant than the positive reasons Americans feel an affinity for Israelis.

Today, the predominant reasons for support are probably the shared values of the two societies. Israel's military strength displayed in the Lebanon war has altered the perception of Israel as an underdog, for the time being, but there remains a desire to insure that Israel retains a qualitative military superiority over its neighbors. The view that Israel is a strategic asset has also acquired increasing support as the other reasons begin to lose their appeal. *Jerusalem Post* correspondent Wolf Blitzer explains:

> A new generation of lawmakers has taken charge here in Washington. These Senators and Representatives—unlike the Henry Jacksons and Hubert Humphreys and the Jacob Javits'—do not have the personal, first-hand experiences of living through World War II, the Holocaust and the birth of Israel. For many of them, Israel is simply another country in the world.[5]

A less visible means of influence employed by the Israeli lobby on Capitol Hill is a network of pro-Israel congressional aides. Both the current executive director of AIPAC and his predecessor were legislative aids who had been active on Israel-related issues. While he was still working for Senator Ribicoff, Amitay discussed the behind-the-scenes activity of the aides:

> There are a lot of guys at the working level up here . . . who happen to be Jewish, who are willing to make a little bit of extra effort and to look at certain issues in terms of their Jewishness, and this is what has made this thing go effectively in the last couple of years. These are all guys who are in a position to make the decisions in these areas for those senators. You don't need that many to get something done in the Senate. All you need is a certain commitment to get something done and, if the guys are willing to put time into that instead of a million other things they have to do, if they're willing to make a couple of calls, if they're willing to get involved, you can get an awful lot done just at the staff level. . . . The senators have a million things to do and they'll take the recommendation [of their aides] most times.[6]

After he became executive director of AIPAC, Amitay tried to discount the influence of the network, but it remains an important component of the Israeli lobby and one that has no rival.

One Jewish leader, Earl Raab, has formulated what he calls the "Law of Marginal Jewish Power" which states that "As a political force, the Jews will be able to exert influence over American foreign policy to the extent that their influence is wielded in the direction of what American public officialdom already considers the best interests of the United States."[7] The fact that the lobby succeeds so infrequently when opposed by the president, and virtually every time the president supports it, suggests that this is true to a large extent; nevertheless, there are cases when the lobby is able to overcome presidential opposition. In addition, there are cases where the lobby is able to exert influence by stimulating legislation that would not be proposed in its absence.

The first case study in part I provides a control case to illustrate that the lobby is not able to reach its objective just because a decision requires congressional involvement. Chapter 2 describes the efforts of two successive presidents to sell sophisticated weapons to Saudi Arabia, which the lobby believed not only threatened Israel, but risked the compromise of American technology. The presidents argued, however, that the sales were in the interests of national security and, due to the reluctance of Congress to rebuke the president on security issues, we see that the lobby was ultimately defeated. Many congressmen were willing to challenge the presidents' interpretation of U.S. national security interests. In fact, the House disapproved the 1981 AWACS sale, and would have disapproved the 1978 F-15 sale, had the issue come to a vote. Although the lobby was unable to stop the sales, it did succeed in forcing both presidents to modify the terms of the agreements and place restrictions on the type and use of the equipment transferred to the Saudis. These compromises, it will be shown, were forced upon the president by pressure from the Israeli lobby.

The arms cases challenge the leadership model by demonstrating that two presidents with completely different ideologies and policies toward the Middle East can adopt almost identical positions. This can be explained in terms of the realist model; that is, the two leaders arrived at the same policy in this instance because they shared a perception that the U.S. national interest required the arming of Saudi Arabia. On the other hand, the difficulty each president encountered in Congress, and the bargaining they were forced to engage in, also provides evidence of the influence that pluralist forces exert, even on security-related issues in the legislative branch.

Chapters 3 and 4 present even better examples of lobby influence. In both the Jackson-Vanik and antiboycott bill cases, it is clear the issues were placed on the agenda as a direct result of lobby pressure, and would never have been considered in the absence of the lobby. Once again, presidents opposing the lobby's position argued that the national interest would be undermined by the adoption of the bills; however, these arguments were far weaker because the two cases were only indirectly related to security issues. Both the Jackson-Vanik and antiboycott bills involved essentially economic issues that had security and political overtones. Since economic issues are thought to be subject to lobby influence, it is not surprising that this is found to be the case.

Chapter 4 also supports the leadership model. We shall see that the change, from the rigid opposition of Gerald Ford to antiboycott legislation, to the supportive administration of Jimmy Carter, guarantees that the lobby's goal will be achieved. The difference in the two presidents' positions is partly a function of differences in ideology, but also partly due to lobby influence, as we will see when Carter makes the Arab boycott a campaign issue to attract the support of Jewish voters.

Thus, part I will show that the Israeli lobby's influence and access to the legislative branch does result in the adoption of the legislation it supports. Pluralist forces do play a role in each of these policy outcomes, but the predominance of the realist model on security issues and the importance of leaders will also be demonstrated.

Notes

1. David Truman, *The Governmental Process* (NY: Alfred A. Knopf, 1962), 506–7.
2. Paul Light, *The Presidential Agenda* (MD: Johns Hopkins University Press, 1982), 94.
3. Robert F. Trice, "Congress and the Arab-Israeli Conflict: Support for Israel in the U.S. Senate, 1970–1973," *Political Science Quarterly* (Fall 1977), 445.
4. For example, see George Kent, "Congress and American Middle East Policy," Willard A. Beling, ed., *The Middle East—Quest for an American Policy* (NY: State University of New York Press, 1973), 287–8.
5. Wolf Blitzer, "The AIPAC Formula," *Moment* (November 1981).
6. Stephen Isaacs, *Jews and American Politics* (NY: Doubleday, 1974), 255–6.
7. Earl Raab, "American Jewish Attitudes on Israel: Consensus and Dissent," *Perspectives* (November 1981), 18.

2

The Sale of Arms to Saudi Arabia

Jimmy Carter was a source of anxiety for many in the Jewish community when he became a serious candidate for president. As a "born-again" Christian, Carter was associated with those "spiritual headhunters out to nail Jewish scalps on the wall like coonskins."[1] After winning the Democratic nomination, Carter began to try to use his religion as an asset with Jewish voters, stressing the sameness of the God of Israel and Christendom and asserting his commitment to American pluralism. He also began to make the kinds of statements Israel's supporters expected to hear. "The survival of Israel," he said in a speech on 6 June 1975, "is not just a political issue, it is a moral imperative." In addition, he was very critical of Ford's Middle East policy, including the president's willingness to sell arms to Egypt and Saudi Arabia. With regard to the latter sale of missiles, Carter said, "There is no reason to think these missiles will increase security and stability in the Middle East. There is no reason to think they can be used only for defense. There are only reasons to fear that we will increase the chance of conflict." He scolded Ford for adding arms to Arab countries "without limit on quantity or quality" because "it undermines our commitment to Israel."[2]

The combination of disenchantment with Ford, loyalty to the Democratic party, and a willingness to "trust Jimmy" led nearly three-quarters of the Jewish voters to cast their ballots for Carter. Only blacks were more loyal to the Democratic ticket than Jews, but signs of wariness within the Jewish electorate were evident as preelection polls showed their percentage of "undecideds" was twice the national average.[3]

Carter recognized that the United States was committed to maintain Israel's military superiority and admitted that hurting Israel was "political suicide."[4] Nevertheless, when Israel submitted a secret proposal in July 1977, for 150 F-16s and 25 F-15s, Carter and his advisers feared that such a large infusion of new weapons would undermine the administration's efforts to reconvene the Geneva peace talks. In addition, there was concern that the cost of the weapons requested by Israel ($4.8 billion) would be seen as contrary to the administration's new arms transfer policy, which was designed to reduce U.S. arms sales. The Pentagon gave the administration an excuse not to fulfill the request when it suggested that Israel did not need the additional planes.

The decision was further complicated by the requests of both Saudi Arabia and Egypt for sophisticated weapons. In the summer of 1976, President Ford's Deputy Secretary of Defense, William P. Clements, Jr., travelled to Saudi Arabia and promised that the United States would replace its obsolete planes with any American fighter plane they wanted. The Saudis chose the top American plane, the F-15. Tom Gervasi asserted that it was not the Saudis who chose the F-15, but the Americans. He argues that without the Saudi sale, U.S. procurement schedules would fall behind; thus, the F-15 was pushed, particularly by the Air Force, to lower production costs and accelerate procurement.[5] The Ford administration was favorably disposed to the request but did not have an opportunity to act on it. William Safire later accused Ford of deliberately withholding information during the campaign about the proposed arms sales to the Saudis.[6]

When Carter visited Riyadh after his election, he was reminded of what the Saudis considered the commitment to receive the F-15s. The president returned with the intention of making good on that promise, especially after being told that unless the deal was concluded soon, Saudi Arabia would look to the French to meet their military needs. Some within the administration opposed the sale on the ground that it would undermine the arms transfer policy, while others argued that the Saudis should be either sold the less sophisticated F-16s, or at least be required to contribute to peace negotiations before receiving the F-15s. The Saudis rebuffed all such efforts to modify or put conditions on the sale.

In November 1977, Anwar Sadat made his dramatic journey to Jerusalem, initiating the peace process that was to culminate in the Camp David Treaty. The administration recognized the need to offer some evidence of support for Sadat's move and the sale of fighter planes, the first such sale to an Arab "confrontation state," was chosen as the means of doing so.

Even before any of the sales were formally announced, six members of the Senate Foreign Relations Committee wrote to Carter and asked him to reconsider the sale to the Saudis. The administration was undaunted by such concern, and announced on 14 February 1978 the intention to sell sixty F-15s to Saudi Arabia, fifty F-5Es to Egypt, and fifteen F-15s and seventy-five F-16s to Israel. Anticipating opposition, the administration submitted the sales as a package, and repeatedly stressed that no sale would be permitted unless they were all approved. The administration knew that it would be difficult to obtain congressional approval to the sales for the Arab states, so it intentionally held the jets for Israel hostage in an attempt to insure that Saudi Arabia and Egypt would receive arms.

There were several controversial aspects of the proposal, but the bulk of the opposition centered around the sale of weapons to the Saudis. First, it was argued, the Saudis did not need America's most sophisticated fighter, and its introduction into the Arab arsenal would have a negative impact on the qualitative edge enjoyed by Israel over its antagonists. Secondly, the Saudis had led the Organization of Petroleum Exporting States (OPEC) cartel's efforts to raise oil prices. Third, the Saudis had not demonstrated any commitment to peace and had actually opposed Sadat's initiative.

Despite the opposition of eleven of the fifteen members of the Senate Foreign Relations Committee, the Saudi sale was included in the package. Secretary of State Cyrus Vance explained that Saudi Arabia "is of immense importance in promoting a course of moderation in the Middle East, with respect to peacemaking and other regional initiatives and more broadly in world affairs, as in petroleum and financial policy."[7]

There was not only opposition to the substance of the proposal, but also to the form in which it was presented; that is, the "package." Vance and his congressional liaisons opposed the linkage tactic because they believed Congress would see it as a "neo-Nixonian effort at compliance by circumvention." The proposal would thereby be transformed from a debate on the merits of the arms sales to a "confrontation over the President's duty to obey the Nelson-Bingham [Arms Export Control] law."[8] White House advisers, however, were looking for a showdown and insisted that the State Department use the word "package" in its announcement of the proposed sales.

For the Israeli lobby, the package had ominous implications: "By placing Israel in the same category as Saudi Arabia and Egypt, the administration is obviously trying to make the Arab sales more acceptable to the Congress, but the administration is also abandoning America's traditional special relationship with Israel."[9] Speaking for the administration, Robert Lipshutz, the president's counsel, reaffirmed the commitment to Israel, but acknowledged that the Carter administration was interested in developing special relationships with the "moderate" Arab states. "It has always been done surreptitiously, with Nixon, Ford, Kissinger and the workings of 'shuttle diplomacy,' but now we are *openly* trying to strengthen those relationships," Lipshutz said.[10]

To a certain extent the arms sale was a no win situation for the United States. Rep. Henry Waxman explained that even if Congress vetoed the sale, as he believed it should, "it would upset the expectations of Egypt and Saudi Arabia, thus undermining the Administration's credibility." Blocking the sale, he noted, would not undo the damage that had already been done to United States-Israel relations. If Congress failed to veto the sale, however, "the Arabs will ultimately gain greater military power, and the Israelis, weighing the potential threat arrayed against them, will be further inhibited from making strategic concessions for intangible assurances."[11]

The Pluralist Dimension

The debate pitted the Arab and Israeli lobbies in direct competition with little involvement by other interest groups. The opponents of the sale faced, not only the precedent that no arms sale had ever been vetoed by Congress, but also a determined administration that had just won a major foreign policy victory in Congress—the ratification of the Panama Canal Treaty. In addition, the Arab lobby made a dramatic appearance on to the Capitol Hill scene. As a congressional aide later told Hoag Levins:

> The Arabs just suddenly appeared in Washington in 1978. It was that quick. Boom! . . . The progress they made was incredible. Four years before, the Arab lobby was a joke. You had maybe two people here who knew what they were doing. The others were all very polite and basically nice guys, but basically dumb as shit about the system. They were tiptoeing around like nuns in a whorehouse, afraid of offending anybody. They didn't know what they were doing or even how to find out. They didn't even understand the theory of the system, let alone how it works here on the Hill on a day-to-day basis. And then, Wham! Arabs are everywhere; know exactly what they are doing; are very slick about doing it. It was amazing.[12]

Part of the reason for the change was the Arabs' investment in foreign agents. There were twenty-five agents lobbying on the Saudis' behalf for the F-15 sales. These agents added their knowledge of the American system to the lobbying efforts of the mostly Western-educated Saudi royal family who had their own skills of persuasion. Rep. Benjamin Rosenthal vouched for their abilities:

> "I just had a member of the royal family in here and he was really quite a charming guy. His argument made some sense. I don't happen to agree with it, but it made some sense. All in all, I think he was pretty effective."[13]

This testimonial comes from a Jew who was one of Israel's staunchest supporters, so it might not be unreasonable to expect that the Arab lobbying effort might have had some impact on the less committed members of Congress.

The Saudis did not rely entirely on charm, however, they also threatened to go elsewhere for their military needs. In a letter to all the members of Congress, Saudi Ambassador Ali A. Alireza warned that his country would replace its old U.S. Lightnings one way or the other, and would consider buying French planes, or helping to finance the development of aircraft comparable to the F-15.[14]

The Israeli lobby effort was further complicated by the resignation of Carter's liaison with the Jewish community, Mark Siegel. In his resignation letter Siegel expressed "strong and personal reservations about the wisdom of your [Carter's] arms sales decision, the 'packaging' of that decision, and its timing." He added that he was "concerned about amending U.S. commitments to Israel as part of the Sinai Disengagement Agreement by making the fulfillment of our commitments predicated on approval of arms sales to other nations, two and a half years after the fact."[15] Many people saw the Siegel resignation as proof of the administration's confrontational attitude toward the Israeli lobby. (Although there was no formal liaison with the Arab-American community, Carter did "confess" that he met with Arab leaders from all over the country.)

At about the same time, there was a lot of publicity given to an angry meeting between the chairman of the Conference of Presidents of Major American Jewish Organizations, Rabbi Alexander Schindler, and National Security Adviser (NSA) Zbigniew Brzezinski. After the meeting, Schindler met with Carter's political adviser, Hamilton Jordan, and Robert Lipshutz (the President's counsel) to complain about the administration's harsh rhetoric toward Israel and the Jewish community. He said that "all the anger and mistrust is toward the National Security Council and toward Brzezinski."[16]

The Israeli lobby's anger was directed at Brzezinski because he was believed to be responsible for the arms sale package. In some of his writing prior to becoming the NSA, Brzezinski had expressed the need to use American leverage over Israel to force territorial concessions that amounted to almost total withdrawal to the 1967 borders. He had also suggested that Israel should talk to the PLO, and that a Palestinian state would have certain benefits.[17] These views alone were anathema to the Israeli lobby, but it was his alleged comments about the lobby itself that generated the most anxiety. Brzezinski was reported to have said that the F-15 vote would "break the back of the Israeli lobby" and, a year earlier, he was supposed to have said that American Middle East policy could not succeed until the American Jewish community had been confronted on a major issue and defeated. AIPAC's executive director, Morris Amitay believed that Brzezinski was out "to cripple the pro-Israel forces."[18]

Despite the acrimony, President Carter remained committed to the arms sale. At his March press conference he said:

> I have no apology at all to make for this proposal. It maintains the military balance that exists in the Middle East. I can say without any doubt that the superior capabilities of the Israeli Air Force, compared to their neighbors, is maintained, and at the same time, it reconfirms our own relationship with the moderate Arab leaders and nations for the future to insure that peace can be and will be maintained in the Middle East.[19]

Tension between Israel and the United States increased throughout March, beginning with the 11 March PLO attack on two civilian buses in Israel that killed thirty-six people, and was hailed by Saudi State Radio as a "courageous operation."[20] Israel responded three days later by launching an invasion of Lebanon under the name "Operation Litani."

Despite some uneasiness over Israel's actions, most members of Congress remained sympathetic to Israel's arguments against the plane sales, and majorities of both foreign affairs committees sent letters to the president opposing the sale of F-15s to Saudi Arabia and objecting to the package.[21] Carter was urged to delay the sale, but Saudi Arabia told U.S. officials that "a delay is just as bad as a rejection" and the president refused to withdraw the sale, although he did delay submitting the proposal to Congress until after the Panama Canal Treaty vote. The administration also hoped to avoid the likely embarrassment of losing in the House.[22]

At the end of April, Carter again asserted that the sale was "in the best interests of the nation" and spokesman Jody Powell reiterated the administration's unwillingness to sell jets to Israel if the Saudi sale was blocked. Carter was under increasing pressure, however, from Congress to modify the sale. Senator Jacob Javits said the "fatal defect is that it is a package." Senator Frank Church argued that linking the sales together "violates the intent and spirit of the congressional review procedures." Finally, when Senator Robert Byrd told the president that even supporters of the sale would vote against the package on the legal grounds outlined by Church, the White House relented and offered a compromise. The president was particularly receptive to the concerns of Church and Byrd because they had just led the successful fight for passage of the Panama Canal Treaty. The day after speaking to Byrd, Carter sent him a draft of a letter Vance would send to Church "unlocking the package." By including Byrd in the consultation process and offering a compromise, Carter was able to "unruffle feathers" in the Senate. The letter itself was ambiguous:

> In submitting these proposed sales to Congress on the same day, the Administration is not attempting to place conditions or inhibitions on the scope of Congressional review or the action of Congress. Indeed, we understand that the Congress will want to review these important transactions separately and with great care, and we stand ready to facilitate that process.[23]

The letter assuaged the concerns of some, but the leaders of the move to block the sales saw the compromise as so ambiguous as to have no meaning. Nevertheless, it did quiet most of the debate over the form of the proposal, and discussion shifted to more substantive issues after being formally submitted to Congress on 28 April.

Two days later, the president reiterated his belief that the proposal was "best for Israel," and that in his discussions the previous month with Prime Minister Menachem Begin, the Israeli leader never mentioned any concern over the sale.[24] On the contrary, Begin told the Knesset that he objected to the sale of "the most advanced planes on earth to Saudi Arabia" because it would make that country a confrontation state.[25] Carter was more concerned, however, that the United States "keep that sense in Saudi Arabia that we are their friends" and that "they can trust us when we make a commitment." He added: "I believe that it's best for Israel to have this good, firm, solid, mutually trustful, friendly relationship with the moderate Arab leaders."[26]

Meanwhile, Vance was testifying that the Saudis were working to support Anwar Sadat's peace efforts. Congress was also reminded that the Saudis were likely to go elsewhere for weapons if they were denied F-15s. Secretary of Defense Harold Brown emphasized the Soviet threat to Saudi Arabia and thus to American oil supplies. He also assured senators that "Israel could defeat any combination of likely opposing forces, and will continue to be able to do so for quite a few years to come." He wrote a letter to the chairman of the House International Relations Committee telling him that the Saudis had assured the United States that it had no aggressive intentions against any state and that it would only use the F-15s for "legitimate self-defense." The Saudis also promised not to transfer the planes to a third nation or allow nationals of another country to train, pilot, or gain access to the aircraft without consent from the United States.[27] Administration officials also intimated that the continuation of Saudi Arabia's "favorable" oil policy was tied to the sale, a notion disputed by Saudi Oil Minister Sheik Ahmed Zaki Yamani, who said that "linking the F-15 with oil sales is not justified."[28]

The National Association of Arab Americans' (NAAA) Hisham Sharabi told Congress that the sale was necessary to give the United States the leverage to play the role of peacemaker. Another Arab lobby group, the Federation of Arab American Organizations called for an arms embargo to the Middle East, but, short of that, advocated a two-thirds reduction in the arms for Israel.[29]

Opponents of the sale had a different outlook. Representative Rosenthal pointed out that, contrary to the president's statements, the Israelis were very concerned about the sale of F-15s to the Saudis, especially in such large numbers. Former Secretary of State Henry Kissinger also noted the military threat the weapons posed to Israel and criticized the administration for its hypocrisy: "One cannot say that they have no military impact on Israel but they can have a military impact on threats from the Soviet side."[30] Senator Javits also ridiculed the idea that the Saudis could defend the Middle East against the Soviets, suggesting that "we had better triple the population in the first place" because Saudi Arabia is an enormous area.[31]

The sale's critics also found the reported Saudi assurances unconvincing, especially in view of the expansion of Saudi bases near the Israeli border. In addition, Saudi leaders had repeatedly made statements contradicting Brown's report of the Saudis willingness to restrict the use of the F-15s. For example, Crown Prince Fahd was quoted in the *New York Times* two years before the proposed sale as saying: "All of our nations' armed forces are a force in the defense of the Arab nations and the Arab cause." In April 1978, Fahd told *Paris Match*:

> Saudi Arabia allocated all its forces and strength to bring about victory
> of the Arab rights, their honor and all that is sacred in their eyes.
> . . . This means that the task entrusted to our army is not only to
> protect the kingdom, but that it could intervene anywhere that our
> national duty commands. Our army was in Syria; we have units in
> Jordan. . . . All this shows our readiness.

Foreign Minister Saud ben Faisal told *Newsweek* that the kingdom
would "use whatever resources we have to hurt the enemy" and
Defense Minister Sultan ben Abdul Aziz pledged that "All our
weapons are at the disposal of the Arab nations and will be used
in the battle against the common enemy."[32] The Saudi statements,
combined with that country's past history of support for Arab
armies in wars against Israel, were a source of anxiety for both
the Israelis and their American supporters.

Finally, the argument that the Saudis would buy arms from
France if they didn't get the F-15s from the United States was
dismissed by Javits who asked rhetorically: "Do you think they
are going to lean on France for their security for the next five
years? They are not crazy, believe me."[33] Another witness pointed
out that the Saudis were likely to buy French arms regardless of
whether or not they received the F-15s. The difference was not
only a matter of quality, the American aircraft being the most
advanced fighter in the world, but also the likely impact of the
sale on the arms race. If the Saudis purchased French planes,
Steven Rosen said presciently, there would be no pressure to
follow up the sale with a request for AWACS or Hawkeye radar
planes "which almost surely would be the next thing the Saudis
would want to go with the F-15s."[34] Senator Daniel Patrick Moy-
nihan summed up the sale as "a rationalization of American
nervelessness in the area of international economic policy as well
as political and military policy."[35]

The sale's opponents forced a compromise. The idea, ironically,
was suggested by a Republican whose views on the Middle East
had been repudiated by Carter—Henry Kissinger. On 8 May,
Kissinger, who supported the sale of arms to Saudi Arabia, told
the Senate Foreign Relations Committee that Israel should be
sold more planes and that constraints should be imposed on the
deployment and equipment sold to Saudi Arabia. According to
the former secretary, the Ford administration had discussed sell-

ing Israel a number of planes that "were several orders of magnitude above" those offered by the Carter Administration. He suggested selling Israel an additional twenty F-15s. Carter was reluctant to increase the number of jets for Israel, but was hoping to avoid a confrontation with Congress, so Vance told the committee the next day that Israel would be offered twenty more F-15s to bring the total to thirty-five. With previous sales of twenty-five F-15s, Israel now would receive the same number Saudi Arabia was obtaining.[36] The administration also gave the Israelis private assurances that additional arms would be forthcoming. In the following months, Israel completed arms transactions worth nearly $900 million, signed a memorandum of understanding that called for cooperative research and development projects, and secured an agreement to have the delivery of F-16s accelerated.[37]

Kissinger's suggestion that limits be placed on the use of the F-15s was also accepted by the administration, and Secretary Brown presented the Senate with assurances that Saudi Arabia accepted the restrictions. The concessions won over some of the undecided, but did not dampen the Israeli lobby's resolve to block the sale. Representative Rosenthal, for example, said the additional airplanes for Israel were not really a concession because they would have gotten them anyway. AIPAC's Amitay told the Senate Foreign Relations Committee that no sale was preferable to the package, and Senator Javits called for a reduction in the number of F-15s for Saudi Arabia.[38] The opponents succeeded in passing a resolution of disapproval in the House International Relations Committee, but the real showdown was expected in the Senate.

As the vote of the Senate Foreign Relations Committee approached, both sides hardened their positions. The Conference of Presidents sent a telegram on 10 May to every member of Congress, opposing both the original and the compromise package as harmful to the national interest, a threat to the security of Israel, and an impediment to peace negotiations.[39] Meanwhile, the White House was not too quietly framing the issue as a test of who would determine U.S. foreign policy, the Prime Minister of Israel and the Israeli lobby, or the president.[40]

On 11 May, prior to the vote of the Senate Foreign Relations Committee, President Carter promised to sell, or even grant Israel the additional twenty F-15s. In addition, he gave assurances that he would not sell Saudi Arabia auxiliary fuel tanks that would allow the Saudi F-15s to fly to Israel, or bomb racks and air-to-air missiles that could give the F-15s offensive capabilities. The Saudis, he said, had agreed not to base the airplanes within striking distance of Israel. Finally, he said that he would not sell AWACS or "any other systems or armaments that could increase the range or enhance the ground attack capability of the F-15."[41]

Despite these assurances, the Senate Foreign Relations Committee vote on the resolution of disapproval ended in a tie, 8-8, with six Democrats voting against the administration, including Senator Church who had taken the lead in negotiations with the White House. The committee then made the unusual decision to send the package to the floor despite the fact that the tie vote had meant the resolution of disapproval had been defeated. The decision was dismaying to the administration because it had hoped to avoid a floor fight.

The day after the committee vote, Saudi Foreign Minister Saud told Walter Cronkite that "Saudi Arabia would only accept a limitation of F-15 deployment 'that is of general applicability' and is not aimed individually at Saudi Arabia for a specific requirement."[42] The next day, the administration again claimed that Saudi Arabia would not base its planes within striking distance of Israel, despite Saud's statement to the contrary. Carter sent a letter to every senator in which he said that a veto would be a "devastating blow" to Sadat, and would undermine the forces of "moderation" in the region. Carter also tried to persuade senators that the sale was really in Israel's best interests because of the need to fulfill prior commitments and to prevent "the intrusion of hostile influences" into the region.[43]

In what was no doubt an effort to support the president's case, Saudi King Khalid wrote a letter to Carter claiming the need for F-15s to blunt "Communist expansion in the area" and assuring the president that they would only be used to defend the kingdom. "I believe the Kingdom's long and increasingly close relationship with the United States is," the king said, "even with all its proven mutual benefits, still at only an early stage of reciprocal worth."[44] Ironically, one of the "benefits" the sale's supporters claimed America derived from this relationship, moderation of oil prices, was shown to be of dubious value two days earlier when Sheik

Yamani announced that his country had reduced oil production to absorb the market surplus, and thus prevent the decline of petroleum prices.[45]

The day before the vote, Brown, Vance, and Carter all called wavering senators, and the Israeli Embassy countered with a statement reiterating the view that the planes posed "a serious danger to Israel's security." Meanwhile, 66 percent of the public opposed the sale, according to a Harris poll.[46]

Finally, on 16 May, in what Senator Mike Gravel described as a "litmus test" for future support from Jews, the Senate voted 54–44 against the resolution to block the sale. The Republicans voted 26–11 with the president, but a majority of the Democrats, 33–28, voted *against* Carter. Perhaps the most important vote for the sale was cast by Senator Abraham Ribicoff. As a Jew and a liberal, Ribicoff's vote was seen as providing a protective cover for other liberals favoring the deal but concerned about the reaction of Jewish constituents.[47] In fact, Ribicoff's vote was only one example of how divisive the issue had been. Not only had Jews taken opposite sides, but also conservatives like James Allen and Harry Byrd, liberals such as George McGovern and Frank Church; and the Majority Leader Robert Byrd and Majority Whip Alan Cranston. The Israeli lobby had taken on the administration, the Arab lobby, and much of the Senate, including some traditional supporters, and lost the battle.

After the vote, former Israeli Prime Minister Yitzhak Rabin, in the tradition of the "out" party, called the sales to the Arabs the "greatest setback" for Israel in the United States in more than a decade. Begin saw it as an attempt to impose peace terms on Israel.[48] Sadat, on the other hand, saw the sale as "proof of the American people's support for President Carter's peace efforts in the Middle East." Saudi Arabia's state radio said the vote indicated "the Jewish lobby in the United States is weakening"[49] and the NAAA declared victory over its nemesis:

> The political conclusion to be drawn from the vote is that the Israeli lobby lost its first major fight and its apparent veto over American policy toward the Arab world. . . . The vote confirmed that the Israeli lobby is subject to political limits. This reality opens the door to a more constructive and balanced American approach to the Middle East.[50]

The statement was correct in regard to the demonstration of limitations, which, in fact, always existed, to the Israeli lobby's influence. But it was mistaken, as subsequent events have shown, in assuming this meant a change in U.S. policy toward the Middle East. True, this was the biggest arms sale, with the most sophisticated weapons ever offered to an Arab nation, but the Israeli lobby *had* forced a compromise on its content. The United States also remained committed to Israel's security. It should be remembered that the arms package also included fifteen F-15s (and the promise of twenty more) and seventy-five F-16s for Israel.

The Saudis Come Back For More

In order to persuade Congress to accept the sale of F-15s to Saudi Arabia in 1978, the Carter administration had to offer the compromise that the package would not include bomb racks or missiles. On 6 March 1981, the State Department explained that it was reneging on the Carter administration's earlier commitment because the instability of the region had increased the danger of Soviet penetration. In order to forestall opposition, President Reagan agreed to drop the sale of bomb racks, and offer Israel an additional $600 million in credits and the opportunity to buy more F-15s.[51] This mollified Israeli officials who were not anxious to pick a fight, especially one they were likely to lose, with a president considered to be a close friend.

In a demonstration of its independence, the Israeli lobby challenged the idea of selling additional weapons to Saudi Arabia on the grounds that it would be "harmful to American interests, dangerous to the cause of Middle East peace and threatening to our country's friend and fellow-democracy, Israel. . . . "[52] Opposition to the sale of F-15 enhancements remained relatively muted, however, until 2 April when the administration decided to add Airborne Warning and Control System (AWACS) radar planes to the deal. After press leaks revealed the new proposal, over 100 congressmen made speeches opposing the sale and an Associated Press poll found only 20 senators willing to support it.[53]

The State Department tried to allay congressional fears by claiming that AWACS would not threaten Israel, because they would be used primarily to protect Saudi oil fields and would have various restrictions placed on their use, but it was hard for the Israeli lobby to accept the argument that the AWACS were not a threat to Israel. Moreover, the lobby feared the precedent of providing the Arabs with a weapons system superior to anything provided to Israel. The Israeli government also reversed its earlier position and vocally opposed the sale after the AWACS were added. With the prospect of an all-out fight over the sale looming, Senate Majority Leader Howard Baker advised the president to postpone the sale until after the president's economic package was passed. This provided the Arab and Israeli lobbies time to mobilize their supporters.

Lobbying Fervor

Despite a deterioration of United States-Israel relations, caused by Israel's bombing of Beirut and an Iraqi nuclear reactor during the summer, AIPAC succeeded in collecting signatures from majorities in both Houses opposing the AWACS sale. Proponents of the sale were equally active. In an exhaustive investigation of the AWACS debate, Steven Emerson concluded:

> The Saudi lobbying campaign resulted in one of the most successful manipulations of American business and American foreign policy ever attempted by a foreign power. Saudi Arabia demanded and received the aggressive support of the most powerful corporations in America. Scores of other business interests joined the campaign in order to protect existing petro-dollar contracts or to obtain new ones. Still thousands of others were indirectly induced to join by pressure from their own domestic suppliers, purchasers, or business partners. And many others with no commercial stake in the sale, or even in Saudi Arabia, jumped into the lobbying fray because they were prevailed upon to believe that not upsetting the Saudis was vital to the U.S. economy.[54]

The oil industry lobbied hard for the sale, with Mobil spending more than a half million dollars on full page advertisements extolling the virtues of the economic partnership between the United States and Saudi Arabia. By far the biggest lobbying effort, however, was orchestrated by Boeing, the main contractor for AWACS, and United Technologies, which had $100 million at stake. The presidents of Boeing and United Technologies sent out more than 6,500 telegrams to subsidiaries, vendors, and suppliers all over the country urging them to support the sale.[55]

The single most effective lobbyist for the sale was probably Frederick Dutton. His most significant contribution was to transform the debate on AWACS from substantive issues to a personal one; that is, he was able to frame the issue as a fight between the president of the United States and the prime minister of Israel. As he told the *New York Times*, senators who opposed the sale would have to explain "how they will run foreign policy now that they have chosen Begin over Reagan."[56]

Despite the Arab lobby's efforts, there was strong congressional opposition to the sale. The sale's opponents initiated a resolution of disapproval, which said that the sale could lead to the compromise of American technology, would reward Saudi Arabia for its refusal to join the Camp David peace process and financial assistance of the PLO, and contradict earlier assurances that the capabilities of Saudi F-15s would not be enhanced. That same week, Prime Minister Begin arrived in Washington. The president made another attempt to hold out a carrot to stifle Israeli opposition to the sale. In this case, the two leaders reached a "strategic understanding" said to consist of naval exercises, storage of medical supplies in Israel, and joint planning against an outside attack.[57] Although strategic cooperation implicitly depended on the AWACS deal being approved, Begin remained adamantly opposed to the sale.

On 14 September, Reagan became personally involved in the lobbying effort and met with twenty-seven senators at the White House and, on 1 October he held a press conference in which his statements of support of AWACS were seen as a direct challenge to the Israeli lobby. "American security interests must remain our internal responsibility," he said. Then, in an obvious reference to Israel, he added: "It is not the business of other nations to make American foreign policy." He also tried to reassure Israel's supporters that the sale posed no threat to Israel, contradicting the statements of Israel's Prime Minister, Defense Minister, and military experts.

The Israelis listened closely to the president's views and some Foreign Ministry officials recommended that Israel avoid an all-out fight with a president considered to be a friend of Israel. AIPAC, American Jewish leaders, and congressional opponents of the sale conveyed their concern about the apparent weakening of the Israeli position, directly to the government. "They did not want to see the rug pulled out from under their feet."[58] Thus, the battle lines were drawn in what became widely seen as "Reagan vs. Begin."

Let The Hearings Begin

In his Senate testimony, Secretary of State Alexander Haig argued the sale was important for the administration's desire to "develop a strategy that can move the peace process forward and protect our vital interests in an unstable area exposed not only to historic Arab-Israeli rivalries, but increasingly to threats from the Soviet Union and its proxies." With regard to those who feared AWACS posed a threat to Israel or might fall into enemy hands, Haig assured the Foreign Relations Committee that there would be limitations placed on their use, and that elaborate security measures would be employed to safeguard the equipment.

During the hearings, Middle East events helped complicate the domestic issue. The administration claimed that an Iranian air attack on the oil facilities in Kuwait provided evidence of the need to provide the Arabs with the capacity to defend their petroleum resources. The assassination of President Anwar Sadat was also seen as a reminder that U.S. policy should be based on a foundation of a mutuality of interests and could not depend on particular leaders.[59]

Although there was an intense lobbying campaign taking place behind the scenes, few of the participants in that battle testified at the hearings on the sale. The NAAA's representatives reiterated the administration line that the sale would not threaten any other countries, that Saudi Arabia played a major peacemaking role in the Middle East, and that Saudi Arabia was "the major force for price moderation within OPEC."[60] AIPAC's Thomas Dine countered that:

1. There has been and is no Saudi quid pro quo to U.S. foreign policy in the Middle East.

2. It is dangerous to the United States to transfer sophisticated defense technologies to arm an inherently unstable government.
3. An unbridled arms race involving the most advanced weaponry that now exists in the American, European, and Soviet arsenals is unfolding, which undermines all peace efforts.
4. Selling F-15 enhancement items, such as the AIM-9L Sidewinder missiles, would violate explicit assurances provided to the Congress.
5. The sale is a threat to Israel's security.[61]

As expected, the sale was overwhelmingly rejected by the House 301–111. In the Senate, it also appeared that the sale was in serious trouble. As late as 23 October, the *New York Times* counted fifty senators opposed to the sale and only forty in favor, with the rest undecided. The day before the Senate vote, however, in the most dramatic reversal of the debate, Roger Jepsen, one of the original sponsors of the resolution of disapproval, announced he was switching his vote, and eight other senators announced they were voting for the sale.

The final vote was 52–48, rejecting the resolution of disapproval and thereby permitting the sale to proceed. Eight senators, one a Democrat who had co-sponsored the resolution of disapproval, switched their votes. Edward Kennedy commented afterwards: "In my 19 years up here I have never seen such 180 degree turns on the part of so many senators."[62]

The Arab lobby hailed the AWACS sale as a major victory over the Israeli lobby. According to Levins: "That AWACS vote represented nothing less than a revolution within the Capitol's established order. Things were not likely ever to be the same again. The Arab lobby had established itself as a major force in American politics and was continuing to consolidate and strengthen its position."[63]

Was the outcome really a victory for the Arab lobby? Strictly in terms of obtaining the desired outcome it would have to be classified as such, but it was not the Arab lobby that was responsible for the result, it was the president.

The Power of Executive Persuasion

"AWACS: He Does It Again" was the caption accompanying the president's picture on the cover of *Time* magazine the week after the vote. The president had indeed done it again, snatching victory from what appeared just a few days earlier to be certain defeat. Even AIPAC's Dine admitted that it was the president who was responsible for the sale's passage, calling it "a vote of confidence in President Reagan himself," and a response to the president's "appeal that if the sale were defeated, his effectiveness would be impaired."[64]

The turning point occurred when James Baker began to shuttle senators in to see the president. Beginning in September, the president met with seventy-five senators and held private discussions with twenty-two Republicans, fourteen of whom voted for the sale. He also met with twenty-two Democrats and convinced ten to vote his way. In the week before the vote, Reagan made twenty-six telephone calls to plead his case and had private meetings with seventeen senators between Monday morning and 2:00 P.M. the day of the vote.[65] "When the President started calling up senators and inviting them down to the White House," Senator Robert Packwood said, "they came back converted."[66]

One of the most important factors in persuading uncommitted senators to support the sale, and opponents to switch, was the letter Reagan sent to Congress promising that before delivering the AWACS to Saudi Arabia he would "certify" to the Senate that he had obtained agreements from the Saudis that would prevent the use of the planes against Israel or the compromise of its technology. The letter also appeared to commit the president to obtaining "substantial assistance" from Saudi Arabia in moving the peace process forward.

There were also counter-pressures. Of the twenty Republicans who signed the resolution of disapproval, six were up for reelection in "Jewish" states; two were Jews; and two were from New York and Florida. Of those ten, only one (Hayakawa of California) voted for the sale. This supports the argument that the informal component (i.e., public opinion and voting behavior) of the Israeli lobby does exert influence, even on Republicans.

There were ten other Republicans who had signed the letter of disapproval. Except for Robert Packwood, all were first term senators who had been swept into office by Reagan's victory. Besides this electoral debt, the senators were subject to various pressures, and all but Robert Kasten and opposition leader Pack-wood succumbed.

Several senators announced they were supporting the president after receiving "top secret" assurances regarding Israel's security. Others were given more tangible reasons to switch their votes. For example, Slade Gorton received a promise from the White House to support an appropriation to renovate a public health hospital in Seattle, Charles Grassley found that his request for the appointment of his candidate for U.S. Attorney in Iowa was being expedited, and Montana's John Melcher was enticed by support for a coal conversion facility near Butte. When William Cohen of Maine told his colleagues that he was switching his vote to help Israel, everyone laughed. "Come on, Bill," one senator replied, "just say you sold out, but don't give me that stuff about saving Israel."[67]

By far the most important and surprising reversal was made by Roger Jepsen, who had given an eloquent speech to AIPAC's policy conference explaining the religious and political basis for his support for Israel and opposition to the AWACS sale. A week before the vote, Jepsen broke into tears when explaining the conflicting pressures on him to his colleagues. The day before the vote, he switched because he said he has received "highly classified" information from the president that eased his fears about the AWACS' threat to Israel. "A vote for the sale," he said, "is a vote for my President and his successful conduct of foreign policy."[68]

There was a little more to Jepsen's decision. As one White House official explained: "We just beat his brains out." Jepsen protested that he was one of the president's most loyal followers, but he was told that Reagan had to win the AWACS vote and that his vote was needed. If he did not vote with the president, he would get no further cooperation from the White House. "We stood him up in front of an open grave and said he could jump in if he wanted to," the official said. Meanwhile, the White House was putting out calls to people in Iowa that, in turn, generated calls and letters to Jepsen. Additional pressure was put on Jepsen indirectly by Iowa's other senator. When Grassley switched his vote, Jepsen faced the prospect of becoming the junior senator from Iowa. Although the change would have been only in the eyes of the administration, that would be enough to deny Jepsen the patronage and ceremonial advantages of being the leader of the state's delegation.[69]

The administration also tried to obtain Democratic support. The only Democrat to switch, Nebraska's Edward Zorinsky, had refused to accept a telephone call from the president before the Foreign Relations Committee vote. He said he did not "want to get caught with the Gipper in the locker room at half time." Later, he did meet with the president who told him that King Hussein was coming to visit in a few days and asked: "How can I convince foreign leaders that I'm in command when I can't sell five airplanes?" Zorinsky left saying he had never been subjected to a "full-court press like this before." There were other pressures on Zorinsky as well, such as the discovery that the lampposts in Riyadh were made in Nebraska. Demonstrating that being Jewish does not guarantee support of the Israeli lobby position, Zorinsky also voted for the sale.[70]

The administration was not always successful in its lobbying campaign. Dennis DeConcini of Arizona, for example, was told that Reagan would not campaign against him, but he voted against the sale anyway.[71] Democrat Patrick Leahy was subject to pressure from both sides because he had remained uncommitted. After a forty-five minute discussion at the White House, Leahy told Reagan that he would go home to Vermont and consider his vote. "When you're walking those fields and looking over those beautiful mountains," the president said, "think of my face up there in the sky looking down on you." Leahy replied: "I'll have to go to the Capitol physician first to get my arm put back in the socket."[72] Leahy voted against the sale.

The president did not restrict his lobbying to the use of positive reinforcement; he also tried punishment. For example, about fifteen minutes after Rudy Boschwitz of Minnesota cast the only Republican vote against the AWACS sale in the Senate Foreign Relations Committee, he learned that an Air Force base in Duluth would be closed.[73]

In the end, the president succeeded in swaying enough senators to win the vote. What other evidence is there that the Arab lobby was not responsible? Perhaps the strongest evidence is that the lobby has failed to achieve any of its objectives since the AWACS vote. Contrary to Levins' analysis of the outcome, there was no revolution in the balance of lobbying power, with the Israeli lobby not only achieving several of its objectives, but also succeeding in stopping the Reagan administration from selling any additional weapons to Arab states for the remainder of the president's first term.

Summary

The two cases examined here provide excellent examples of the interaction between the three models of decision-making. The realist model is represented by the efforts of both Carter and Reagan to frame the issue of arms sales to Saudi Arabia in terms of national security interests of the United States. Traditionally, Congress is reluctant to deny the president what he feels is necessary to protect American national security and, in fact, had never disapproved a proposed arms sale. These cases illustrate, however, the differences in perception of the national interest, with majorities in the House in each instance on record opposing the sales, and near majorities in the Senate ultimately voting against them. The realist model does not explain this opposition or the bargaining process that the administrations were forced to engage in to assure approval of the sales.

In order to understand the willingness of the Congress to challenge the president in each instance, it is necessary to take into account the role of domestic politics in the decision-making process. In the absence of the Israeli lobby it is highly unlikely that there would have been the same degree of opposition to the proposed sales. Although congressmen, like the president, phrased their opposition in terms of various security concerns, the primary source of opposition was from supporters of the lobby who saw the sales as threats to the U.S. interest in maintaining the security of Israel. The existence of this opposition, along with the fact that the presidents in each case, particularly the AWACS sale, were barely able to get their proposals approved, also provides evidence of lobby influence.

The exercise of influence on both sides was most clearly demonstrated in the AWACS case, where several senators were induced to switch their intended votes within days of the vote. The three main reasons that senators switched their votes from disapproval in the AWACS case were deference to the president's foreign policy-making prerogative, the conviction by Republicans that they should support "their" president, and deals made by the president to secure support. The president's capacity to lobby and offer incentives to congressmen to entice their support was evident in the deals struck with senators like Melcher and Gorton, and in the threats applied directly to Boschwitz and less directly to Jepsen. Although there are no specific examples of bargains made by Carter, he was also forced to engage in "logrolling" to obtain the support he needed. In addition, many Senate Democrats felt obligated to support their president, while other senators followed the tradition of deferring to the White House.

In both sales, the fact that there was a controversy and an uncertain vote is testimony to the Israeli lobby's influence. Moreover, that influence was used, not only to force modifications in the proposed sales, but also to induce both administrations to provide compensatory aid to Israel.

The F-15 sale did mark a change in the balance of lobbying power, however, as the Arab lobby became more effective in communicating its position. Although the balance did not shift in the Arab lobby's favor, there was a significant change in the perception of the lobby on Capitol Hill. By 1981, the lobby was even better organized and increasingly active; and therefore would be expected to be more influential than in the past. One of the main reasons the Arab lobby was more successful in getting its message across in 1981, was the unprecedented involvement of business groups in lobbying activities. Not only did the business component of the lobby take a more visible role, but there was also a successful campaign to build a coalition of businesses normally uninvolved or disinterested in Middle East politics. The Arab lobby has been unable to hold that coalition together on subsequent issues. By contrast, the Israeli lobby in the two arms sales cases was relatively unsuccessful in mobilizing a coalition to fight the sale, but is still able to draw on a wide range of religious, ethnic, and social groups for support on most issues.

The presidents were successful in pushing their proposals through, primarily because they were able to convince a majority of senators that arming the Saudis was in the national interest. International events, the bombing of Kuwait and Sadat's assassination, helped reinforce Reagan's argument. Does this success support the leadership model?

Actually, the outcomes in the arms sales cases were more a reflection of the power of the presidency as an institution, than differences in the leaders occupying the White House. The United States has been supplying Saudi Arabia with weapons since the 1950s, and Gerald Ford sold a large number of Maverick missiles to the Saudis prior to Jimmy Carter's election. Carter represented a different party, had an entirely different ideology, and pursued a completely different foreign policy, yet was consistent in his willingness to sell arms to Saudi Arabia. In his 1976 campaign, in fact, Carter had criticized Ford's sale of missiles to the Saudis, he emphasized Christian values and human rights, neither of which was particularly consistent with Saudi policy, and he had adopted a policy to limit all U.S. arms sales.

In 1980, Ronald Reagan ran a campaign that repudiated Carter's policies. His party, ideology, and foreign policy were also very different from those of Carter. In particular, Reagan was known as a staunch supporter of Israel and was very concerned about possible losses of U.S. technology to American enemies; nevertheless, he too was consistent on this particular policy. Consequently, it would have been difficult to predict in advance that Carter or Reagan would have been willing to sell advanced weapons to the Saudis.

The leadership model tends to rely heavily on ex post facto analyses, so it is possible to explain the willingness of Carter and Reagan to propose the two arms sales, using hindsight. In this case, the two different leaders could arrive at similar policies by different means. Carter, for example, was obsessed with the issue of energy, so his actions might be explained in terms of his belief in the need to insure the security of U.S. energy supplies. Reagan's willingness to risk the loss of AWACS technology, and an increase in the threat to Israel, might be explained by his anti-Soviet foreign policy orientation; that is, the need to improve the Saudis' defense capability to counter a perceived Soviet threat.

We are interested in more than the question of how the policy was arrived at, however; we also want to know if a policy is likely to be adopted. At this point in history, Carter and his staff have been generally considered to have had poor relations and success with Congress, while Reagan was extremely successful. Although both presidents were coming off major legislative victories, Carter on the Panama Canal Treaty and Reagan on his economic policy, Carter's insensitivity toward Congress was reflected by his insistence on presenting the Saudi sale as a package, something even members of his own party opposed. In addition, Carter was very unpopular at the time of the sale, his popularity having reached its nadir, so it would have been difficult to predict Carter's success on the basis of his leadership. Ronald Reagan's ability to push the sale through might have been easier to predict, given not only his legislative momentum, but also the fact that his public approval rating was well over 50 percent, and that many of the freshman Republican senators owed their seats to the president and could be called upon, as they were, for their support.

In the cases of arms sales to the Saudis, then, the realist model was the most useful in explaining the presidents' victories, but the pluralist model helps explain the degree of opposition the presidents faced and the compromises they were forced to make. The leadership model provides some insight into the motivations of each president for their proposals, but does not provide a reliable means of predicting their ability to overcome the opposition those proposals encountered.

Notes

1. James Barber, *The Pulse of Politics* (NY: W.W. Norton and Co., 1980), 204.
2. *Near East Report* (22 February 1978), 29; Steven L. Spiegel, *The Other Arab-Israeli Conflict* (IL: University of Chicago Press, 1985), 347.
3. Melvin Urofsky, "President Carter—A New Era?" *Midstream* (January 1977), 47.
4. *New York Times* (20 October 1977); Spiegel, *The Other Arab-Israeli Conflict*, 1985, 326.
5. Rehavia Yakovee, "Arms for Oil—Oil for Arms: An Analysis of President Carter's 1978 Planes 'Package Deal' Sale to Egypt, Israel, and Saudi Arabia," Claremont, Ph.D. Diss., 1983, 26–8 and 99–100; Congressional Quarterly, "New U.S. Plane Sales to Middle East Will Test Hill Feeling on Peace Moves," *Weekly Report* (8 April 1978), 837.

62   The Water's Edge and Beyond

6. *New York Times* (1 May 1978).
7. *New York Times* (15 February 1978); *Near East Report* (15 February 1978), 29; *State Department Bulletin* (March 1978), 37; Spiegel, 1985, 347.
8. Thomas Frank and Edward Weisband, *Foreign Policy By Congress* (NY: Oxford University Press, 1979), 107.
9. *Near East Report* (22 February 1978), 29.
10. William Lanouette, "The Many Faces of the Jewish Lobby in America, *National Journal* (13 May 1978), 749.
11. Henry Waxman, "Making A Mess of the Middle East Stew," *Los Angeles Times* (23 February 1978).
12. Hoag Levins, *Arab Reach* (NY: Doubleday, 1983), 10–11.
13. Lanouette, "Many Faces of the Jewish Lobby," 753.
14. Rehavia Yakovee, 84; *New York Times* (2 April and 12 May 1978).
15. *Near East Report*, (15 March 1978). See also Siegel's op-ed piece written after his resignation: "Security Means Life," *New York Times* (26 March 1978).
16. *New York Times* (19 March 1981); Lanouette, "Many Faces of the Jewish Lobby," 752.
17. Zbigniew Brzezinski, "A Plan for Peace in the Middle East," *New Leader* (7 July 1974); Brzezinski, et al, "Peace in an International Framework," *Foreign Policy* (Summer 1975).
18. Rehavia Yakovee, 60–1 from the *Los Angeles Times* (19 May 1978) and *Jerusalem Post* (21–27 December 1980).
19. *State Department Bulletin* (April 1978), 22.
20. *Near East Report* (15 March 1978), 41.
21. *New York Times* (11 March 1978); *Near East Report* (15 March 1978), 41. Twenty-one of thirty-seven members of House International Relations Committee, fifteen Republicans and six Democrats, signed the letter, as did twelve of sixteen members of the Senate Foreign Relations Committee.
22. *New York Times* (16 and 23 March 1978).
23. *New York Times* (22, 23, 25, 29 April 1978); Frank and Weisband, *Foreign Policy by Congress*, 108.
24. *New York Times* (30 April 1978).
25. Rehavia Yakovee, 32–3. Speech on 15 February 1978.
26. Carter speech, 5 May 1978. *State Department Bulletin* (July 1978), 20.
27. Rehavia Yakovee, "Arms for Oil," 72–74, 83, 311.
28. *New York Times* (8 May 1978).
29. Rehavia Yakovee, 72–3, 81–3, 221–2; *Near East Report* (10 May 1978), 79.
30. Rehavia Yakovee, "Arms for Oil," 75–76, 86.
31. Congressional Quarterly, *Almanac* (DC: CQ, 1978), 410.
32. Rehavia Yakovee, "Arms for Oil," 86.
33. *CQ Almanac*, 410–411.

34. Rehavia Yakovee, "Arms for Oil," 86.
35. *CQ Almanac*, 410–411.
36. *New York Times* (9–10 May 1978); Frank and Weisband, *Foreign Policy by Congress*, 109.
37. David Pollock, *The Politics of Pressure* (CT: Greenwood Press, 1982), 239–44.
38. *New York Times* (11 May 1978); *Near East Report* (10 May 1978), 80.
39. Presidents Conference, *Annual Report* (Year ending 31 March 1979), 5.
40. Pollock, *The Politics of Pressure*, 239; Ghassan Bishara, "The Middle East Arms Package," *Journal of Palestine Studies* (Summer 1978), 78.
41. Steven Emerson, *The American House of Saud* (NY: Franklin Watts, 1985), 174; Congressional Quarterly, "Congressional Role in Arms Sales . . . Has Become Scrutiny But Not a Veto, *Weekly* (10 April 1982), 799; Yakovee, "Arms for Oil," 65–7.
42. Ibid., 313.
43. *New York Times* (13 May 1978).
44. *New York Times* (14 May 1978).
45. Anti-Defamation League, *The U.S.-Saudi Relationship* (NY: ADL, Spring 1982), p. 12 quoted from the *Washington Post* (11 May 1978).
46. *New York Times* (14, 15, 17, 24 May 1978).
47. Frank and Weisband, *Foreign Policy by Congress*, 108.
48. Pollock, *The Politics of Pressure*, 239.
49. *Near East Report* (17 May 1978), 85.
50. Congressional Quarterly, *The Washington Lobby* (DC: CQ, October 1979), 150.
51. Pollock, *The Politics of Pressure*, 277; Steven Emerson *The American House of Saud*, (NY: Franklin Watts, 1985), 177–8; *New York Times* (26 February 1981).
52. Presidents Conference *Annual Report* (Year ending March 31, 1981), 18.
53. Emerson, *The American House of Saud*, 178–9.
54. Steven Emerson, "The Petrodollar Connection," *The New Republic* (17 February 1982), reprint; also Emerson, *The American House of Saud*.
55. Emerson, *The American House of Saud*, 213.
56. *New York Times* (18 September 1981); *Near East Report*, (25 September 1981), 178.
57. *New York Times* (11 September 1981).
58. Wolf Blitzer, "The AIPAC Formula," *Moment* (November 1981), reprint.
59. James Buckley, Under Secretary of State testimony, U.S. Congress. Senate Foreign Relations Committee, Hearings, October 1981 [henceforth SFRC], 32.

60. Ibid., 145–52.
61. Ibid., 159.
62. Emerson, *The American House of Saud*, 182.
63. Hoag Levins, *Arab Reach* (NY: Doubleday, 1983), 3.
64. *Near East Report* (6 November 1981), 203.
65. Walter Isaacson, "The Man With The Golden Arm," *Time* (9 November 1981), 25; George J. Church, "AWACS: He Does It Again," *Time* (9 November 1981), 12–3.
66. *New York Times* (29 October 1981).
67. Isaacson, "Man With Golden Arm," 25–26; John Rourke, *Congress and the Presidency in U.S. Foreign Policymaking* (CO: Westview Press, 1983), 260; James Kelly, "In A World Without Sadat," *Time* (26 October 1981), 21; John Hyde, "How the White House Won Jepsen's AWACS Vote," *Des Moines Register* (29 October 1981), 1; *New York Times* (29 October 1981).
68. Isaacson, "Man With Golden Arm," 25; Church, "AWACS," 13.
69. Hyde, "How the White House Won," 1.
70. Isaacson, "Man With Golden Arm," 25; Emerson, *The American House of Saud*, 208–9.
71. Kelly, 21.
72. Isaacson, "In A World Without Sadat," 26–31.
73. *New York Times* (18 October 1981).

3

The Jackson-Vanik Amendment

The "twin pillars" of detente, according to Henry Kissinger, were "resistance to Soviet expansionism and a willingness to negotiate on concrete issues, on the concept of deterrence and a readiness to explore the principles of coexistence."[1] The development of economic relations were seen as a means of promoting coexistence and easing tensions. It was also hoped that by encouraging the Soviet Union to become more dependent on the international economic system, it would have an incentive to moderate its political activities.

As Soviet behavior began to meet the requirements of "moderation," negotiations on East-West trade started to expand. The pace of negotiations accelerated as the 1972 presidential campaign approached, with Richard Nixon conscious of the desire of U.S. businessmen to increase trade with the Soviet Union. More importantly, Kissinger hoped to obtain Soviet cooperation in his efforts to negotiate a peace settlement in Vietnam by holding out the carrot of increased trade. Less than two weeks before the election, the United States signed a trade agreement with the Soviet Union providing, among other things, Most Favored Nation (MFN) status. Despite the fact that the agreement represented the break in the Cold War long sought by many members of Congress, it was to undergo a two-year fight for approval.

Congress was reluctant to support the Trade Reform Act because it considered the Soviet Union a repressive regime that denied basic human rights to its citizens. There was a particular concern for Soviet Jews who were not only persecuted within the country, but also prohibited from immigrating to Israel or, for that matter, anywhere else.

In February 1972, a bill was introduced to authorize $85 million to help Israel absorb Soviet Jews. The issue of Soviet Jewry was further spotlighted by a resolution adopted in a lopsided vote (359–2) by the House, calling on the Soviet Union to permit the free expression of ideas, the exercise of religion, and the right of emigration.[2] On 30 April there were large demonstrations in ninety cities calling on the president to raise the issue of emigration with Soviet leaders at his forthcoming summit meeting. Over one hundred congressmen signed a letter circulated by Rep. Jack Kemp asking the president to protest the treatment of Soviet Jews.[3] The real catalyst for future legislation, however, was the Soviets' imposition on 8 August 1972 of a "diploma" tax. This tax was to be applied to all emigrants who had received a higher education and was so exorbitant people holding advanced degrees could not afford to pay.

Up until the imposition of the "diploma" tax, Jewish organizations had not given Congress or the administration a clear signal of how they should respond to the persecution of Soviet Jews. This quickly began to change. On 15 August, Soviet Jewish activists warned that the decree would create "a new category of human beings—the slaves of the twentieth century." Senator Abraham Ribicoff was joined by over seventy of his colleagues in protesting against the tax and threatening to oppose trade agreements with the Soviet Union.[4] Sy Kenen, the executive director of AIPAC, meanwhile contacted Morris Amitay, then Senator Ribicoff's aide, and suggested that he invite the legislative assistants in both Houses to develop a proposal in conjunction with Jerry Goodman of the National Conference on Soviet Jewry (NCSJ), and Yehudah Hellman of the Presidents Conference. It was at this meeting that Senator Henry Jackson's aide, Richard Perle, suggested an amendment denying Most Favored Nation status to a nation that denies its citizens the right to emigrate, and which imposes more than nominal exit fees.[5]

The idea quickly became a campaign issue. At a Soviet Jewry rally (30 Aug.), Democratic presidential candidate George McGovern said that Soviet Jews "should not be forgotten when talking about peace and economic agreements."[6] Later he told the Presidents Conference he would fight to prevent granting MFN to the Soviet Union unless they changed their emigration policy. Nixon, meanwhile, was interested in preventing the Soviet Jewry issue from becoming a factor in the campaign. The president's campaign strategists had been confident that Nixon could double the 17 percent share of the Jewish vote he received in 1968, but after McGovern's salvos and the adoption by thirty-five states of legislation denouncing Soviet persecution, Nixon found himself scrambling to short-circuit the issue. At the end of September, the president met with a group of thirty-two Jewish supporters and assured them he was working through diplomatic channels to ease the plight of Soviet Jews and that he would not engage in "harsh confrontations."[7]

After the September meeting of legislative aides, when the decision to tie emigration to MFN was finalized, Senator Henry Jackson addressed the NCSJ and received their endorsement for the proposal. "The Jewish organizations entrusted their cause to Jackson," Stern explains. "Clearly it was a reversal of the popular image of the Jewish lobby twisting a Senator's arm."[8] Perle and Amitay circulated a "Dear Colleague" letter and quickly signed up sixty-two sponsors. "Why did so many people sign the amendment?" one senator asked rhetorically, "Because there is no political advantage in not signing."[9] After reaching seventy-five sponsors, Jackson introduced the amendment.

Kissinger was adamantly opposed to tying the trade agreement to Soviet emigration policies. Instead, he believed in the efficacy of "quiet diplomacy." Ordinarily, Kissinger's foreign policy view would not entertain the possibility of extracting voluntary concessions from the Soviets, but he apparently became quite confident when he saw signs of flexibility. He claims his quiet diplomacy was successful, pointing to the increase in Soviet Jewish emigration from 400 in 1968 to 35,000 in 1973.[10] Talbott suggests the increase was due to Soviet manipulation; that is, "the leaders in Moscow have recognized from the outset that Jewish emigration from the U.S.S.R. is a more volatile, significant, and indeed exploitable issue in the context of *American* domestic politics than in their own." Thus, they decided to help Kissinger undermine opponents of detente by easing emigration and allowing the secretary to take the credit.[11]

There is evidence to support Talbott's contention; for example, the day the trade agreement was signed with the United States, the Soviets allowed 175 Jewish families to emigrate without having to pay the "diploma" tax. The Soviets, and many other observers, apparently thought the Senate legislation was meant to be a warning, rather than a serious initiative. This judgement was based on the expectation that Congress would adjourn before any trade bill could reach the floor of the Senate, and the fact that there had been no serious effort to introduce a Jackson-type amendment in the House. The Soviets took no chances, however, and made an additional gesture in an effort to forestall any legislation in the future. On 29 December, the Kremlin announced that it had modified the "diploma" tax by exempting people fifty-five and older, and by reducing the payment to correspond to the number of years that the would-be emigrant had worked for the state. The indications were, however, that no more concessions would be forthcoming.[12]

The election year ended with Richard Nixon winning in a landslide. The president succeeded in his goal of doubling the percentage of the Jewish vote, receiving 35 percent compared with McGovern's 65 percent. The year also ended without any action being taken on the Jackson amendment. Instead of fading away after the election, as some expected, however, the issue of Soviet Jewry remained an impediment to finalizing the trade agreement with the Soviet Union.

The Debate Begins in Earnest

On 16 March 1973, Senator Jackson reintroduced his amendment even though the administration had not yet sent the trade agreement to Congress. Korey suggests that he did so because of the efforts of the Soviets to mobilize opposition to the amendment.[13] The effort was made by a Soviet delegation led by V.S. Alkhimov, Deputy Minister of Foreign Trade, which had come to the United States ostensibly to participate in a U.S.-Soviet trade conference sponsored by the National Association of Manufacturers (NAM) in Washington on 27 February.

The Soviets warned that if Congress frustrated the normalization of trade relations, there would be "serious political repercussions," including the possibility of renewed anti-Semitism in the Soviet Union because of the special status Soviet Jews would acquire. Congressmen who met the Soviets were equally blunt, telling them that their emigration policy was a major impediment to the expansion of trade. Senator Edmund Muskie warned that "Soviet leaders would be profoundly mistaken if they underestimated American feelings on the exit visa question."[14]

Meanwhile, Secretary of the Treasury George Shultz met with Premier Leonid Brezhnev in Moscow and came away with the impression that trade and banking officials, at least, were willing to rescind the "diploma" tax in order to facilitate trade negotiations. Four days after Shultz's meeting, forty-four Soviet Jews were permitted to leave without paying the tax, an event which received an unusual degree of publicity.

Soon after, a Soviet journalist frequently used by the Kremlin to leak information to the West, wrote an article saying the "diploma" tax would no longer be enforced. The Nixon administration saw the Soviet move as a vindication of the policy of quiet diplomacy. Senator Jackson was not satisfied, however, and said he would push his amendment to insure the Soviets do not "relapse into old patterns."[15]

Several reasons have been advanced for why Jackson was so persistent in pushing for his amendment. Stern has suggested that he was primarily interested in acquiring Jewish support for his planned presidential bid. He was successful in this regard, although probably no more so than had he simply continued to support legislation favored by the Israeli lobby as he had done in the past. Another possible reason is Jackson's desire to obstruct, if not prevent, the implementation of detente because, in his view, the Soviet Union was a threat to the free world.[16] The most altruistic reason is that he was simply concerned about the fate of Soviet Jews. This last reason is probably the least plausible, at least as Jackson's primary motivation, since he had questioned in the past the role of morality and human rights in the conduct of foreign policy, and because there were other senators who could make similar arguments.[17] What distinguished Jackson from most of his colleagues was that most of the other senators with such humanitarian concerns were liberal Democrats who eschewed Cold War approaches to dealing with the Soviet Union. "To all of them but Jackson, Kissinger-style detente seemed to be worth a longer trial."[18]

On 26 September 1972, Jackson again twisted the lobby's arm when he addressed a group of 120 Jewish leaders brought together by the NCSJ, telling them: "The time has come to place our highest human values ahead of the trade dollar. . . . You know what you can do? I'll give you some marching orders. Get behind my amendment. And let's stand firm!"[19] For the next two-and-a-half years Jackson gave the orders and the lobby, with only occasional deviations, followed.

The effort to link MFN and emigration in the House was led by Charles Vanik. Vanik was a supporter of East-West trade, but he also had a district with a large percentage of people of East European descent, and an estimated 11 percent of his constituents were Jewish.[20] In the previous Congress, Vanik had introduced his bill as a companion to Jackson's, but was unsuccessful in lining up cosponsors. This time he got an early start, with his aide Mark Talisman telephoning all 435 representatives in January. Vanik reintroduced his bill in February, and by the middle of the month, the Jackson-Vanik amendment had 72 Senate and 272 House sponsors.[21]

There had been a tendency to disregard the amendment until Rep. Wilbur Mills became its chief House sponsor.[22] Mills dominated trade debates because he was practically the only one who knew anything about trade policy;[23] consequently, his support was sought out by the amendment's backers. The Israeli lobby used its resources first, to acquire Mills's support and, after he began to waver by offering the Soviets a compromise if they dropped the "diploma" tax, then to maintain it. According to Kenen, obtaining Mills's support was relatively straightforward: "We called an old friend, Phillip Back, in Little Rock. On Monday morning, 6 February, he telephoned me to say that Mills had agreed."[24]

Part of the reason for the Israeli lobby's failure to take the lead was the lack of political activism on the part of the Soviet Jewry movement. The formal lobby, primarily AIPAC, was still in a relatively undeveloped stage with a small staff and budget. The established Jewish organizations, the Conference of Presidents and the American Jewish Congress in particular, opposed tying Soviet trade to emigration. Israel's ambassador to the United States, Yitzhak Rabin, argued that "United States interference in Soviet internal affairs—no matter how warranted by the injustice of the exorbitant emigration tax—would be counter-productive."[25] Prime Minister Golda Meir was in a re-election fight of her own and preferred not to choose between two friends—Nixon and Jackson—or to interfere in Soviet affairs. Since Israel was not providing any guidance, Jewish leaders found themselves forced to choose between supporting the president's quiet diplomacy, and the Jackson amendment. It was a rare instance of the Israeli lobby lacking cohesion.

The Administration Initiative

The Nixon administration was, in 1973, well aware of the threat to its trade agreement and its policy of detente posed by the Jackson-Vanik forces. In February, Nixon dispatched Charles Colson to Russia where he told Deputy Foreign Minister Vasily Kuznetsov that the Soviet "diploma" tax was an impediment to granting the Soviet Union MFN.[26] On 1 March, Nixon requested that Israeli Prime Minister Meir make an effort to find a compromise on the issue and apparently was assured that Israel would "cool it."[27] At the end of the month, the administration received an even bigger break when Nixon was informed that the tax was being lifted.[28] Given this assurance, Nixon submitted the Trade Reform Act to Congress on 10 April with the message that he understood the Congress' concern about the "diploma" tax, but reasserting the administration's position that denying MFN to the Soviet Union was not the "proper or even an effective way of dealing with this problem."[29]

Those who had previously been sympathetic to the administration position were impressed by the news of the tax being lifted. The leaders of the opposition, however, remained skeptical of Soviet intentions and committed to their current course of action. When Nixon suggested that there was no longer any reason to block the trade bill, Jackson reportedly replied: "Mr. President, if you believe that, you're being hoodwinked." Jackson insisted that he would continue to support his amendment "in the hope that it won't apply to the Soviet Union because they will be in compliance with the free emigration provision."[30]

The president's difficulties with Congress were compounded by

Nixon's admission, the day before meeting with Jackson, that Watergate involved high officials in the administration. The administration went from the position of great political advantage enjoyed at the time of the Strategic Arms Limitation Treaty (SALT) deliberations, to the point where Congress was consciously seeking opportunities to prove its independence. Kissinger saw the congressional pressure as an effort "to extend criticism of Nixon's alleged moral insensitivity into foreign policy, an area where the president's competence had previously gone unchallenged."[31]

Having failed to persuade his congressional antagonists, Nixon met with a group of fifteen Jewish leaders. What was interesting about the meeting was that *it was the president who was lobbying the interest group*, rather than the other way around. Nixon told the group that he had made a commitment to the Soviets to provide MFN, and that this was an integral part of detente. The Jackson-Vanik amendment, he said, would negate the commitment. Moreover, he told them, the Kremlin walls are very thick. "If you are inside they will listen to you; if you are outside you are not even going to be heard."[32]

After the meeting, Jacob Stein, chairman of the Conference of Presidents, Charlotte Jacobson, vice-chairman of the NCSJ, and Max Fisher, former president of the Council of Jewish Federations and Welfare Funds, issued a statement which omitted any reference to the Jackson amendment. The statement created the impression that the Jewish community was not firmly committed to the amendment. The constituents of the Israeli lobby immediately pressed for clarification. The Greater New York Conference on Soviet Jewry responded to an urgent call from Perle by reaffirming its support for Jackson-Vanik. On 26 April, the Executive Committee of the NCSJ met and decided to issue a statement supporting the amendment, but action was postponed until the following week when the Presidents Conference was scheduled to meet. After "a clash bordering almost upon open insurrection," Stein agreed to the demands of the "grassroots" for a statement supporting the amendment. A statement was issued on 2 May expressing continued support for the Jackson amendment, while also expressing appreciation for the efforts of the president.[33]

The declaration reflected the dilemma confronting the Israeli lobby, whereby the leadership was being asked to choose between supporting the president or the Jackson-Vanik amendment. They considered Nixon a friend of Israel, and his continued support was required to insure a continuation of aid. Moreover, the leaders knew that only the executive branch could extract concessions from the Soviets. Finally, some Jewish leaders who supported detente feared that the amendment would undermine the negotiations to ease superpower tensions. On the other hand, the Jackson amendment was seen as a unique weapon that might not receive support in the future. The threat of the amendment had already had an effect on Soviet behavior, so some leaders were unwilling to be charged with premature capitulation.[34] The choice was effectively made for the Israeli lobby by an unexpected group— Soviet Jewish activists.

A week before the Jewish leaders met with Nixon, 105 leading Soviet Jews wrote an open letter to Congress warning against being misled by the suspension of the "diploma" tax. There still was no such thing as free emigration, they said, rather "everyone's fate is determined by unknown people acting on unknown considerations in a totally arbitrary way." This was followed by an appeal to Jewish leaders by over 100 activists in the Soviet Union, urging them to stand firmly behind the Jackson-Vanik amendment. While the *Washington Post* called the Kremlin assurances a "major breakthrough" that should "melt support for the Jackson amendment," the appeals of the Soviet Jews insured that no such thaw would occur.[35]

Brezhnev came to the United States in June and took the opportunity to personally lobby the Congress. On the 19th he met with seventeen members of the Senate Foreign Relations Committee and eight other congressmen, and presented his optimistic vision of future trade relations while, at the same time, emphasizing the importance of the Soviet Union receiving MFN status. In anticipation of a confrontation on the emigration issue, Brezhnev offered the congressmen statistics which purported to show that 97 percent of all applicants for exit visas were allowed to emigrate. In addition, he said that over 60,000 Soviet Jews had been permitted to leave. This contention was vigorously denied by the NCSJ, which said the number was actually 31,700 and that

100,000 applications were still pending. The *Washington Post* (24 June) concluded that "the figures and assurance Mr. Brezhnev offered on emigration were at such variance with the facts as previously understood that he may not have helped much his own case."[36]

Whatever good Brezhnev may have accomplished through his lobbying efforts in Moscow and in Washington was subverted by a series of what Kissinger called "heavy-handed blunders."[37] During the summer, two dissidents were put on trial, historian Andrei Amalrik was sentenced to two years in prison, and Alexander Solzhenitsyn was being harassed, while physicist Andrei Sakharov was detained and warned about his political activities. Sakharov became directly involved in the debate over the Jackson-Vanik amendment on 14 September when he wrote an open letter to Congress calling the amendment an indispensable first step for assuring detente. Rejecting the arguments advanced by the Nixon administration, Sakharov warned that abandoning the Jackson-Vanik amendment would be "a betrayal of the thousands of Jews and non-Jews who want to emigrate, of the hundreds in camps and mental hospitals, and of the victims of the Berlin Wall."[38]

Just as the Soviet Jews helped persuade the American Jewish community to unite behind the Jackson-Vanik amendment, the Sakharov letter had the effect of activating a large group of non-Jews. The issue now took on a "transcendent character involving universal morality. . . . Many militant doves, hitherto suspicious of Senator Jackson's hawkish record, now began echoing the Sakharov 'letter' urging support of his amendment. The coalition, in consequence took on an increasingly humanist edge; no longer could it be challenged as merely hardnosed and anti-detente."[39] Kissinger called it a rare convergence, "like an eclipse of the sun."[40]

Besides liberal groups like Americans for Democratic Action (ADA), and the scientists' associations, labor was also a vigorous opponent of the Trade Reform Act. Labor was opposed because of the perceived threat to American jobs, as George Meany testified: "We're not interested in seeing American workers displaced by slave labor."[41] Unlike the other groups, however, labor supported the Jackson-Vanik amendment, not because it was interested in Soviet emigration, but because it saw the legislation as a means to block the expansion of trade altogether. Since labor was determined to block the trade bill and made no attempt to present alternatives or compromises, its lobbying efforts were ineffective. From the perspective of the Israeli lobby, however, labor support was helpful in providing a counter to business opposition to the Jackson-Vanik amendment.

Conservative Republicans were also attracted to the Jackson-Vanik amendment "because they shared Meany's suspicion of Soviet motives, and perceived that the best way of preventing United States trade concessions altogether was to tie them to the issue of Jewish emigration."[42] Ethnic groups from Eastern Europe were also supportive, since the amendment encouraged freedom of emigration for all people, without specifying Jews.

There was relatively little opposition outside the administration to the Jackson-Vanik amendment. The main opponents were leaders of the business community who feared the amendment might jeopardize the long-desired expansion of trade with the Soviets. The newly formed Emergency Committee on American Trade (ECAT) was actively lobbying against the legislation, as was the vocal chief executive of Pepsico, Donald Kendall, who wrote a letter to sixty-five chief executives asking them to pressure the Ways and Means Committee to kill the Jackson-Vanik amendment. Someone leaked the letter to Morris Amitay who, in turn, gave it to the *Washington Post*. The *Post* ran the story "Big Firms to Press Hill on Soviet Trade Benefit" on page one, undercutting the lobbying effort.[43] Nevertheless, the members of ECAT were able to put together a last minute lobbying campaign with 1,200 corporate leaders to push for the adoption of the *trade bill*. The opposition to the Jackson-Vanik *amendment* was much more limited; in fact, very little was written, either at the time of the debate, or since, to suggest that business interests were a factor in the attitudes of decision-makers. Korey suggests, moreover, that Sakharov's involvement changed the nature of the debate by charging it with moral overtones that "all but neutralized the commercial and business arguments."[44]

The administration position on the issue remained consistent throughout the debate. The Jackson-Vanik amendment was seen as a threat to detente and, by extension, to world peace. In June, 1974, Nixon said in a speech that "we cannot gear our foreign policy to transformation of other societies" and that "we would not welcome the intervention of other countries in our domestic affairs and we cannot expect them to be cooperative when we seek to intervene directly in theirs."[45]

The administration's arguments became increasingly irrelevant as Nixon was progressively rendered politically impotent by the revelations of Watergate. Nixon blamed his political troubles for his inability to overcome opposition to the trade bill: "The convergence of antidetente forces would have existed regardless of any domestic political problems. But Watergate had badly damaged my ability to defuse, or at least to circumvent, them as effectively as I otherwise might have been able to do."[46]

The Russians Blunder Again

Five days before the final House Committee vote, Henry Kissinger was named Secretary of State. The secretary, according to Korey, "deliberately" waited until the hour before the Ways and Means Committee voted on the Vanik amendment to hold his first press conference as Secretary of State. Hoping that the timing would maximize the impact of his argument, Kissinger said that U.S. credibility would be harmed if the nation did not fulfill its obligations. Detente, he said, was in such a fragile position that "overt acts" of pressure might jeopardize its implementation.[47] Despite the Secretary's protestations, the Ways and Means Committee retained the Vanik amendment and voted 20–5 to report the Trade Act on 3 October 1973.

The discussions about defeating the amendment were quickly made irrelevant by the surprise attack of Egypt and Syria against Israel on 6 October. The Soviets' support for the Arab attack infuriated Congress, and virtually assured that the Jackson-Vanik amendment would be adopted. The war also, paradoxically, undermined Jewish support for the amendment.

When the war broke out the Israeli lobby was afraid the state of Israel was threatened with defeat. The war effort was the highest priority for Israel, and Ambassador Simcha Dinitz gave American Jewish leaders the impression that nothing, including the Jackson-Vanik amendment, should be allowed to interfere with Israel's pursuit of additional weapons. Other leaders, who apparently had direct contact with the prime minister's office, were convinced there had been no change in Israel's interest in aiding Soviet Jews.[48]

On 25 October, Jacob Stein, Max Fisher, and Richard Maas met with Kissinger, and were told that Moscow's cooperation was needed to bring about a cease-fire, and that continued support for Jackson-Vanik imperiled negotiations. Fisher, in particular, was persuaded by the secretary's arguments, but even staunch supporters of the amendment were admittedly "diffident" about pressuring the Soviets. The delegation made a tentative decision to ask Jackson to avoid a showdown in the House. Maas raised the issue first with the executive committee of the NCSJ, and was instructed to give Jackson a neutral account of the Kissinger meeting, but not to suggest delaying action on the amendment.[49]

Jackson had been warned that some Jewish leaders were wavering, so he invited Senator Ribicoff and B'nai B'rith president David Blumberg to attend the meeting. Jackson and his supporters argued that there was no relationship between his amendment and aid to Israel. Moreover, if the Vanik amendment was adopted by the House, he said, not only would Soviet Jews be helped, but the United States would also have a lever to use with the Soviets in Middle East negotiations. Afterward, the Jewish leadership issued a statement reaffirming support for the amendment, while also praising the Nixon administration for its quiet diplomacy and aid to Israel. From then on there was no wavering of support.

The administration tried a different strategy after the war broke out and persisted for a time after the cease-fire. Since Kissinger feared that the Jackson-Vanik amendment would complicate his efforts to negotiate a cease-fire, he advised the president to work to delay the House vote until enough support could be mobilized to defeat the measure. Treasury Secretary Shultz and other administration officials disagreed and urged immediate action to facilitate trade negotiations with Japan and Europe. They believed the MFN issue could be dealt with separately, and did not want to risk losing the entire agreement.

After Wilbur Mills advised the president that further delay would increase that risk, Nixon gave his approval to bring the bill to a vote. The president, according to Kissinger, had put his prestige on the line, instructing House Speaker Carl Albert to either defeat the Vanik amendment or delete MFN from the trade bill. "But by that time, the President had little prestige left."[50] One of the administration's supporters, Rep. Barber Conable, said the administration's difficulties stemmed from the failure of the president and Kissinger to realize that MFN was being opposed, not just by the American Jewish community, but by a very impressive coalition. "The so-called Jewish lobby . . . is only the cutting edge. And therefore, it's not an easy proposal to turn around."[51]

The administration could not turn the proposal around. The House voted 319–80 on 11 December to refuse credits, credit guarantees and investment guarantees to non-market countries which deny their citizens the right to emigrate. The administration's effort to delete the MFN provision from the bill was also defeated by the overwhelming margin of 298–106. The entire Trade Reform Act was then adopted by a vote of 272–140, the smaller margin being at least partly attributable to labor opposition. That same day, Congress also approved the emergency assistance bill providing $2.2 billion in aid to Israel, demonstrating that Jackson was correct in saying the two issues were not linked.

Jackson applauded the vote as a clear message to the Soviet government that the American people are committed to the free movement of men and ideas on which a more stable and lasting peace must be based.[52] Kissinger's view was that the bill "would do serious and perhaps irreparable damage to our relations with the Soviet Union."[53] The stage was set for a battle royale in the Senate.

A New Year—The Same Fight

Senator Jackson, on 23 January 1974, criticized the Soviets for their continued "capricious cruelty" and warned that as long as emigration is prevented by ransom taxes and other measures, he would fight to amend the trade bill.[54] The administration, meanwhile, was trying to negotiate with some key senators to kill or modify the Jackson amendment. It was not until February that Kissinger passed the word to a group of Jewish leaders that he was interested in working out a compromise with Jackson.[55]

When Jackson and Kissinger met on 6 March, the secretary

proposed a compromise that would allow the Senate to review Soviet emigration policy at some agreed intervals after MFN was granted. Jackson was less impressed with Soviet concessions than Kissinger, however, and would only accept a written guarantee of increased emigration. Frustrated, Kissinger said: "Our dialogue was beginning to resemble negotiations between sovereign countries."[56]

At their second meeting, on the 16th, Jackson wanted a written guarantee of 100,000 exit visas, a demand Kissinger knew would be unacceptable to the Soviets. A third meeting was set up during April with Ribicoff and Javits also in attendance. In that meeting, Jackson said the 100,000 figure was only a target, a concession offset by a new demand that visas be granted to Jews in large cities, rather than just people of low educational and cultural levels in the provinces. Kissinger was exasperated:

> I was being asked to triple emigration from the Soviet Union (on top of the hundredfold increase we had already achieved before Jackson entered the lists) and to specify from what regions emigrants should be drawn—all in return for giving the Soviets the same trade treatment already enjoyed by over 100 other nations.[57]

At the end of April, Kissinger went to Geneva to discuss the Syrian-Israeli peace negotiations with Foreign Minister Andrei Gromyko and reminded him that there was no legal prohibition against emigration from the Soviet Union except for people with security clearances. In view of this fact, Kissinger suggested that he be allowed to express assurances to Congress that 40 to 45,000 emigrants would be permitted to leave the Soviet Union. Gromyko agreed to let Kissinger pass on the number 45,000 "as a trend," but not as a commitment.

The president's domestic problems were a major complication. Watergate was progressing inexorably toward its denouement as Nixon prepared for his last summit meeting with Brezhnev. Two days before Nixon left, Jackson announced his intention to attach new conditions to the trade agreement, and to hold steadfast in opposition to granting concessions to the Soviets.[58]

When Nixon met Brezhnev at the end of June, he pointed out "that if detente unravels in America, the hawks will take over, not the doves," and suggested that he make a concession on

Jewish emigration "if only to pull the rug out from Jackson and some of the media critics." At the end of the summit Brezhnev appeared to give in: "As far as I am concerned, I say let all the Jews go and let God go with them."[59] Unfortunately for the would-be emigrants, the premier's apparent enthusiasm for ridding himself of an irritating problem soon passed.

The Beginning of the End

Less than two months after returning from Moscow, Nixon resigned from office and, on 9 August 1974, Gerald Ford became president. Based on his past record, Ford's coming to power might have been expected to signal a change in the administration attitude toward the Jackson-Vanik amendment, but it did not.

In 1967, Ford was one of over 300 congressmen who signed a letter condemning the suppression of Soviet Jews, and the following year he said in a speech that "when the next measure comes before the Congress involving East-West trade, or a similar appropriate bill, I will advocate an amendment, I hope with bipartisan support, to express the sense of the Congress that the Soviet Union should display concern for American opinion in Soviet policies affecting the Jews."[60] Five years later, however, Representative Ford was willing to support the Jackson amendment only in principle, while opposing it in practice.[61]

Once he became president, Ford adopted the Nixon-Kissinger policy of quiet diplomacy. He considered the trade agreement "the most significant trade legislation in the last 40 years" and was determined to save it.[62] On 14 August Ford met with Ambassador Anatoly Dobrynin and obtained an oral guarantee that 55,000 Jews would be allowed to leave annually. The following morning, the president conveyed this guarantee to Jackson, Ribicoff, and Javits and warned that the agreement would fall through if they insisted on a written guarantee. The president apparently made an impact on the participants. Even Jackson said afterwards that Ford's "direct intervention in this matter has given it new momentum and new movement."[63]

Kissinger and Jackson renewed their compromise talks and reached an agreement whereby they would exchange three letters. In the first, Kissinger would list Soviet assurances, then Jackson would issue a reply with his understanding of the first, and, finally, the third letter would accept Jackson's letter on behalf of the president.

Kissinger's letter said the administration had been assured by the Soviets that "unreasonable impediments" would be removed from the path of emigrants, and that people holding security clearances would be prevented from emigration only for a limited time period. The rate of emigration was to "begin to rise promptly above the 1973 level. . . ." Jackson's response said that he understood the Soviet assurances to mean the end of intimidation of visa applicants, and that security clearances would be valid excuses for holding up emigration for only three years from the time the person was exposed to sensitive information. Furthermore, he set 60,000 emigrants per year as a "minimum standard of initial compliance."[64]

On 30 September, a complication arose when Jackson was informed there would be no third letter. This infuriated the senator. Stanley Lowell, chairman of the NCSJ, then intervened. He asked twenty-five Jewish leaders to telegram the White House and warn the president that he would be held responsible if the compromise fell apart. Lowell also sent a message to Jackson's office urging him to continue the negotiations with Kissinger. "This," according to Albright, "was the hardest Jackson's office had ever been leaned on by the National Conference, which had for two years gone along faithfully with Jackson's tactical judgements."[65] Senator Javits came up with the compromise of adding the operative paragraph from the third letter to the first and Jackson accepted it in a meeting with Kissinger on 8 October.

Another disagreement arose over Ford's desire to have the agreement last for two years, subject to a congressional veto if the assurances on emigration were not implemented. Jackson preferred one year and renewal only after congressional approval. The president gave Jackson his "word of honor" that he would cancel the agreement if the Soviets failed to carry out their promises. A few days later an agreement was reached on the length of the trade agreement, splitting the difference at eighteen months. Under the agreement, the president could waive restrictions on MFN for a period of eighteen months. This authority could be renewed afterward on a yearly basis by concurrent resolution. If

Congress withheld approval, and the president continued the waiver, then either House could veto the president's action within forty-five days.[66] The letters were then formally exchanged on 18 October.

Kissinger implied in his Senate testimony that Ford had received assurances from Brezhnev during the summit accepting the terms used in the letter to Jackson. On the basis of that testimony the Senate voted 88–0 on 13 December to approve the provision of the Jackson amendment allowing the president to grant the Soviet Union MFN status. The Trade Reform Act then was adopted 77–4. The House version of the bill did not have the waiver, so it was added in conference; the Senate version was then approved by both Houses on 20 December.

Soon after the Senate vote, the Soviets began a propaganda blitz denouncing American "intervention" in Soviet domestic affairs and denying that any concessions on emigration had been made. Although Ford expressed reservations about the amendment when he signed the trade bill on 3 January 1975, the Soviets were not appeased and, on the 10th, told Kissinger they were abrogating the trade agreement.[67] The Soviets had complained throughout the two-year debate on the issue about interference in their internal affairs, but it was another amendment, unrelated to emigration, that passed with little public notice, and was the real cause of the trade agreement's undoing.

Stevenson Throws in a Wrench

Earlier in the year, on 30 June, the president's authority to use the Export-Import Bank came up for its bi-annual renewal. The administration had not expected a problem, so it was caught flat-footed by the opponents of the trade agreement. According to Kissinger, Jackson's forces saw the bill as a means of putting a "double lock on East-West trade" along with the Jackson-Vanik amendment, and also as a back-up just in case the other amendment failed.[68] An amendment was offered by Senator Adlai Stevenson with the cooperation of Jackson, but without the knowledge of the Israeli lobby, that set a $300 million limit on credit for the following four years.

The amendment had serious repercussions because the United

States had provided $469 million in credits to the Soviet Union since October 1972. The emigration issue was only of symbolic importance, but credits were seen as a necessity if the Soviet Union was to obtain access to American technology.[69] In addition, the Soviets saw the denial of credits as another manifestation of United States discrimination. When the Stevenson amendment passed, it vitiated any hope of the Jackson-Vanik amendment succeeding.

Immediately after the abrogation of the trade agreement, emigration from the Soviet Union began to decline and did not increase again until Jimmy Carter began arms control negotiations. A record number of Soviet Jews were allowed to leave in June 1979, coinciding with the signing of the SALT II treaty. Since the passage of Jackson-Vanik, over 200,000 Jews have emigrated from the Soviet Union, but this number has little to do with the amendment; rather, it has been a function of the state of U.S.-Soviet relations. In the Ford years, as detente began to unravel, emigration declined. The level increased with the improvement in bilateral relations under Carter, and then decreased as relations deteriorated again after the Soviet invasion of Afghanistan. Under the initial Cold War-like relations of the Reagan administration, emigration was reduced to a trickle. The ascension of Mikhail Gorbachev, and his implementation of *glasnost* and *perestroika*, brought about a revolution in U.S.-U.S.S.R. relations. As the Cold War receded, emigration began to increase to unprecedented levels.

Summary

The Jackson-Vanik amendment, Orbach suggests, satisfied a number of American interests: "It represented toughness, it allayed the Christian conscience, and it demanded Soviet concessions."[70] At the same time, its adoption represented a rejection of the realist argument made by the administration that the measure would undermine detente and hence national security. The U.S. interest in freedom of movement and the promotion of human rights were perceived by most congressmen to be more applicable in this case than security concerns, and therefore were willing to oppose the president. The arguments in favor of supporting the amendment were persuasive, but they would never have been raised had it not been for the Israeli lobby.

The lobby was indeed influential in putting the Soviet Jewry issue on the legislative agenda, encouraging congressional support, and inducing Jackson to accept a compromise. The issue had, in fact, been on the agenda periodically for about 100 years, but Soviet "blunders" served as catalysts for the Soviet Jewry movement and, at the same time, opponents of detente. The combination of Soviet repression of dissidents, the diploma tax, and support for the Arab attack on Israel in October 1973, reinforced lobby arguments that the Jackson-Vanik amendment would not undermine detente since the Soviets were not exercising much restraint in their behavior. In addition, the Soviet actions highlighted their antagonism toward values, such as freedom of emigration, which were held to be in the national interest. Contrary to Stern's implication that a minority frustrated the will of the majority, public opinion polls and overwhelming congressional support indicate that the principles embodied in the Jackson-Vanik amendment were not a minority view.[71]

In pluralist terms, it is also possible to see that the Israeli lobby succeeded in building a broad coalition of liberal and conservative organizations that supported the amendment in the hope of promoting freedom of emigration. Many of the conservatives did accept the realist argument that detente would be undermined, but that possibility served as a motivation for them to support the amendment, because of their fear that the policy of detente would shift the balance of power in favor of the Soviet Union.

The formal lobby component was active, although it was primarily Jewish organizations other than AIPAC that did the lobbying. In addition, the lobby network, particularly aides Amitay, Perle, and Talisman, were extremely influential in the outcome. Not only did the lobby enjoy access to Congress, but also, to a surprising degree, to the White House, where Jewish leaders met on several occasions with the president and secretary of state. What was interesting about these meetings is that they were initiated by the White House, and not the lobby, and exemplified one of the peculiarities of the debate; that is, the tendency of decision-makers to lobby the Israeli lobby.

The Israeli lobby coalition also enjoyed the balance of lobbying power on the issue since there was little opposition to the amendment. Business interests represented by the National Association of Manufacturers (NAM), ECAT, and individual corporate executives, opposed the bill, but accounts of the debate suggest that these interests had little influence on the outcome. Congress seemed to dismiss business arguments, especially after Sakharov's letter was published, as blatant profit-seeking at the expense of fundamental principles of human rights.

What remains difficult to explain is the behavior of Senator Henry Jackson. On the one hand, he was under pressure from his labor supporters to block the trade agreement and, on the other hand, he was being asked by the Israeli lobby to use MFN status as bait to increase emigration. If Jackson was really interested in preventing the trade agreement from being ratified, he should not have been willing to compromise; that is, unless he anticipated that the Soviets would abrogate the treaty. There is no evidence, however, that he expected the Soviets' response. By compromising, Jackson insured that the agreement would pass, thereby alienating labor. Stern's explanation for Jackson's willingness to compromise was the fear that Congress would no longer support his amendment after the 1974 elections.[72] Since the bill did not pass until after the elections, this reason is probably only partly responsible. Jackson also acted in accordance with the wishes of the Israeli lobby, which for really the first time, pressured Jackson to compromise to avert further antagonism of the new administration.

As was the case in the arms sales, the administration decision to seek a compromise came about in response to the lobby's pressure and the likelihood that the president's position would otherwise be defeated. The negotiations between Kissinger and Jackson, moreover, exemplified the political bargaining expected to take place when an issue is decided in the legislative branch. When the compromise appeared to be unravelling, it was lobby pressure that forced the parties to reach a final agreement.

The informal lobby was also influential because the issue spanned two elections. When McGovern made Soviet Jewish emigration a campaign issue in 1972, Nixon was forced to give the matter his attention. In addition, Nixon's desire to improve his standing with Jewish voters motivated him to make supportive statements, although he never changed his substantive policy. The decision to finalize an agreement with Jackson was made partly because Ford wanted to resolve the matter prior to the midterm elections.

The difficulty of using the leadership model for predicting outcomes is apparent once again in this case. On the one hand, the Nixon-Kissinger foreign policy maintained that achieving detente was the most important goal of U.S. policy, a position that would lead to opposition to the Jackson-Vanik amendment, but, on the other hand, the administration believed in linkage, which would have suggested that improvement in U.S. trade relations could only occur after a moderation of Soviet policy. If the trade agreement was a purely executive decision, there would have been no problem predicting the outcome, since the administration believed Soviet behavior had indeed moderated. The agreement required congressional approval, however, and Congress did not consider the actions of the Soviets to have improved. Thus, we see why evaluation of the models requires analysis of legislative as well as executive cases.

The change in leaders also had an ambiguous impact on the outcome. If Ford's record is analyzed, one can see that he had been one of the first congressmen to suggest linking emigration and trade, yet when he became president he adopted Nixon's opposition to the amendment. This might be explained by proponents of the leadership model in terms of the continuity of the foreign policy-making establishment; that is, the architect of detente, Henry Kissinger, was still responsible for formulating U.S. foreign policy. In addition, as Senator Jackson noted, Ford did bring new momentum to the compromise negotiations, but, as suggested above, this may have been more a function of concern with the upcoming elections than a change in policy.

Another component of the leadership model, which actually overlaps with the pluralist model and demonstrates that leaders cannot be evaluated in a vacuum, is the domestic political environment the president faced. The emigration issue arose at the end of President Nixon's first term when he was faced with an increasingly hostile Democratic majority (as well as opposition within his own party) in Congress and declining public approval. Nixon was interested not only in reducing this opposition but attracting substantial support from Jewish voters. He was very successful in the latter, but only marginally successful in the former, losing three Senate seats and picking up twelve House seats. Throughout the remainder of his term, Nixon's political capital dissipated and, with the revelations of Watergate, his popularity declined to an eventual low of 24 percent. Given his political vulnerability and the failure to make a credible realist argument against the amendment, it is not surprising that Congress was willing to oppose Nixon. Even if Nixon had not resigned, however, he still would probably have been defeated on the issue because large majorities were already on record in support of the measure.

When Gerald Ford assumed the duties of president, he inherited the hostile Democratic majority faced by his predecessor, but he did enjoy the confidence of the public initially (71 percent approval), and a desire shared by governed and governors alike, that the country needed a period of healing. Thus, Ford enjoyed a honeymoon prior to the elections, which allowed him to intercede with Senator Jackson and stimulate the movement toward a compromise. As was the case with Nixon, however, a majority of Congress had already been lined up by the lobby in support of the amendment, so compromise was his only opportunity to avoid an outright defeat.

The Jackson-Vanik case cannot be explained by the realist model. The issue was economic and political rather than security-related, and therefore, Congress was less inclined to defer to the president. The pluralist model illustrates how the issue reached the legislative agenda, explains congressional support, and accounts for the administrations' failure. There was very little difference in the policies of the two leaders, primarily because there was no change in the Secretary of State. The greater willingness of Ford to compromise was less a function of his ideology, than the political constraints that he faced.

Notes

1. Henry Kissinger, *Years of Upheaval* (Boston: Little, Brown and Co., 1982), 982.
2. I. L. Kenen, *Israel's Defense Line* (NY: Prometheus, 1981), 281.
3. *Near East Report* (10 May 1972), 77.
4. *Near East Report* (20 Sept 1972), 165.

5. Kenen, *Israel's Defense Line*, 285.
6. William Korey, "The Story of the Jackson Amendment, 1973–1975," *Midstream* (March 1975), 9; *Near East Report* (6 September 1972), 158; *Near East Report* (27 September 1972), 171.
7. *Near East Report* (4 October 1972), 173.
8. Paula Stern, *Water's Edge* (CT: Greenwood Press, 1979), 33.
9. Stern, *Water's Edge*, 35.
10. Kissinger, *Years of Upheaval*, 249–250, 986.
11. Strobe Talbott, "Social Issues," in *The Making of America's Soviet Policy* Joseph S. Nye, ed. (CT: Yale University Press, 1984), 198.
12. Korey, "Story of the Jackson Amendment," 9–10.
13. Ibid., 11.
14. Ibid., 11.
15. Ibid., 12–14.
16. Stern, *Water's Edge*, 21.
17. Ibid.
18. Joseph Albright, "The Pact of the Two Henrys," *New York Times Magazine* (5 January 1975), 20.
19. Albright, "Pact of the Two Henrys," 20; Stern, *Water's Edge*, 21.
20. John Rourke, *Congress and the Presidency in U.S. Foreign Policy-making* (CO: Westview Press, 1983), 269.
21. Albright, "Pact of the Two Henrys," 22; Dan Caldwell, "The Jackson-Vanik Amendment," in *Congress, the Presidency, and American Foreign Policy*, John Spanier and Joseph Nogee, eds., (NY: Pergamon Press, 1981), 5, 1P. *Near East Report* (4 March 1973), 42; Kenen, *Israel's Defense Line*, 286.
22. *Near East Report* (21 March 1973), 45.
23. Robert A. Pastor, *Congress and the Politics of U.S. Economic Policy* (CA: U.C. Press, 1980), 151–2.
24. Kenen, *Israel's Defense Line*, 286.
25. Stern, *Water's Edge*, 22, 75.
26. Albright, "Pact of the Two Henrys," 24.
27. Stern, *Water's Edge*, 66.
28. Kissinger, *Years of Upheaval*, 252.
29. Korey, "Story of the Jackson Amendment," 14.
30. Kissinger, *Years of Upheaval*, 253; Korey, "Story of the Jackson Amendment," 14–15; Albright, "Pact of the Two Henrys," 24; *Near East Report* (28 March 1973), 49.
31. Kissinger, *Years of Upheaval*, 252–4.
32. Korey, "Story of the Jackson Amendment," 21–22; *Near East Report* (25 April 1973), 66; Richard M. Nixon, *RN* (NY: Grosset and Dunlop, 1978), 876.
33. Korey, "Story of the Jackson Amendment," 22–4; Albright, "Pact of the Two Henrys," 26.
34. Korey, "Story of the Jackson Amendment," 23; Stern, *Water's Edge*, 73.

35. *Near East Report* (25 April 1973), 67.
36. Korey, "Story of the Jackson Amendment," 15; *Near East Report* (27 June 1973), 101.
37. Kissinger, *Years of Upheaval*, 988.
38. Korey, "Story of the Jackson Amendment," 17–18.
39. Ibid., 18.
40. Nixon, *RN*, 875.
41. Dan Caldwell, "The Jackson-Vanik Amendment," in *Congress, the Presidency, and American Foreign Policy*, John Spanier and Joseph Nogee, eds. (NY: Pergamon Press, 1981), 5, 11.
42. Albright, "Pact of the Two Henrys," 22.
43. Ibid., 26; *Near East Report* (19 September 1973), 150.
44. Korey, "Story of the Jackson Amendment," 18.
45. *Near East Report* (12 June 1974), 144.
46. Nixon, *RN*, 1024.
47. Korey, "Story of the Jackson Amendment," 18–19.
48. Albright, "Pact of the Two Henrys," 26.
49. William Orbach, *The American Movement to Aid Soviet Jews* (MA: University of Massachusetts Press, 1979), 145–6; Albright, "Pact of the Two Henrys," 28; Korey, "Story of the Jackson Amendment," 25.
50. Kissinger, *Years of Upheaval*, 991.
51. Richard S. Frank, "Administration's Reform Bill Threatened by Dispute Over Relations with Russia," *National Journal* (24 November 1973), 1750.
52. Korey, "Story of the Jackson Amendment," 21.
53. Pastor, *Congress and Politics of U.S. Economy*, 174–5.
54. Korey, "Story of the Jackson Amendment," 10.
55. Kissinger, *Years of Upheaval*, 991.
56. Ibid., 992–3.
57. Ibid., 993–5.
58. Ibid., 995–7.
59. Nixon, *RN*, 1031, 1034.
60. *Near East Report* (14 August 1974), 179.
61. *Near East Report* (16 May 1973), 79.
62. Gerald R. Ford, *A Time to Heal* (NY: Berkeley Books, 1980), 219.
63. Korey, "Story of the Jackson Amendment," 26.
64. Ibid., 26–7; Albright, "Pact of the Two Henrys," 30–1, 34.
65. Albright, "Pact of the Two Henrys," 31; Caldwell, "Jackson-Vanik Amendment," 14.
66. Albright, "Pact of the Two Henrys," 34; Korey, "Story of the Jackson Amendment," 27.
67. Korey, "Story of the Jackson Amendment," 35–6.
68. Kissinger, *Years of Upheaval*, 996–7.
69. Daniel Yergin, "Politics and Soviet-American Trade: The Three

Questions," *Foreign Affairs* (April 1977), 532; Korey, "Story of the Jackson Amendment," 20.
70. Orbach, *The American Movement*, 154.
71. Stern, *Water's Edge*, 212.
72. Rourke, *Congress and the Presidency*, 269. Rourke concludes that Jackson supported labor and abandoned Soviet Jewry, but the opposite was true. Frank, "Administration's Reform Bills," 1750; Stern, *Water's Edge*, 103, 150–153.

4

The Antiboycott Bill

The Arab boycott was formally declared by the newly formed Arab League Council on 2 December 1945: "Jewish products and manufactured goods shall be considered undesirable to the Arab countries" and all Arab "institutions, organizations, merchants, commission agents, and individuals" were called upon "to refuse to deal in, distribute, or consume Zionist products or manufactured goods."[1] The boycott is divided into three components: the *primary* boycott, the *secondary* boycott, and the *tertiary* boycott. The primary boycott is simply the refusal of Arab states to trade with Israel. Beginning in April 1950, the boycott was extended to include the refusal by Arab states to trade with third parties— non-Israelis—which are thought to contribute to Israel's military and economic power. This is the secondary boycott. The tertiary boycott then prohibits trade of goods containing components made by blacklisted firms.

The objective of the boycott has been to isolate Israel from its neighbors and the international community, as well as to deny it trade that might be used to augment its military and economic strength. The Arab nations apply the laws selectively, with exceptions made on the basis of a calculation of whether the potential harm to the Arab countries outweighs the expected benefits of the boycott.[2] Egypt stopped enforcing the boycott altogether after signing the Camp David Peace Treaty.[3]

Legislative History

The first reaction to the Arab boycott apparently came from the State Department on 22 May 1956: "[We] are obliged to

91

recognize that any attempt by this country to force our views on a foreign national would be considered intervention in the domestic affairs of that nation and therefore greatly resented."[4] The reaction of Congress, spurred by American Jewish organizations, was to adopt a resolution condemning discrimination against Americans. Similar resolutions were routinely attached to foreign aid legislation, but no real effort to combat the boycott was taken until 1964. The combination of U.S. government laxity and heavily publicized instances of discrimination against American individuals and firms then led to a serious push for antiboycott legislation.

The Israeli lobby, via AIPAC's 1964 policy statement, condemned the Arab boycott and the continued restrictions on Israeli shipping.[5] A resolution opposing restrictive trade practices or boycotts and prohibiting action supporting such practices was introduced but did not pass. It was reintroduced the following year over the opposition of the administration, which argued "it might be counter-productive and provoke the Arabs to intensify their boycott practices."[6] President Johnson also thought that a strong congressional stand against the Arab boycott might lead to similar opposition to U.S. embargoes against Cuba, China, Vietnam, and Korea.[7] An amendment to the Export Control Act was adopted after the administration forced a compromise whereby the president was given the discretion to decide whether to prohibit boycott compliance.

The Arabs were incensed by the legislation, which they denounced as a "Zionist maneuver" instigated by "Zionist legislators."[8] Arab anger died down, however, after it became apparent that the Commerce Department left companies to themselves to decide whether or not to comply with the boycott. In each of the next five Congresses efforts to make the antiboycott provisions of the Export Control Act mandatory failed.

The Emergence of Arab Power

Prior to 1973, the Arab boycott was regarded as a "toothless and gutless" propaganda device.[9] After the oil embargo, however, it was seen as a tool to force the United States to reduce its support of Israel. The Arab world was becoming an increasingly significant economic market; in fact, it represented the fastest-growing American export market. Arab investment in the United States, meanwhile, was somewhere around $20–25 billion. The most important statistics, however, were probably the quadrupling of the price of crude oil and the dramatic increase in the level of U.S. oil imports from the Arabs from 30–45 percent of total crude imports.[10]

One of the consequences of the oil embargo was to stimulate American initiatives to improve U.S.-Arab relations, particularly with Saudi Arabia. In June 1974, Henry Kissinger signed an economic cooperation agreement with the Saudis designed to allow the United States to "be helpful in the realization of Saudi aspirations," which meant channeling billions of dollars of new business into Saudi Arabia. "All of it however has been on Saudi Arabia's terms—meaning exclusion of hundreds of blacklisted U.S. companies plus discrimination against American Jews."[11]

Also in 1974, the chief executives of seven blacklisted American firms including Ford, RCA, and Coca Cola urged Kissinger to use his "best efforts to persuade the Arab nations that the new role of the United States and the Middle East and the new climate of diplomatic accommodation in the region would be well served by an end to these discriminatory barriers."[12]

By 1975, it became increasingly clear that the boycott was more far reaching than originally thought and that the government was not doing much either to enforce existing law or encourage Arab moderation. In February, Senator Frank Church made public for the first time a list of fifteen hundred American firms on the 1970 Saudi blacklist.[13] Publication of the blacklist made the public aware, for the first time, of the scope of the boycott. What was more shocking, however, were revelations of U.S. government complicity in the boycott. The most serious was probably the admission by representatives of the Army Corps of Engineers that Jewish soldiers and civilian employees were excluded from projects the corps managed in Saudi Arabia.[14] The administration's response was that the State Department was pursuing a "low-key approach" to the problem.

The administration was further embarrassed by the discovery that the United States held shares in an investment company which had been involved in boycotting Jewish banks. Soon after, the government announced plans to sell its interest.

Meanwhile, the furor over the Army Corps of Engineers continued. On 26 February, President Ford had told a press conference the discrimination of Jews by the corps "is totally contrary to the American tradition and repugnant to American principles. It has no place in the free practice of commerce and in the world. . . . "[15] Soon after, however, it was revealed that the Pentagon had signed an agreement with a company to train Saudi national guardsmen that contained a clearly discriminatory clause. In testimony before a House subcommittee, an Army spokesman argued it was "the responsibility of the Corps of Engineers to adhere to the laws and customs of that country in performing its mission." Requests for Saudi visas, he said, had to be accompanied by a certificate showing some evidence of the person's religion, such as a baptismal certificate, marriage license, or birth certificate.[16]

In the month of February 1975, when a number of boycott-related incidents occurred, the House Armed Services Committee went to the Middle East on a fact-finding tour and Henry Waxman was denied a visa because of being Jewish. After the State Department intervened, Waxman obtained a visa and attended an audience with King Faisal during which he heard the King say that "the Jews have no business in Saudi Arabia. . . . They are our enemies. Jews from America and around the world support Israel. Friends of our enemies are our enemies." When Waxman asked Faisal about his attitude toward Israel, the king said: "Palestine is an *Arab* country." He added that it was "his deepest hope and prayer to pray at Muslim holy places in a *Muslim* Jerusalem."[17]

The impact of the various incidents was to create the impression that discrimination against Jews was an integral part of the Arab boycott. Boycott report statistics showed, however, that a small number, less than one percent, of business transactions could be labeled as discriminatory on religious or racial grounds. In addition, after the public outcry, Saudi Arabia stopped requiring certificates of religion with visa applications, but about half of the Arab League nations continued to require applicants to reveal their religion. By the time Saudi Arabia acted, it was too late; the damage had been done.

Israel Takes A Stand

Israel had been unhappy about the boycott but did not feel overly threatened by it. The Director General of the Ministry of Finance said the problem was primarily a result of American companies' lack of understanding of the boycott. U.S. businessmen simply did not realize that they could do business with Israel if they wanted.[18] After the oil embargo, however, the Israelis' attitude changed. As Deputy Prime Minister Yigal Allon told the Knesset in February 1975: "The instrument of war this time [is not] the tank and the concentration camp but the check and the petrodollar."[19]

After a banking scandal erupted in Europe involving Arab discrimination against Jewish-owned firms, President Ford condemned the boycott during his 26 February 1975 press conference and thereby gave new urgency to the issue. As the *Chicago Tribune* (28 February) wrote: "President Ford's statement Wednesday, the strongest public denunciation of the boycott by a Western head of state since it was imposed in 1946, was a deliberate escalation of U.S. policy on the issue, . . . " although, the *Jewish Post and Opinion* (7 March) pointed out it had not used the words "Arab boycott." Given the president's lead, the Israeli lobby became active.

In February, the staff directors of the Anti-Defamation League (ADL), American Jewish Committee, and American Jewish Congress arranged a conference at Harvard with a group of economists. In an unprecedented move, the three directors decided to coordinate their activities to maximize their effectiveness. The three also decided that AIPAC should be excluded to prevent the antiboycott effort from being confused with the effort to win American support for Israel.[20]

There was some concern that support for antiboycott legislation would undermine the Israeli lobby's position on other issues or prompt some form of Arab retaliation; nevertheless, nearly a dozen antiboycott amendments to the Export Administration Act were proposed during the ninety-fourth Congress. On 5 March

Senator Adlai Stevenson introduced an amendment that increased reporting requirements for firms that receive boycott requests, and gave the president the authority to reduce economic transactions with boycotting countries. The amendment was primarily directed toward the tertiary boycott.

In the House, Jonathan Bingham introduced a much more stringent bill, which attempted, according to the Senate Banking Committee's staff expert, Stanley Marcuss, "to end compliance with the boycott, whatever the consequences." The difference between the two bills, Marcuss said was that "the Senate viewed the legislative issue as primarily one of U.S. sovereignty and the rights of American citizens, [while] the House viewed the issue as primarily a foreign policy matter, requiring the United States to counter and undermine the boycott of Israel itself. . . . "[21]

The Israeli lobby, meanwhile, addressed the issue in both chambers with an emphasis on the discriminatory aspects of the boycott. Thus, while Stevenson and Marcuss were arguing for free trade, the American Jewish Congress' Paul Berger was claiming the boycott "demands that companies doing business in Arab lands, including American companies, must make themselves 'judenrein'—with respect of officers, employees, and those with whom they do business. . . . " This theme was echoed in speeches by members of both Houses, leading the Israeli government to worry that, by focusing on discrimination, the secondary boycott might be ignored and legislation would only be offered to deal with the religion issue.[22]

There was some opposition from the business community, but business, in general, maintained a low profile during the early part of the antiboycott debate. Raymond Garcia, president of the Emergency Committee for American Trade (ECAT), which represents sixty-five multinational corporations, explained why: "Kissinger and Simon and Ford said the legislation would be harmful to the Mideast peace effort. Under those circumstances, the business community felt if that was U.S. policy, the business community would let the executive branch state those views." Teslik adds: "This strategy had worked in 1965 and was backed by the threat of a presidential veto. Moreover, it looked better for antiboycott legislation to be opposed by government officials than by businessmen getting rich off of Arab contracts."[23]

In November, the administration moved to forestall antiboycott legislation. On the twentieth, Ford issued an executive order strengthening the Commerce Department's reporting requirements and proposed a comprehensive package to prevent discrimination against Americans. The package included orders for agencies making overseas assignments not to take into account the exclusionary policies of host countries; instructions to the State Department to take diplomatic action on behalf of individuals denied visas because of these policies; and orders for the Commerce Department to prohibit firms from complying with boycott requests which could cause discrimination against Americans.[24]

These were just the kind of cosmetic changes the Israeli government had warned would be adopted if the Israeli lobby insisted on emphasizing the discrimination issue. For its part, the ADL welcomed the president's package as a first step, but maintained that it "fails to come to grips with the full scope of Arab boycott operations in the United States."[25] Less than one month later, in fact, the American Jewish Congress revealed that Saudi Arabia had informed ARAMCO that it would not issue visas to "undesirable persons, it being understood that the undesirable persons include the Jews."[26] Nevertheless, the administration continued to stand by its policy of quiet diplomacy and to stress the need to support "legitimate U.S. interests in the Middle East."[27]

Ford's Last Year

At the beginning of 1976, the Saudis reacted to the antiboycott proposals with a mixture of indignation and resignation. Farouk Akhdar, a planning official, expressed the former sentiment when he said that Congress "might put us in a position where we receive [business] from elsewhere. No country will dictate to us what we will do." The Planning Minister, Hisham Nazer, laid the burden of opposing the legislation on American companies, which he said had to "safeguard their right to work and earn."[28] On the other hand, the Saudi Commerce Minister, Suleiman al-Salayim, expressed an understanding of American domestic politics and was confident "things will be cleared up in a year—once the elections are over." [29]

Despite the implicit Arab threats, most U.S. companies were hesitant to enter the fray. They were no doubt discouraged further by the Justice Department's decision to charge Bechtel with the suppression of competition by excluding blacklisted individuals and firms from subcontracting contracts the company had with the Arabs. The State Department was afraid the suit would alienate Saudi Arabia. The business community, along with the federal bureaucracy, thought the United States would lose billions of dollars of potential Arab business and asked the Attorney General to withdraw the lawsuit. He refused and the case dragged on until January 1977, when the Justice Department and Bechtel signed a consent decree prohibiting the company from refusing to deal with blacklisted American firms, and from requiring other companies to do the same. The order was only binding on Bechtel. The Israeli lobby was dissatisfied, arguing that the agreement not only failed to prohibit Bechtel from participating in the Arab boycott but "in effect explains to Bechtel how to continue to participate." [30] The resolution of the Bechtel case helped convince many in Congress that existing law was inadequate for dealing with the boycott.

Business, in general, remained sensitive to the appearance of cooperating with the boycott and stayed in the background of the legislative battle. Some feared a counter-boycott and, although the Israeli lobby had decided against such a tactic, there were no doubt memories of past lobby-led boycotts. An aide to the House International Relations Committee complained: "We had tried early to get business comment on the bill, but they were reluctant because they did not want to offend either side." [31]

Many American companies supported the principle of anti-boycott legislation and refused to bow to the Arab blacklist. The response of RCA's Eugene P. Seculow was typical when he called the boycott's effect on American business "capricious and insidious" and said: "Our position has been very simple. We believe in free trade and we are attempting to do business everywhere in the world where it is not against U.S. laws. But we won't comply with the boycott to negotiate our way off the list." [32]

The only major business group to testify against the antiboycott proposals in 1976 was the Associated General Contractors of America (AGC) whose members had substantial building contracts in the Middle East. Their spokesman, Edwin Jones, claimed that the construction industry would lose more than $200 million in potential foreign business and 80,000 American jobs over a five year period if the antiboycott legislation was adopted.[33]

The National Association of Arab-American's (NAAA) did not even oppose the legislation during Ford's tenure. In fact, executive director Michael Saba said the organization wanted to see an amendment to end the boycott. In 1975, the NAAA was not yet registered as a lobby and, moreover, preferred to focus its energies on increasing representation of the Arab lobby's interests in Congress.[34]

The nature of the debate changed in 1976 from the previous year's emphasis on the discrimination issue, to a more general concern with American complicity in the boycott. "There is a strong feeling," Senator Stevenson said, "that Congress should not permit American companies to be enlisted in a war against Israel."[35] The issue was reduced to a choice between principle and corporate greed.

By the summer of 1976, the legislative momentum was nearing its peak. The House International Relations Committee had adopted an amendment that prohibited U.S. agencies from cooperating with discriminatory practices of foreign governments when assigning personnel abroad, and the full House passed an amendment preventing American universities from receiving federal aid to fulfill discriminatory foreign contracts.

A major conflict erupted between the administration and Congress in July when the chairman of a House subcommittee tried to obtain copies of the boycott reports filed by American companies with the Commerce Department. There were thousands of reports on file, three-quarters of which were filed by firms that declined to reveal whether they had complied with boycott demands. The reports, therefore, were thought to be "loaded with dynamite."[36] The committee concluded that the Commerce Department had deliberately misled Congress about the extent of U.S. companies' compliance with the boycott and had actually encouraged compliance.

On 24 July, Commerce Secretary Rogers C.B. Morton sent the

committee a summary of the reports, but refused to provide the reports themselves because they had been submitted to Commerce under a pledge of confidentiality. After being threatened with a contempt citation, Morton agreed to turn over the reports in return for a promise of confidentiality. The nearly five month fight kept the boycott issue in the limelight and made it appear the administration was protecting companies guilty of boycott complicity, and "smacked of the secrecy and distrust of Congress that had loomed large in the Watergate episode and Richard Nixon's resignation." Substantively, the Commerce reports indicated the participation of American businesses was much greater than previously thought. Instead of the $10 million Commerce said was involved in boycott-related trade, the figure was $4.5 billion, with a 94 percent rate of compliance reported by exporters for the period of March–September 1976.[37]

The main arguments in the debate surfaced in House testimony. The American Jewish Congress' Will Maslow said that the businessmen were "willing to defy the boycott if only they were given some statutory authority to do so." Federal Reserve Board Chairman Arthur Burns testified that "it is unfair to expect some banks to suffer competitive penalties for responding affirmatively to the spirit of U.S. policy, while others profit by ignoring the policy."[38] The administration's main argument was expressed by Treasury Secretary William Simon:

> We believe that peace in the Middle East is the only ultimate answer. In the administration's view, heavy-handed measures which could result in confrontation with the Arab world will not work. A far more constructive approach, we believe, is to work through our growing economic and political relations with the Arab states, as well as our close relations with Israel, and the broad range of contacts which the executive branch and the regulatory agencies maintain with the U.S. business community to achieve progress on the boycott issue.[39]

The Secretary added that the Arabs would simply go elsewhere to trade if the United States enacted antiboycott laws.

The Israeli lobby answer to this line of argument was that administrations had claimed that antiboycott legislation would undermine peace negotiations for more than a decade, and yet peace was still a remote possibility. The ADL's Seymour Graubard remarked that "we cannot work passively any longer for final peace in the Middle East before seeking to halt Arab coercion of American business firms."[40]

Another argument used by the legislation's opponents was that it would have serious political and economic repercussions. Rep. Delbert Latta, for example, asserted that the Arab response would be an oil embargo and, although the Saudis denied it, they were hurt by reports that they had threatened an oil embargo.[41]

As the House vote approached, the Arab lobby began a concerted effort to defeat the legislation. Mobil Oil ran ads warning against the passage of antiboycott legislation, and Exxon took what the *Wall Street Journal* (30 September) called "one of the strongest stands it has ever taken on a controversial public issue." The Arab Information Center distributed copies of its *Arab Report* dealing with the boycott issue, and the U.S.-Arab Chamber of Commerce sent telegrams to all the members of Congress as well as the president and vice-president. The NAAA also ran advertisements opposing boycott legislation. In addition, the Saudi Foreign Minister, Prince Saud ben Faisal spoke with the president and lobbied members of Congress.[42] Despite the last-minute efforts, the Export Administration Act with the Bingham amendment was adopted by the full House 318–63 on 22 September. The Arab reaction was again threatening. "Damn American law!" Kuwait's Finance Minister said, "We will boycott and we will continue to boycott, and we will never import anything from the U.S.!"[43]

The overwhelming vote should have given the administration a good idea of the depth of congressional support for the measure, but Ford remained stubbornly opposed to any antiboycott legislation. The House bill was especially strict, banning a wide range of boycott-related activities and imposing civil and criminal penalties on violators. The administration also opposed Senator Stevenson's amendment, however, which was much more moderate, calling only for public disclosure of compliance with boycott requests. The administration was not persuasive and the Senate passed the Stevenson amendment by the comfortable margin of 65–13. In retrospect, had the administration been willing to compromise, it is very likely that a relatively weak bill would have emerged from Congress.

Since the bills passed just a week before the existing law expired, there was a sense of urgency surrounding efforts to reconcile differences in the two bills. Although a compromise was worked out by an "unofficial" conference committee, it was never approved because a Senate filibuster prevented the conference committee from being appointed.

While the Senate was tied up, the administration decided to make an effort at a compromise of its own. Two days before Congress was to adjourn, the administration proposed an antiboycott bill that was weaker than either of those passed by Congress. Ford's motivation for the initiative was primarily to shift the blame for the failure to adopt antiboycott legislation onto Congress, which he did in the subsequent presidential debate. Knowing this to be the case, Democrats in Congress were unwilling to let the president off the hook. "The Democrats had a good issue and they knew it. There was no chance," Moses added, "that they would fritter it away by agreeing to a half measure at the behest of a campaigning Jerry Ford."[44] Consequently, Ford's efforts failed and the Export Administration Act expired on September 30. The same day, the president issued an Executive Order extending the Act, while reducing some of its penalties, until the 95th Congress could enact a new bill.

Another source of pressure on the president was his opponent, Jimmy Carter, who made the boycott a campaign issue by raising it during the foreign policy debate (6 October) with the president. "I believe," he said, "that the boycott of American businesses by the Arab countries because those businesses trade with Israel or because they have American Jews who are owners or directors in the company is an absolute disgrace," and promised "I'll do everything I can as President to stop the boycott of American business by the Arab countries."[45]

President Ford, meanwhile, was prepared with a rebuttal to Carter. He had already set up Congress by trying to force a compromise and now tried to take advantage of the tactic by announcing that since "*Congress* had failed to act" he was ordering Secretary of Commerce Elliott Richardson to disclose the names of companies that had participated in the boycott.

For the first time, the business community became frightened. *Newsweek* (25 October) reported that businessmen preferred risking fines for failure to file reports, to having their companies' names disclosed. "What really seems to concern the business community," *Newsweek* reported, "isn't so much the new disclosure policy itself but the growing antiboycott sentiment it reflects."

Despite Richardson's failure to carry out Ford's order, the threat this sentiment represented stimulated business opposition on a scale unseen previously. Given his campaign position on the boycott, the election of Jimmy Carter convinced many businesses that had stayed on the sidelines in 1976 to join the battle, and induced those that had participated in the debate to intensify their efforts.

Although the disparate views of its members prevented the Chamber of Commerce from taking a position, its president, Richard Lehmann, and ECAT's Raymond Garcia chaired a weekly meeting of the Trade Action Coordinating Committee that became increasingly concerned with the boycott. The argument that the U.S. economy would suffer became an increasingly popular theme of the opponents of antiboycott legislation. Reflecting that theme, the Arab lobby created a boycott task force—Full Employment in America Through Trade, Inc. (FEATT)—on 11 November 1976, at a meeting sponsored by the NAAA. FEATT claimed that antiboycott legislation would cause the United States to lose $30–50 billion and 800,000 to one million jobs over a five-year period. Congress did not find these warnings of dire consequences to the U.S. economy convincing, especially since organized labor supported the legislation. As it turned out, the FEATT quickly fell apart.[46]

A "Friendly" Administration Takes Over

Jimmy Carter said in June 1977 that his strong stand against the boycott "was one of the things that led to my election," and this may very well have been true. His position had been drafted by Representative Rosenthal's office and was designed, at least in part, to attract Jewish voters. The strategy paid off because it was the Jewish vote that helped Carter defeat Ford in key electoral college states. For example, if only one in nine of the New York Jews who voted for Carter had voted for Ford, he would have lost New York and the presidency.[47] As a result, Carter theoretically had a campaign debt to repay.

The antiboycott issue provided Carter with a relatively costless means of repaying the debt. The legislation had overwhelming support in the last Congress and had not lost any momentum, even though the election had come and gone. An additional stimulus was provided when several state legislatures adopted their own antiboycott laws. Pressure was thus put on the federal government to pass a law that would create a uniform policy on the boycott, and prevent some states with tough antiboycott laws from being put at a competitive disadvantage to those with no laws. The announcement of the consent decree between the Justice Department and Bechtel on 10 January, combined with increasing evidence of business compliance with the boycott publicized by the Israeli lobby as a result of the Commerce Department's disclosure of its reports, added fuel to the antiboycott fire. The most important change in 1977, however, was the support of the president replacing the Ford threat of a veto. Given this support, antiboycott legislation was reintroduced in Congress.

Despite the legislative momentum, public support, and his own campaign promises, Carter began to back away from his support for antiboycott legislation. This might be partly explained by the general tendency of presidents to take positions in their campaigns to attract Jewish votes, which they cannot or will not stand behind once they are elected. In addition, one of the themes of the Carter administration was to be the need to escape dependence on Middle East oil. The knowledge that the United States was dependent on foreign oil tempered his support for policies opposed by the Arabs. The president was also obsessed with the desire to apply his belief in mutual cooperation to the Middle East. Thus, the effort to negotiate a comprehensive peace in the region was a focal point of the administration's early foreign policy initiatives. The antiboycott legislation was seen as having the potential to upset the Arabs and thereby endanger both American oil supplies and Carter's peace efforts.

Early in January 1977, the administration expressed support for antiboycott legislation. In February, however, Secretary of State Cyrus Vance said that both antiboycott bills were flawed and should be replaced by new legislation. He subsequently presented Congress with a set of amendments that significantly weakened the existing proposals. This retreat was primarily due to Carter's peace efforts. To play an active role in the search for Middle East peace, the administration had to consider the effect of a race to enact antiboycott legislation, on its perception as an "honest broker" in peace negotiations.[48]

For their part, the Arabs renewed many of their old threats. Prince Fahd told the *Sunday Times* (4 April) that antiboycott legislation might be met with an increase in oil prices. Sheik Ahmed Zaki Yamani, the Saudi petroleum minister, told sixteen senators on 4 April that the Saudis would continue to fight Israel with the boycott. The following month, the Arab chambers of commerce and industry urged that foreign firms that refuse to cooperate with the boycott be blacklisted, and called antiboycott efforts a "further example of imperialist interference with the exercise of the sovereignty of independent states."[49]

Despite sometimes harsh rhetoric, the business community was well aware that some form of antiboycott bill would be adopted. Thus, even the U.S. Chamber of Commerce had issued a policy statement supporting legislation that would "eliminate or reduce any restrictive trade practices impeding the freest flow of international trade." In addition, corporate executives like C. L. Whitehill of General Mills remained vigorous supporters of the Israeli lobby position.[50]

On 5 April, the Senate Banking Committee reported out an antiboycott bill that included amendments permitting boycotters to make unilateral selections of goods that are easily identifiable by source, and allowing subsidiaries of U.S. companies to abide by the laws of host countries. The Israeli lobby was disappointed by the weakening of the bill and a joint statement was issued by several Jewish organizations applauding the essentials of the bill, but condemning its loopholes. The statement also expressed dissatisfaction with Carter's retreat from his previous commitment to effective legislation. The business lobby was also dissatisfied, but recognized that it was not going to be able to weaken the legislation any further. Both sides became increasingly convinced that further confrontation would have little benefit, and that each might suffer substantially higher costs in terms of hostility from the other, as well as the administration and Congress if the battle was prolonged. The Israeli lobby was given further incentive by the Israeli government's interest in a compromise.[51] As a result, the two sides entered into negotiations to resolve their differences.

Negotiations between the two lobbies actually began in 1976, when a meeting was arranged between George Shultz of Bechtel, Irving Shapiro of DuPont, several other business leaders, and officials of the ADL to discuss a compromise. The ADL was apparently unwilling to make any concessions to the businessmen because Shapiro said he and his colleagues "ran into a brick wall." In late November, Shapiro was at an ADL dinner and mentioned to the ADL's national director Benjamin Epstein that it was unfortunate the antiboycott battle was causing a rift between business and the Jewish community. Shapiro pointed out that American investments had helped build up the Israeli economy and that it was a mistake for the Israeli lobby to confront the business community. Shapiro suggested that the ADL and business leaders get together to try to work out a compromise. Epstein agreed and a meeting was set for January 28.

There were a number of reasons why both parties were anxious to negotiate. Teslik explains:

> business wanted to minimize the damage to United States-Arab trade that antiboycott legislation implied; and the ADL knew that an endorsement from big business would expedite the passage of a veto-proof bill. But both also wanted to protect the public images and political influences of the institutions they represented. . . . The Business Roundtable feared looking money-hungry in a public debate, an image that plagues the oil industry, and the ADL did not want to look like it cared more about a foreign country, Israel, than about full employment, American economic growth, and American foreign policy objectives.[52]

In addition, the election of Jimmy Carter had eliminated any possibility that the bill would be vetoed.

The January meeting was held at the Seagram Building in New York. The organization ostensibly representing business was the Business Roundtable (BR), a group founded in 1972 and representing 170 corporations. What made the BR powerful was the combination of the involvement of corporate executives and access to the resources of member companies. Shapiro, the BR chairman, had particularly close ties to the administration and was considered "the unofficial chairman of the board of American business." Moreover, he had "unimpeachable credentials as a concerned and active member of the American Jewish community."[53] The main negotiator for the Israeli lobby was the ADL's Burton Joseph. It was not until much later in the talks that the American Jewish Committee and American Jewish Congress (AJCs) became actively involved.

The initial meeting succeeded in producing a task force which received encouragement from both Congress and the administration. Several weeks later (on 2 March), a Joint Statement of Principles was announced in which the parties agreed that American companies *should not* be free to comply with the boycott by discriminating against Americans nor by boycotting Israel or blacklisted U.S. companies. The statement also provided for certain exceptions, the most important being an allowance for "unilateral selection"; that is, the Arabs' prerogative to choose which suppliers should provide component goods and services.[54] Three members of the BR expressed reservations about the agreement and the chairman of Mobil, Rawleigh Warner, Jr., dissented. In addition, the AJCs and other Jewish organizations had not been directly involved in the negotiations and were not asked to stand behind the statement.[55] Thus, the less than unanimous support of the respective constituencies was to make implementation of the agreement difficult.

On 8 March, Alfred Moses of the American Jewish Committee told the House International Relations Committee that the principles in the joint statement were embodied in the language of an amendment proposed by Representative Rosenthal. This shocked the BR, which had negotiated the compromise to avoid the strict House bill. Two days later, Shapiro sent letters to President Carter, Senator Adlai Stevenson, Representative Clement Zablocki, and other officials objecting to Moses' testimony.

On 14 March, Shapiro, Joseph and other negotiators met to try to repair the damage done by Moses' testimony. Whatever progress was made was undone the very next day when the two men gave contradictory testimony before the Stevenson Subcommittee.[56] Thus, the ADL-BR negotiations resulted in mistrust, misunderstanding, and bitterness between the parties. Worse yet, the Israeli lobby found itself with little support from other interest groups. "Although American principles and ideals are at stake in the boycott controversy," the *Congressional Quarterly* reported, "the issue has been pursued almost exclusively by the nation's Jewish community."[57]

Since it appeared the ADL-BR agreement had broken down, the White House pressed the House to come up with a compromise of its own. At the end of March, an unofficial subcommittee of the International Relations Committee met and agreed to amendments permitting U.S. companies to comply with unilateral selection requirements, if they did not know the sole purpose of the selection was to implement the boycott, and also giving the president authority to grant exception from antiboycott prohibitions to allow companies to comply with local laws. The administration accepted the amendments and the bill was reported out of committee. The business community still thought the bill was too strict, while the Israeli lobby complained that it was too weak. What the amendments really represented was the influence of the Carter administration which, for the first time in the long debate, asserted its will.[58]

The President had stayed in the background for almost the entire debate, but on 9 April his political adviser, Stuart Eizenstat, called in the Israeli lobby's negotiators and told them "the president wants this resolved" and that they needed to compromise. Business groups that had been denied access to the president were told the same thing. The president was willing, Eizenstat told both parties, to accept whatever they were able to work out.[59]

On 19 April, the two sides resumed negotiations. Paul Berger of the American Jewish Congress, Max Kampelman of the ADL, and Alfred Moses of the American Jewish Committee now represented the Israeli lobby, and a group of Business Roundtable lawyers led by Hans Angermueller of Citibank represented the business community. An agreement was reached that tightened various provisions and limited exceptions to the antiboycott proposal. In return for these concessions, the Israeli lobby negotiators accepted a broader version of the unilateral selection exception and a weaker ban on negative certification.[60]

The following week, at the AIPAC policy conference, Jewish leaders argued over the agreement. Morris Amitay, the executive director of AIPAC, wanted his organization to enter the fray and lead a floor fight for a stricter bill. The American Jewish Congress' Phil Baum agreed. They already had the support of Senators William Proxmire and Paul Sarbanes for such a fight, but the Israelis and the other leaders succeeded in persuading the others to accept the compromise.

The business lobby also was having difficulty reaching a consensus on the compromise. Dresser Industries and Mobil led a campaign against the agreement, returning to the scare tactics of previous months, claiming that 500,000 American jobs would be lost, oil prices would rise, and an anti-Semitic backlash would result from the adoption of antiboycott legislation.

The divisions within the business lobby were evident up to the final vote, as various corporations maintained their opposition. There was only one company that concerned Shapiro, however, and that was Exxon. Since Exxon had the largest investment in the Middle East, he believed that other companies would support the agreement if he could get Exxon to approve it.

In another example of government officials lobbying an interest group, Vance and Eizenstat contacted Exxon's chairman Clifton Garvin, and told him the president wanted the agreement approved and that the compromise would help his efforts to achieve peace in the Middle East. These admonitions, along with those of other business leaders, persuaded Garvin to go along with the compromise. The BR's forty-two member policy committee then approved the agreement, after receiving mailgrams from Garvin, Shapiro, Shultz, Reginald Jones of General Electric, and Walter Wriston of Citicorp.[61]

The Israeli lobby was successful in framing the debate in terms of U.S. domestic policy rather than U.S. Middle East policy. The press went along with this understanding, printing editorials supporting antiboycott legislation as a means of upholding American principles. For example, the *Washington Post* (17 April) wrote: "No realistic person would assert that an antiboycott law will not cost something. . . . But if there is a price to keep foreigners from compelling Americans to trample on their own basic values, surely it is worth paying and, as surely, thoughtful and responsible Americans will be willing to pay it." Opponents of the measure saw things differently; for example, Robert Michel complained: "There is fear, a very real fear, present in the House that those who question or vote against . . . [antiboycott legislation] will be labeled less than friendly to the nation of Israel." Rosenthal's rebuttal was that the issue was not whether to vote for or against Israel, "It is a vote for or against fundamental American principles."[62]

The House voted overwhelmingly (364–43) for the antiboycott legislation. Whether the vote was for Israel or "fundamental American principles" is impossible to say, but the fact that the two motivations were compatible no doubt influenced the outcome and the size of the majority.

The House vote was taken *before* the ADL-BR agreement was announced, indicating not only that the legislation had a certain degree of momentum, but also that the arguments of the Israeli lobby had the upper hand. In the Senate, there was little suspense after President Carter gave his blessing to the ADL-BR agreement on 3 May. Senator John Heinz introduced the amendments agreed upon by the negotiators and, in a speech approved by the ADL, said: "It is somewhat unusual for us to consider intact actual language developed outside the Congress, but in this case I believe the circumstances clearly warrant it." What was unusual was not that interest groups had written the legislation, but that Congress and the president had encouraged them to do so, and also had accepted the negotiators' appeal not to add amendments.[63] The Senate then adopted the bill by a vote of 90–91. This time there were no parliamentary obstacles to the Conference Committee's deliberations, and the Senate version of the bill was approved by both Houses.

The Arab League responded in typically bombastic fashion. During the 8 June boycott conference in Alexandria, Mohammed Mahgoub said the League would take a decisive stand against the new law, which he regarded as part of "a campaign of hysterical laws and bills . . . which Israel and world Zionism are trying not only to enforce on the U.S.; but also in some countries of western Europe."[64] Mahgoub also reiterated the now routine threats that the Arabs would buy their goods elsewhere, as well as a new policy of keeping the names of companies removed from the blacklist a secret to protect them from pressure.

The law as finally adopted encourages, and in some specified cases, requires U.S. companies to refuse to take actions that have the effect of supporting the restrictive trade practices or boycotts fostered or imposed by any foreign country against a country friendly to the United States or against any American. The law permits U.S. companies to comply with the primary Arab boycott. They are also allowed to comply with requirements forbidding the shipment or transshipment of Arab exports to Israel. Positive certificates of origin may be issued and unilateral selection by Arab customers is permitted. Violation of the Act is punishable by a $25,000 fine and/or one year in prison. The Commerce Department may also impose a civil penalty of not more than $10,000 for other violations.

Contrary to the claims that the bill would lead to a drastic reduction in trade with the Arab world, trade has substantially increased. In fact, from the time the law went into effect, 1978, through 1982, U.S. exports to the boycotting nations rose from $9.4 billion to $18.5 billion, almost a 100 percent increase.[65] Although it is impossible to prove that U.S. trade would not be greater in the absence of the law, the data indicates that U.S. business has not suffered too much damage as a result of its adoption.

Summary

Senator Adlai Stevenson said the antiboycott issue "has generated as much emotion and pressure as I have seen generated by any issue since I came to Congress."[66] That pressure emanated from the Israeli lobby. Although the Ford administration attempted to frame the issue in realist terms; that is, the proposed legislation threatened U.S.-Arab relations and the flow of oil, large majorities in Congress interpreted the issue differently. Since the issue was essentially economic (and political), Congress was not as likely to defer to the president; moreover, congressmen perceived the boycott as a threat to other national interests—freedom of trade and antidiscrimination—which were at least as important as those allegedly threatened by the legislation. Thus, the realist model alone again fails to provide guidance as to whose perception of the national interest will prevail.

In fact, there was a fairly long history of congressional concern with the boycott. In 1960 and 1965, the president succeeded in emasculating legislative remedies, but the laxity of enforcement that followed sowed the seeds for stronger legislation in the future. By 1976, Congress had become unhappy with the Commerce Department's implementation of the 1965 antiboycott provisions, but this was probably less important than revelations of U.S. complicity with the boycott and the blatant discrimination practiced by the Arab League. These events served as catalysts for legislative action and reinforced the lobby's arguments that American principles were at stake.

The Israeli lobby was successful in putting an issue of concern on the legislative agenda. As Steiner points out, if some other nation instituted a boycott, for example, India against Pakistan, it is unlikely that there would be any public outcry, but because Israel was the target of the boycott, and there is a domestic lobby concerned about Israel, this boycott became an issue.[67]

As the pluralist model suggests, the Israeli lobby benefitted from the absence of competition from other interest groups. In 1976, both the Arab lobby and the business lobby, in general, were content to let the Ford administration fight its battle. The business community was hesitant to actively oppose the legislation because it did not want to appear to be cooperating with the boycott. In addition, as is the case with the business lobby in general, there were splits within the ranks. Many large and influential corporations actually supported the legislation.

After Carter's election, when it became evident that some antiboycott legislation was inevitable, both the Arab and business lobbies intensified their lobbying activities. In order to cut their losses, businessmen decided to negotiate with the Israeli lobby and a compromise was ultimately reached. Nevertheless, the debate represented a fairly close approximation to the outcome anticipated by the pluralist model. In this case, there were two competing lobbies, and the dominant one's interest was adopted with modifications forced upon it by the opposition. The Israeli lobby held the balance of lobbying power; that is, it built a stronger coalition, was more unified, and could count on its informal component to exert pressure on congressmen. The way the issue was presented by the lobby—principles over profits—was also difficult for its opposition to counter. In addition, both houses of

Congress were on record in favor of the legislation in 1976, and the House passed its 1977 bill *before* the Israeli and business lobbies negotiated the compromise that resulted in the final bill. It was the business lobby, then, that was under greater pressure to make concessions in order to prevent more stringent legislation from being adopted.

Although the boycott was a campaign issue in 1976, the election did not have the impact the lobby's critics allege. If politicians were as concerned about the "Jewish vote" as they say, then Ford would not have opposed what was obviously an extremely popular measure during the election year, and the issue would have faded away after the election. The fact that neither of these results occurred suggests that electoral concerns are not paramount. This is not to say they have no impact whatsoever, however, as we saw, Ford did take some action to strengthen the monitoring of compliance of existing legislation, and offered a last minute compromise bill after he was criticized by Carter for failing to confront the boycott. For his part, Carter made the boycott a campaign issue and promised to take action once he became president.

Since Carter expressed a different position from Ford on the boycott, the leadership model should help explain the outcome. Given Ford's opposition, the bill should have been defeated if the president's position is the dominant criterion for policy outcomes; however, both houses of Congress did pass bills over his opposition. The fact that the antiboycott bill did not become law under Ford, was more a matter of luck than design, since Congress failed to pass the final bill because it ran out of time. Had Ford been re-elected, the bill would almost certainly have been adopted.

In order to understand how the lobby could overcome Ford's opposition, it is necessary to look at the domestic political context. By 1975, Congress was in a skeptical mood and was willing to challenge the executive. In the aftermath of Watergate, the controversy over Commerce Secretary Morton's unwillingness to release department boycott reports fed congressional suspicions. Given Congress' foreign policy assertiveness during the Ford Administration, then, we would expect a greater likelihood that a measure proposed by the Israeli lobby would attract congressional support. Even if members of Congress support the lobby's position, however, the president might still be able to win as we saw in chapter 2. One difference in the two cases is that the arms sales were administration initiatives, and therefore a defeat would have meant a rebuke of the president, while the antiboycott bill represented a legislative policy the adoption of which would not necessarily repudiate the president's policy.

The probability that the president would be defeated on the issue was also increased by the decline in Ford's political capital. Unlike President Johnson, Ford had little political capital with which to oppose the bill. In 1965, Johnson was not running for reelection, in fact he had just been elected in a landslide. His popularity stood at an incredible 80 percent and he enjoyed the support of large majorities in Congress. Ford, on the other hand, suffered the quickest and most severe decline in public approval ever recorded during his first three months in office. In addition, there were only 37 Republican senators and 144 congressmen, the lowest level of support for a sitting president in this century. Given that Ford was up for re-election, it is hard to understand why he did not support the legislation. Congress supported it, his opponent supported it, and a majority of Americans seemed to support it. Ford does not even mention the issue in his memoirs. It may have been, at least partly, a case of a Republican not being concerned with the Jewish vote, as well as the expressed view that antiboycott legislation would hurt U.S.-Arab relations.

When Jimmy Carter was elected president, he not only had campaign promises to keep regarding the boycott, but also had a debt to repay to his Jewish constituents whose support helped put him in the White House. When he came into office, he enjoyed the usual presidential honeymoon and had the popular support of about 75 percent of the public. In Congress, Carter had a presumably friendly majority of 61 senators and 292 representatives. Given Carter's political capital, and the fact that Congress was already on record in support of boycott legislation, the question was no longer whether there would be a bill, but what shape it would ultimately take.

After the business community began to take a more active part in lobbying against the bill, the administration became less involved in pushing the issue, preferring to leave it to the antagonists. When it appeared that negotiations between the parties might not lead to a resolution, however, the president, through his advisers, exerted enough pressure to force a compromise. It was the strength of Carter's political position and the presidency in general, rather than any ideological differences with Ford that led to the outcome. Carter apparently did not consider the issue much more important than Ford, since he only devotes one paragraph of his memoirs to expressing his outrage toward the boycott and claiming credit for the legislative outcome.[68] In fact, the fear that antiboycott legislation might hurt his two major obsessions: pursuit of a Middle East peace agreement and alleviation of U.S. energy dependence on OPEC, led Carter to back away from his prior support for strong legislation. It was Israeli lobby pressure that insured, however, that the bill would not be abandoned.

Notes

1. Terence Prittie and Walter Nelson, *The Economic War Against the Jews* (London: Corgi Books, 1977), 1; Dan Chill, *The Arab Boycott of Israel* (NY: Praeger, 1976), 1.
2. Chill, *The Arab Boycott of Israel*, 5, 80; Hilmny, *National Journal* 1090; Prittie and Nelson, *The Economic War Against the Jews*, 123.
3. Kennan L. Teslik, *Congress, the Executive Branch and Special Interests* (CT: Greenwood Press, 1982), 11.
4. Chill, *The Arab Boycott of Israel*, 47.
5. *Near East Report* (5 May 1964), 38.
6. *Near East Report* (23 March 1965), 21.
7. Chill, *The Arab Boycott of Israel*, 49; Teslik, *Congress, the Executive Branch and Special Interests*, 57.
8. Ibid., 50.
9. Prittie and Nelson, *The Economic War Against the Jews*, 37; Teslik, *Congress, the Executive Branch and Special Interests*, 69.
10. Robert J. Samuelson, "As the Oil Flows, So Flows the Trade," *National Journal* (29 January 1977), 161; Teslik, *Congress, the Executive Branch and Special Interests*, 6; Mitchell Bard, "The Myth of the Middle East Triangle," *Midstream* (October 1985), 7–10.
11. Sol Stern, "On and Off the Arabs' List," *The New Republic* (27 March 1976), 8; Samuelson, "As the Oil Flows," 162.
12. Teslik, *Congress, the Executive Branch and Special Interests*, 71.
13. Ibid., 5.
14. Prittie and Nelson, *The Economic War Against the Jews*, 80; Will Maslow, "The Struggle Against the Arab Boycott," *Midstream* (August–September, 1977), 12.
15. Prittie and Nelson, *The Economic War Against the Jews*, 82.

16. Ibid.
17. *Near East Report* (26 February 1975), 33; Teslik, *Congress, the Executive Branch and Special Interests*, 136; Interview with Rep. Waxman.
18. Nancy Turck, "The Arab Boycott of Israel," *Foreign Affairs* (April 1977), 479.
19. Teslik, *Congress, the Executive Branch and Special Interests*, 91–92.
20. Maslow, "Struggle Against the Arab Boycott, 11–12.
21. *Near East Report* (12 March, 1975), 46; Teslik, *Congress, the Executive Branch and Special Interests*, 82–97.
22. Teslik, *Congress, the Executive Branch and Special Interests*, 111.
23. Ibid., 132.
24. Prittie and Nelson, *The Economic War Against the Jews*, 194–5; Turck, "The Arab Boycott of Israel," 485–6.
25. Teslik, *Congress, the Executive Branch and Special Interests*, 105.
26. Chill, *The Arab Boycott of Israel*, 6–7.
27. Stern, "On and Off the Arabs' List," 8.
28. *Near East Report* (14 January 1976), 7.
29. Teslik, *Congress, the Executive Branch and Special Interests*, 136.
30. Ibid., 175; Turck, "The Arab Boycott of Israel," 487; Prittie and Nelson, *The Economic War Against the Jews*, 104; *Near East Report* (7 April 1976), 57.
31. Richard E. Cohen, "The Anti-Arab Boycott Bill—Welcome to Business's Hard Times," *National Journal* (29 January 1977), 166.
32. Stern, "On and Off the Arabs' List," 11.
33. Paul Lewis, "Administration is Boycotting Anti-Arab Boycott Bills," *National Journal* (19 June 1976), 858.
34. Teslik, *Congress, the Executive Branch and Special Interests*, 135.
35. Ibid., 125.
36. Prittie and Nelson, *The Economic War Against the Jews*, 197.
37. Teslik, *Congress, the Executive Branch and Special Interests*, 99–102; Prittie and Nelson, *The Economic War Against the Jews*, 198.
38. Lewis, 858–9; Teslik, 130.
39. Teslik, 131; Prittie and Nelson, 200; Lewis, 858.
40. Lewis, "Administration is Boycotting," 859.
41. Teslik, 140; David Maxfield, "House Approves Strong Anti-Boycott Law," *Weekly Report* (Congressional Quarterly, 25 September 1976), 2623.
42. Teslik, *Congress, the Executive Branch and Special Interests*, 146–7.
43. Prittie and Nelson, *The Economic War Against the Jews*, 212.
44. Teslik, *Congress, the Executive Branch and Special Interests*, 152; Prittie and Nelson, *The Economic War Against the Jews*, 201–2.
45. "Carter Moves Cautiously on Anti-Boycott Proposals," *Weekly Report* (Congressional Quarterly, 12 March 1977), 437.

46. Teslik, *Congress, the Executive Branch and Special Interests*, 158.
47. Ibid., 153–4; Thomas Frank and Edward Weisband, *Foreign Policy by Congress* (NY: Oxford University Press, 1979), 201.
48. *Near East Report* (5 January 1977), 7; Teslik, *Congress, the Executive Branch and Special Interests*, 174–83; Maslow, "Struggle Against the Arab Boycott," 22.
49. Teslik, *Congress, the Executive Branch and Special Interests*, 16, 204; Prittie and Nelson, *The Economic War Against the Jews*, 45, 212–3.
50. Teslik, *Congress, the Executive Branch and Special Interests*, 189, 192.
51. Ibid., 205–8.
52. Ibid., 170.
53. Ibid., 170–1; Edgar M. Bronfman, "Anti-Boycott Legislation," *The New Republic* (4 June 1977), 18.
54. Frank and Weisband, *Foreign Policy by Congress*, 203.
55. Ibid.
56. Ibid., 204–5; Teslik, *Congress, the Executive Branch and Special Interests*, 196.
57. "Carter Moves Cautiously on Anti-Boycott Proposals," *Weekly Report* (Congressional Quarterly, 12 March 1977), 437.
58. Teslik, *Congress, the Executive Branch and Special Interests*, 201–2; Frank and Weisband, 205.
59. Ibid., 203–9; Frank and Weisband, 206.
60. Ibid., 211; Frank and Weisband, 206–7.
61. Ibid., 186–7 and 212; Frank and Weisband, *Foreign Policy by Congress*, 207; Prittie and Nelson, *The Economic War Against the Jews*, 208; Bronfman, "Anti-Boycott Legislation," 19.
62. Teslik, *Congress, the Executive Branch and Special Interests*, 191.
63. Ibid., 214–5; Frank and Weisband, *Foreign Policy by Congress*, 208.
64. Prittie and Nelson, *The Economic War Against the Jews*, 213.
65. Bard, "Myth of Middle East Triangle," 7.
66. Teslik, *Congress, the Executive Branch and Special Interests*, 5.
67. Henry Steiner, "Pressure and Principles—The Politics of Antiboycott Legislation," *Georgia Journal of International and Comparative Law*, (1978), 540.
68. Jimmy Carter, *Keeping Faith* (NY: Bantam Books, 1982), 278.

Part II

LOBBY INFLUENCE AND THE LOCUS OF DECISION 2: THE EXECUTIVE BRANCH

Introduction to Part II

As noted in chapter 1, an interest group must have access to decision-makers if it expects to influence policy. Although Congress has taken an increasingly active role in foreign policy, the basic formulation of policy still takes place in the executive branch. The Israeli lobby's access to this branch is far more limited than its access to Congress: moreover, the lobby rarely has specific proposals to advocate, so it is not expected to be involved in major policy decisions. The consequence has been that major diplomatic and military decisions, such as the Sinai disengagement agreements, the Syrian-Israeli agreement, the American commitment to veto Security Council condemnations of Israel's retaliatory raids, and the Camp David Peace Treaty are thought to have been made with little or no input from the Israeli lobby. This chapter will challenge that view and present evidence from three case studies that the lobby does, in fact, influence executive branch decisions.

The fact that most American policy decisions regarding the Middle East have been favorable to Israel is partly a function of the pro-Israel orientation of American presidents. Every president is constrained by the electoral cycle and public opinion, both of which favor Israel; therefore, it is not surprising that there has never been a president considered hostile toward Israel. Support for Israel can also be seen as an outgrowth of the foreign policy of President Wilson, who articulated the principle of self-determination in his Fourteen Points long before the creation of the State of Israel. This principle was a major reason for Wilson's endorsement of the Balfour Declaration calling for the establishment of a Jewish national home in Palestine. Every president since Wilson has affirmed the right of the Jewish people to self-determination in Palestine and now Israel. More recently, support for Israel has been argued on the basis of its value as a strategic asset, a conclusion that can be derived independent of any outside pressure.

In general, the White House is more susceptible to domestic pressures than the State Department and is also the locus of all major decisions. Prior to 1967, as noted in the introduction, the Israeli lobby's access to the White House was primarily through personal friends of the president. Some of these individuals will play significant roles in the cases examined in this section. The Israeli government consciously sought out such people, as former Israeli Ambassador Avraham Harman explained:

> In the process of persuading, human beings are open to all kinds of influences. One of the most important influences, especially in a large country like the United States, which is struggling with huge problems, is gaining a man's time. It is not that you are trying to persuade him to do something against his will, his interest or the American interest. It is a question of competing *for his time.* If there is somebody like an Abe Feinberg who has access to the President, doesn't overstay his welcome or abuse it, but reserves use of this access to matters of greatest importance, then he has gained Presidential attention on this matter. That is important. If you go through diplomatic channels, the information gets there—eventually. . . . [1]

According to Bick, another Israeli diplomatic staff member made the point that these individual Jews may not always have the necessary information, so they are briefed to insure they understand the importance of a particular issue.

After 1967, the formal lobby became more important, although personal relationships have remained a means of access. There was also a change in attitude on the Israeli side in 1968 when Yitzhak Rabin came to the United States as Israel's Ambassador. Rabin believed the diplomatic corps was responsible for representing Israel to the U.S. government and that it did not need the help of amateurish American Jews.[2] Eventually, Rabin also came to recognize the valuable role the "amateurs" could play.

As a rule, presidents prefer to deny that interest groups have influence because the president is supposed to represent the whole nation and not any special interest. President Carter, after losing reelection, admitted that one of the biggest surprises of his term was the "extraordinary and excessive influence of special interest groups." In an interview Carter complained:

> There is no lobbying effort, there is no interest group, that has any influence in Washington for a calm, measured, long-range, moderate solution to an extremely complicated question. But there are plenty of interest groups on the radical right or the radical left, or the extreme positions, who are fighting for some selfish advantage. And a president has to remember that he himself represents the breadth of America and the best interest of our people. But the demands by special interest groups who are powerful politically are extraordinary, and a president has to say no. And when you say no against massive give-away programs, massive government programs, it doesn't benefit a president politically. And I think that's why the attrition rate among presidents has been so great in the last 20–25 years.[3]

Each of the presidents involved in this section's cases complained about the pressure of the Israeli lobby. Since there was no formal Arab lobby to speak of until fairly recently, there was little reason for presidents to decry their influence. Probably the first exception to this generalization occurred after Egyptian President Anwar Sadat's historic trip to Jerusalem, described in the Camp David case study. The Arab lobby expressed displeasure over United States support for the initiative, leading Carter to complain that Arab-Americans were giving his staff a difficult time.[4]

Paradoxically, almost every president has established a staff person to act as a liaison with the Jewish community. When President Nixon failed to fill the "Jewish portfolio," the move was apparently welcomed by the Israeli Embassy, which at the time, preferred not to deal with a Jewish liaison at the White House. One of the reasons Israel preferred this setup was the fear that the antiwar activities of Jewish liberals might jeopardize administration support for Israel. The president, in fact, not only had a large number of Jews in his administration, but also had a de facto liaison in Leonard Garment.[5] One former member of the AIPAC staff, Michael Gale, served as Ronald Reagan's liaison and explained his role:

> I will try to get anyone meetings with whomever they want. My job is to try to facilitate contact between the Administration and the Jewish community. I can't always deliver the President. I can't always

deliver the Vice-President or the Secretary of State, but I'll try. I have been successful in setting up meetings with Ed Meese and Jim Baker, the National Security Council and the Defense Department. The people in the Administration are eager to talk with the Jewish community for its input. However, there's a limit on how much they can do because they have other constraints on their time. They have to do work. They can't always meet, and the Jewish community constantly wants to meet. There isn't a Jewish organization in this country from the smallest little temple or B'nai B'rith lodge or Hadassah chapter to the national organizations that doesn't want to meet with them and they can't do it all the time, so we try to put it into balance or perspective.[6]

The White House prefers to bar interest group access, but established a mechanism that allows it because influence works in both directions; that is, interest groups may be the target of administration pressure. For example, according to one former liaison, Myer Feldman, Garment "gets instructions from Mr. Nixon and attempts to sell that position to the Jewish community."[7]

The Israeli lobby has enjoyed only limited access to the State Department and has generally been unable to influence policy originating there. Some people in the State Department feel they have a duty to counter the Israeli lobby's influence that exists inside Congress, others simply become "Arabists" to advance their careers. As one foreign service officer explained: "I made a cool calculation about a choice between becoming a Russian expert or an Arabic expert. I counted up the posts where Russian was the language. There were two. I counted the number where Arabic was the language. There were twenty-four. I became an Arabist."[8]

Even when a Jew, Henry Kissinger, was Secretary of State, there was not any change in State Department policy; in fact, many American Jews and Israelis considered Kissinger anti-Israel. Thus, the lobby has a built-in disadvantage when dealing with the State Department. This carries over to executive decisions because the Secretary of State is the president's chief foreign policy adviser.

The State Department has little use for the opinions of interest groups in general and tends to dismiss them as propaganda. The department is keenly aware, however, of Israeli lobby pressure. In fact, it is the one group that is an exception to the generalization that interest groups have little influence on national security problems. That influence has varied over time, however, and was probably weakest during Eisenhower's term.

In the 1950s, the Israeli lobby was not well-received by Secretary of State John Foster Dulles. For example, after receiving a request to meet with the chairman of the Presidents Conference, who was then a European-born rabbi, Dulles reportedly said: "Why should I waste my time meeting with Rabbi X when I can hear the same arguments directly from Israeli Ambassador Abba Eban and in much better English at that."[9] The State Department prefers to work directly with the Israelis knowing that the discussions will be repeated to the lobby's representatives. Former Assistant Secretary of State for Middle Eastern Affairs, Raymond Hare, explained:

> The Israelis we worked with on the whole were more realistic than American Jews. They were closer to it. To them, facts are more clear cut. If there are certain threats to Israel, the Israeli knows what the threat is; he will evaluate the balance of forces. Someone who is not involved in it, only sees the threat and he will be more emotional than the Israeli because he doesn't know all the facts.

Nevertheless, the Israeli lobby was not ignored entirely. Hare adds:

> We were conscious the Israeli Embassy could get out the information to an interested American public. Both sides knew it. We spoke straightforwardly with Abe Harman (the Israeli ambassador to Washington). We understood each other. We battled it out over planes— like with any other country—but always in back of our minds, we remembered there was a tremendous Jewish influence in this country. . . .[10]

The State Department does have an interest in disseminating information about foreign policy to the public and frequently uses interest groups for that purpose. In general, however, the State Department considers itself a nonpartisan, objective formulator of the national interest in foreign policy. The involvement of Congress and interest groups in the foreign policy-making process is seen as unwarranted intrusions into a decision-making area that should be reserved for the experts, who have a better understanding of America's foreign political and strategical objectives.

As noted in the introduction, it is difficult to determine how a president arrives at a decision. We know that the informal Israeli lobby serves as a constant form of background noise, while the formal lobby applies direct pressure. The lobby's ability to influence the president, the pluralist model holds, will be affected by the competing interests and the domestic political context (i.e., presidential popularity, election campaigns, congressional support).

The primary sources of competing influence in the case of executive decisions are the president's advisers. Presidents receive advice from experts, bureaucrats, and friends, and must somehow sort out often conflicting opinions to reach a decision that must balance political risks with perceptions of the national interest. The realist model suggests that the president will choose the position which reflects the national interest and will be particularly unwavering in policies with clear security implications.

The leadership model asserts that the president will adopt the position advocated by his advisers, but, as we shall see, presidents often receive conflicting advice, and it is not clear whose advice the president should or will accept. If the president possesses a strong personal opinion on an issue, I will suggest, it is difficult to persuade him to change that view, although it is sometimes possible to force some modification in his position. When the president lacks a strong position, he is particularly susceptible to outside influence, but even then, will be expected to choose the alternative that most closely approximates his own general ideology. The more compatible the Israeli lobby's position is with the president's, the greater the likelihood that it will be adopted. The following case studies are included in an effort to obtain some insight into the process by which presidential decisions are made.

Chapters 5 and 6 reexamine the controversy surrounding President Truman's Palestine/Israel policies, and the question of whether his decisions were influenced by domestic political factors. In those cases, Truman's chief foreign policy advisers consistently opposed the Israeli lobby's positions; nevertheless, several of the lobby's positions were adopted, the most important being support for partition and recognition of the new state of Israel. On the other hand, the security-related issue of the arms embargo went against the lobby. As was the case in part I, we will see that the three models interact, and that realism sometimes dominates the decision-making process; at other times the president's personal beliefs are preeminent, and in every case domestic political pressure is felt by the president, who submits to the lobby's influence when it is consistent with his ideology.

The second case, analyzed in chapter 7, has been the subject of much less scrutiny; however, Lyndon Johnson's decision to sell Phantom jets to Israel in 1968 was a turning point in U.S.-Israel relations, establishing the United States as Israel's primary military supplier and diplomatic ally. Once again, we will see that the lobby exerts great pressure on a president who is receiving advice from people who believe the lobby's position is contrary to U.S. interests. The president is much less likely to give in on a security issue like this, but he eventually does agree to make the sale when international events reinforce the lobby's arguments and the sale becomes a campaign issue in the presidential election.

Finally, chapter 8 will investigate the Israeli lobby's role in the peace process, which culminated in the Israeli-Egyptian peace treaty. Since that case is so recent, there is relatively little documentation available beyond the memoirs of the participants. But a recent book on the American side of the negotiations, combined with the pre-existing sources, does provide significant evidence that the Israeli lobby played a role in constraining President Carter's freedom to negotiate, by inhibiting him from pressuring the Israelis or proposing compromises objectionable to the lobby's interests. Since the issue is primarily political, the president is less willing to ignore the lobby's opposition than he would be if it were security related. At the same time, the fact that Carter was inclined to take positions opposed by the lobby will be explained in terms of the leadership model; that is, his own ideology, reinforced by his advisers' positions, led him to policies that conflicted with the interests of the lobby.

Notes

1. Etta Z. Bick, "Ethnic Linkages and Foreign Policy: A Study of the Linkage Role of American Jews in Relations With the United States

and Israel, 1956–1968 (Ph.D. Diss., City University of New York, 1983), 104–5.
2. Bick, "Ethnic Linkages," 105–6.
3. Paul Light, *The Presidential Agenda* (MD: Johns Hopkins University Press, 1982), 79.
4. Jimmy Carter, *Keeping Faith* (NY: Bantam Books, 1982), 299.
5. Andrew J. Glass, "Nixon Gives Israel Massive Aid But Reaps No Political Harvest," *National Journal* (8 January 1972), 57–8.
6. Sue Hoechstetter, "Michael Gale, Jewish Liaison for the White House,"*Congress Monthly* (June, 1983), 13.
7. Glass, "Nixon Gives Israel Massive Aid," 58.
8. Joseph Kraft, "Those Arabists in the State Department," *New York Times Magazine* (7 November 1971), 88–94.
9. Bick, "Ethnic Linkages," 214.
10. Ibid., 214–5.

5

Truman, Israel, and the Jewish Vote Revisited I

One of the long-running controversies in the study of U.S. foreign policy and Middle East policy-making, in particular, has been the question of how much of a role domestic political considerations played in Harry Truman's decision to support the partition of Palestine and recognize the State of Israel. Critics of U.S. policy toward the Middle East have persistently asserted that Truman reacted to Jewish pressure to enhance his chances of being elected, while most scholarly investigations of the issue have found little evidence to support this allegation. Chapters 5 and 6 reopen the issue in an effort to replicate earlier findings, and to examine the role of the Israeli lobby in the formulation of the Truman administration's entire Palestine policy from 1945–1948, starting with the decision to support Jewish immigration into Palestine, and ending with the presidential election held to have been the motivation for Truman's policy.

Conflicting Pressures

There is no question about the pressure that Truman faced throughout the period from his assuming the presidency to his election. In an oft-repeated quote used as evidence that Truman's policy was motivated by electoral considerations. Truman told the ambassador to the Arab-Israeli peace talks in Geneva in 1948: "I won't tell you what to do or how to vote, but I will say only this. In all of my political experience I don't recall the Arab vote swinging a close election."[1]

In addition to the advantage enjoyed by its informal component, the Israeli lobby's formal component held a virtual monopoly in Washington. Many of the Jewish communal organizations had been working independently, but had not developed a means for coordinating political action until the formation of the Emergency Committee for Zionist Affairs (ECZA) in 1939. The committee had twenty-four members taken from the executive boards of the primary Zionist organizations, and was chaired by Rabbi Stephen S. Wise. At that time, the organizations had over 170,000 members, but the ECZA did not have a Washington office or representative, or a public relations department. The former was opened in 1943 and the latter was established in 1941. Later the organization was renamed the American Zionist Emergency Council (AZEC) and Rabbi Abba Hillel Silver was recruited to be co-chairman with Wise, as well as to head the policy-making committee.

Perhaps the most important figures in the nascent Israeli lobby were individual Jews and pro-Zionists who had close contact with Harry Truman. Three men stood out, however, for their roles in lobbying the president. The first was the president's Special Counsel, Clark Clifford, who was primarily concerned with the domestic political implications of Truman's policies and, as we shall see, intervened at critical junctures in the debates over Palestine.

The other "inside lobbyist" for the Zionists was David Niles, who held the title of Special Assistant to the President for Minority Affairs, the so-called "Jewish portfolio." Niles was kept constantly informed by the Zionist leadership and he, in turn, kept the president aware of Zionist concerns. He also kept the Jewish Agency and other Zionists informed and used his influence to moderate their demands. All material pertaining to Palestine passed through Niles's office for his recommendation. "I am one of the instruments of the President who has been privileged to give my opinion to the President on Palestine among other things," he said. That access was crucial for the Israeli lobby and led Chaim Weizmann to credit Niles with helping to "bring about proper understanding of the ideals of our cause in high places in Washington."[2]

The one man most often credited with influencing Truman to support the Zionists was Truman's old haberdashery business partner, Eddie Jacobson. Jacobson's role has long been controversial, with the president's daughter, Margaret Truman, among those who claim that Jacobson's involvement was marginal, dismissing him as "one of hundreds of army friends my father made during World War I."[3] In contrast to his daughter's characterization, Truman called Jacobson "as fine a man as ever walked." When informed of Jacobson's death in October 1955, the former president called him "one of the best friends I had in this world." Finally, although it occurred long after the fact, Truman issued a statement (22 May 1965) applauding the dedication of an auditorium in Jacobson's name in Tel Aviv: "Although my sympathies were already active and present in the cause of the State of Israel, it is a fact of history that Eddie Jacobson's contribution was of decisive importance."[4]

The major turning point in the history of American Zionism took place in 1942, when all of the major Zionist leaders including David Ben-Gurion, head of the Jewish Agency, and Chaim Weizmann, president of the World Zionist Organization, met at the Biltmore Hotel in New York in May. The result of the conference was the adoption of a program calling for the establishment of a Jewish Commonwealth in Palestine. Prior to this time, there had been no consensus regarding the desirability of campaigning for a Jewish state in Palestine, so the Biltmore Program marked the formal beginning of the effort to convince the United States government to support the establishment of a Jewish state.

The Arab Lobby

As disorganized as the Israeli lobby was at this point in time, it far exceeded the capability of the Arab lobby, which for all intents and purposes did not exist outside the State Department and the Pentagon. In 1945, the first Arab Information Office opened in Washington, but contributed little to the debate on Palestine.[5] Although oil company spokesmen like James Terry Duce of ARAMCO were vehemently opposed to a Jewish state, Benjamin Akzin, director of the AZEC's office in Washington, found the oil companies to be neutral on Zionism. They did present a pro-Arab view of the Palestine situation, he said, but they also admitted that Saudi King Ibn Saud was more dependent on the United States than America was on Saudi Arabia. The oil companies, therefore, were not seriously concerned that the Arabs could harm their interests. Then Undersecretary of the Interior, Abe Fortas, supported this conclusion when he told Akzin that "even the oil companies hardly believe that strong American backing of Zionism would result in a permanent endangering of American oil interests."[6] It is in fact striking that no mention is made of oil company lobbying in all that has been written about this period.

The primary sources of opposition to the Zionists were found within the government bureaucracy. The arguments focused on the damage to U.S.-Arab relations that would be caused by supporting a Jewish state and the consequent threat to American oil supplies. The Secretary of Defense, James Forrestal, was an outspoken opponent of Zionist aims because of the threat he believed they posed, not only to oil supplies, but also to America's strategic position in the region. The Joint Chiefs of Staff worried that the Arabs might ally with the Soviets if they were alienated by the West. The defense establishment also bristled at the prospect of sending troops to Palestine to try to enforce a settlement. Opposition was even more vehement within the State Department, where Secretary of State George Marshall took a nonconfrontational, yet negative position with regard to Zionist demands, and undersecretary Robert Lovett, George Kennan, and Dean Rusk all worked to offset the Israeli lobby's pressure. The most vocal proponent of the Arab cause was Loy Henderson, the head of the Near East Bureau.

The president did not find State Department officials' arguments compelling. "Their thinking went along this line," he said. "Great Britain has maintained her position in the area by cultivating the Arabs; now that she seems no longer able to hold this position, the United States must take over, and it must be done by exactly the same formula; if the Arabs are antagonized, they will go over into the Soviet camp. I was never convinced by these arguments of the diplomats," he asserted.[7]

Congressional Influence

Congress is not expected to play a significant role in executive decisions; nevertheless, interest groups will attempt to use their access to the legislative branch to influence the executive branch to as great an extent as possible. The Zionists were successful, for example, in enlisting congressional support for its program. In fact, congressional support for the Zionist program can be traced back to 1922, when Congress passed a resolution supporting the establishment of a national home for the Jewish people in Palestine. Twenty-two years later, the House proposed (27 January 1944) a new resolution endorsing the Biltmore Program, calling for the free entry of Jews into Palestine and the establishment of a free and democratic Jewish commonwealth.[8] By October, the resolution had the support of 411 members. The administration opposed the resolution, however, fearing that it would hurt the war effort. General George Marshall, the chief of staff, urgently requested a tabling or postponement of the resolution for security reasons, and succeeded in persuading his friend Stephen Wise and other Democratic faithfuls to ask for the resolution to be withdrawn on patriotic grounds, while assuring them that he would support their cause after the Allies' victory.[9]

The resolution was shelved for nearly a year as a result of the pressure from the administration. That pressure began to be reciprocated by the Congress as the Potsdam conference approached. On 3 July 1945, Senator Robert Wagner sent a letter to the president signed by 54 senators and 250 representatives, asking Truman to use his influence with Great Britain to open the doors of Palestine to "unrestricted Jewish immigration and colonization," and to urge other governments "to join with the United States towards the end of establishing Palestine as a free and democratic Jewish commonwealth at the earliest possible time."[10]

The president apparently took this advice, and sent Churchill a memorandum prior to Potsdam expressing concern about the restrictions placed on Jewish immigration to Palestine and urging him to lift them. At the conference, Churchill told Truman that he preferred to see the Jewish homeland established somewhere like Tripoli. Then, in a press conference following the meeting, Truman announced that the United States wanted to let as many of the Jews into Palestine as possible, and hoped that a diplomatic arrangement could be reached with the British and the Arabs to set up a state on a peaceful basis.[11] Truman's attitude toward

Jewish immigration to Palestine hardened after receiving a report on the condition of Jewish refugees that summer.

Following a suggestion from Niles, Truman asked Earl Harrison, the former commissioner of Immigration and Naturalization during World War II, to investigate the condition of displaced persons in Europe. In late August, Harrison delivered his report with the startling conclusion that "we appear to be treating the Jews as the Nazis treated them except that we do not exterminate them. . . . They are in concentration camps in large numbers under our military guard instead of S.S. troops. One is led to wonder whether the German people, seeing this, are not supposing that we are following or at least condoning Nazi policy." On the basis of his conversations with the refugees, Harrison reported that most wanted to go to Palestine. "Many have relatives there while others, having experienced intolerance and persecution in their homelands for years, feel that only in Palestine will they be welcomed and find peace and quiet and be given an opportunity to live and work." [12]

After reading the report, Truman sent a copy to British Prime Minister Atlee and told him that "the main solution appears to lie in the quick evacuation of as many as possible of the non-repatriable Jews who wish it, to Palestine." [13] He also ordered General Eisenhower to take the refugees out of the camps and put them into decent houses until they could either be repatriated or evacuated. [14]

The president's reaction to the Harrison report reflected the primary motivation for Truman's Palestine policy; that is, his humanitarian concerns and his personal integrity. The former was reflected in Truman's insistence that a Nuremberg Trial record the crimes of the Nazis. He also led the fight to reform U.S. immigration laws to allow homeless refugees from Europe to move to the United States, and in one specific instance invited 982 Jews from Camp Ontario in New York to remain in America instead of return to Europe as Roosevelt had planned. [15] "The fate of the Jewish victims of Hitlerism was a matter of deep personal concern to me," Truman wrote. "I have always been disturbed by the tragedy of people who have been made victims of intolerance and fanaticism because of their race, color, or religion. These things should not be possible in a civilized society." [16]

Another source of Truman's attitude was his personal integrity; that is, his belief that promises should be kept. As we shall see, his feelings of commitment to Chaim Weizmann were very strong, and Truman was furious when certain State Department actions made it appear that he had deceived the Jewish leader. Truman had a similar view with regard to the commitments of governments, such as the Balfour Declaration. "This promise, I felt, would be kept, just as all promises made by responsible, civilized governments should be kept." [17]

Nevertheless, many Zionists were convinced that Truman was not doing all that he could to influence the British. "What our Government intends to do in the Palestine matter," Rabbi Silver said, "is still a mystery to us." [18] Pressure was again exerted on Truman when a resolution calling on the president to support the Zionist program was reintroduced in the Senate. Senator Wagner told the president that the Republicans would use his opposition against the party if he failed to support the resolution. Truman was also reminded that the Zionist National Committee passed a resolution expressing disgust and resentment toward the president and State Department for their actions toward the Jews, but he remained unmoved. [19]

After Truman raised the immigration issue, the British had felt pressured to either accede to the president's suggestion or provide some justification for ignoring it. On 19 October 1945, the British proposed an Anglo-American inquiry to determine what should be done about the Jews of Europe displaced by the war. Truman continued to oppose the congressional resolution because he said it would undermine the commission's investigation. The Senate adopted the resolution anyway on 17 December. Two days later, the House passed the resolution and "the rebuke of the president was complete." [20]

The following year the political situation deteriorated for the Democratic administration, as the Republicans took control of Congress for the first time in nearly two decades, and began to anticipate recapturing the presidency in 1948. A low cost means of attracting support was to criticize the president's Palestine policy. Thus, the Israeli lobby could count on the support of a majority of the Congress, as well as powerful Senate figures like Robert Taft, and to a lesser extent Arthur Vandenberg. Congress, therefore, provided another source of pressure on Truman.

Riding the Tiger

Truman came to the White House with his own views on the Palestine problem. Whereas "Roosevelt knew the land of the Bible, Truman knew the people."[21] He had grown up knowing Jews in Independence, and his opinions toward them were shaped from his earliest associations with Jewish merchants, and later his friendship with Eddie Jacobson. As a senator, Truman established himself as a champion of the Jewish cause, protesting Great Britain's White Paper almost immediately after it was issued in 1939: "It made a scrap of paper out of Balfour's promise," he said, and "added another to the long list of surrenders to the Axis powers."[22]

Two years later, Truman joined the American Christian Palestine Committee and was later recruited by Peter Bergson to support his idea of a Jewish Army in Palestine to fight with the Allies. In May 1944, he abruptly withdrew his support, Grose claims, because Bergson had placed an advertisement that criticized one of his Senate colleagues. Snetsinger provides evidence, however, that Truman was primarily concerned about the impact of the advertisement on the war effort. In a letter to Stephen Wise, Truman complained that the advertisements were "used to stir up trouble where our troops are fighting" and were being "used by all the Arabs in North Africa in an endeavor to create dissension among them and caused them to stab our fellows in the back." Truman expressed the desire to help the Jews, but not at "the expense of our military maneuvers."[23]

That same year, while the majority of his colleagues were endorsing a resolution supporting the establishment of a Jewish commonwealth, Truman expressed reservations because of his fear that it would jeopardize efforts to finance the war. "I don't want to throw any bricks to upset the applecart," he said, "although when the right time comes I am willing to help make the fight for a Jewish homeland in Palestine."[24] The demands for

Truman to support the Zionist program were to come sooner than he expected.

Soon after becoming president, Secretary of State Edward Stettinius offered Truman his judgement that vital American interests were at stake in the Near East that required careful handling of the Palestine question.[25] Truman was also pressured by those who opposed Zionist demands on the basis of commitments each claimed that President Roosevelt had made. "Although President Roosevelt at times gave expression to views sympathetic to certain Zionist aims," Joseph Grew informed Truman, "he also gave certain assurances to the Arabs which they regard as definite commitments on our part."[26] The evidence of this "commitment" was Roosevelt's promise to Saudi King Ibn Saud, first made in May 1943, and repeated two years later, that "no decision be taken with respect to the basic situation in that country [Palestine] without full consultation with both Arabs and Jews."[27]

Meanwhile, Roosevelt apparently told James Byrnes that he and Saud agreed on everything *except* Palestine, and subsequently wrote to Stephen Wise that he was going to support the Zionist program. When Arab leaders claimed they had received a commitment from the president, Wise released the letter from Roosevelt. Roosevelt reaffirmed his support for the Zionists during the presidential campaign, pledging to support the Democratic plank on Palestine that called for creation of a Jewish commonwealth.[28]

On 27 May 1946, Niles sent Truman a memorandum advising him not to be concerned about the Arab hostility to Zionist aims. He said that Roosevelt had once said that "he could do anything that needed to be done with Ibn Saud with a few million dollars." Moreover, he said that the Arab world posed no real threat to American or Zionist interests, because the Muslims follow Gandhi's philosophy of pacifism. Although he was very wrong on that point, Niles did conclude with a persuasive appeal to Truman that he support the immediate immigration of 100,000 Jews into Palestine.[29]

When Truman began to give public support to Niles' suggestion about immigration, Ibn Saud complained that the president was reneging on his predecessor's commitment. The State Department then released Roosevelt's letter to Ibn Saud to make it clear the administration did not believe its appeals contradicted the earlier understanding. Truman wrote to Saud and said that the United States had a responsibility for the fate of the people liberated in the war and that "these people should be prepared for self-government and also that a national home for the Jewish people should be established in Palestine." It followed, then, that the United States would support the immigration of displaced Jews to Palestine.[30]

The Anglo-American Commission Report

In reply to the president's call for immigration, the British suggested that a committee be set up to study the matter. The Anglo-American Commission issued its report on 20 April 1946, recommending among other things that 100,000 immigrants be immediately allowed admission to Palestine. The committee's findings were essentially ignored, however, and a new commission was appointed made up of higher officials from both governments. The new commission report called for the creation of autonomous Arab and Jewish communities under the control of a central government. Only 1,500 of the area's 45,000 square miles were allotted to the Jewish community, and the central authority was given jurisdiction over Jerusalem, Bethlehem, and the Negev. In addition, Arab approval was to be required before the recommended 100,000 Jews would be allowed to immigrate.

The so-called Morrison-Grady Plan, named after the British and American members of the commission, was blasted by James McDonald who told Truman, at the request of the Zionists, that if this was the price of the 100,000 immigrants, the President would "go down in history as anathema." Truman exploded at that remark and insisted that he had not yet endorsed the plan. The president had hoped that the plan would remove the Palestine problem from his agenda, but it was becoming increasingly clear to him that the problem would not go away. Frustrated, he told McDonald: "Well, you can't satisfy these people . . . the Jews aren't going to write the history of the United States or my history."[31] He complained to another friend at one point that the Jews "somehow expect me to fulfill all the prophecies of the prophets. I tell them that I can no more fulfill all the prophecies of Ezekial than I can of that other great Jew, Karl Marx." In another outburst, the president complained: "I don't believe there is any possible way of pleasing our Jewish friends." At a cabinet meeting, he lamented that "Jesus Christ couldn't please them when he was here on earth, so how could anyone expect that I would have any luck?"[32] Truman was wrong, of course, but it was not yet apparent.

Congressional opposition to the plan also put pressure on Truman. Emanuel Celler, for example, warned the president in June that his actions would "certainly give political ammunition to the upstate Republicans who wanted to attend, and you remember that New York faces a very crucial election."[33] In August, the chairman of the New York Democratic State Committee wrote that "if this plan goes into effect it would be useless for the Democrats to nominate a State ticket for the election this fall."[34] Truman was also advised to reject the plan by a number of congressmen and three of the six Americans from the original Anglo-American Commission.

After the release of an AZEC letter opposing the report, Truman began to back away from the Morrison-Grady plan. At a news conference on 6 June he said that Britain, not the United States, was responsible for preventing the 100,000 Jews from immigrating to Palestine.[35] In response, British Foreign Minister Ernest Bevin accused the president of pushing the 100,000 on Great Britain because he did not want them coming to New York.

Secretary of State Byrnes was virtually alone in urging that the president accept the plan but, in the end, the forces lobbying against it were decisive. It was not only the Zionists, the Americans from the Commission, and Congress that opposed the plan; after all, the Arabs also opposed the plan because it did not advocate an independent Arab state. An additional factor was a change in the substance of the Zionist opposition, that is, Nahum Goldman informed American officials that the Zionists were willing to back away from the maximal objectives of the Biltmore Program and accept a "viable state in an adequate area of Palestine."[36] Thus, while the Morrison-Grady plan was as a whole unacceptable, the notion that the area could be divided into Jewish and Arab territories was now seen as a possible basis for a settlement. This shift toward the acceptance of partition demonstrated that *the White House can influence a lobby*, although here it was a case of indirect influence resulting from Truman's flirtation with the Morrison-Grady plan.[37]

On 12 August, Truman told the British that he could not support the plan. "The opposition in this country to the plan has become so intense," he said, "that it is now clear it would be impossible to give it effective support."[38] It was also clear that Truman remained frustrated by the entire affair, telling the press: "All I was trying to do, was get a hundred thousand Jews into Palestine. [I am] still trying to do that."[39]

Electioneering

The demise of the Morrison-Grady plan signalled the beginning of the campaign for partition. William Clayton, the acting Secretary of State, warned Truman that Wise and others would try to convince him to issue a statement in support of a Jewish state. The State Department opposed such a move and cautioned that a favorable statement would encourage the Zionists "to make fresh demands and to apply pressures in the future." The president replied that he was hesitant to say anything on the subject and that he hoped "it will not be necessary for me to have anything to say."[40]

With Truman apparently ready to wash his hands of the Palestine issue, the Zionists again turned up the pressure by sending Wise to see him. In addition, Republican candidates, particularly in New York, used the Palestine issue to attack the Democrats. In order to counter the attack, influential Democrats lobbied Truman to make a pro-Zionist statement. Niles also worked behind the scenes to persuade Truman to make a statement before Governor Thomas Dewey made one.[41]

Ignoring British appeals to remain silent, Truman issued a statement on 4 October 1946, Yom Kippur, rejecting the Morrison-Grady plan, but suggesting that there was room for compromise with those who favored partition. The president added that a partition plan "would command the support of public opinion in the United States." He also called again for the immigration of 100,000 Jews to Palestine, and said that he would be willing to provide economic assistance to the country once a settlement was reached.[42]

Truman did succeed in preempting Dewey's speech scheduled for two days later. Since Dewey agreed with the president's position, the only criticism he could lodge was that the immigration of 100,000 was insufficient. Thus, the Zionist lobby was in the favorable position of being courted by both candidates, each trying to outbid the other in an effort to win favor among Jewish voters.

The Zionists and their supporters were for the most part ecstatic over the president's statement. Politically, there was no question that it was popular. It allowed the Democrats to steal the Republicans' thunder and it expressed a sentiment generally held by the American people. According to a December 1944 National Opinion Research Center (NORC) poll, 36 percent of the public favored a Jewish state and 19 percent opposed one. A Roper poll taken in October 1945 showed that 80 percent of all Jews believed that the establishment of a Jewish state would be "a good thing for the Jews," and only 11 percent said it "would be bad for the Jews." In December 1945, a poll taken by the American Institute of Public Opinion (AIPO) discovered that 76 percent of the respondents favored permitting the Jews to enter Palestine, and 7 percent were opposed. In the June AIPO poll, 48 percent thought it was a good idea to admit 100,000 Jews into Palestine, while 14 percent thought it was a bad idea. In a January 1946 Gallup poll, 76 percent of those who followed the discussion, favored permitting Jews to settle in Palestine, and only 7 percent were opposed. Even though there was a high degree of support for the Zionists, the issue was not salient for most people. For example, in the 1946 NORC and AIPO (September) polls, almost half the respondents admitted they had not followed the discussion about establishing a Jewish national home.[43]

Congressmen were more attentive to the issue, however, and Representative Celler sent Truman a letter (7 October 1946) complimenting him for his Yom Kippur statement and expressing confidence that it would have a "very desirable political effect upon our chances in New York." Robert Hannegan provided Truman with evidence that his popularity among Jews had improved after the statement to support Celler's optimism.[44]

Other observers were not as complimentary. In an article headlined, "Truman's Palestine Plea Flaunted Foreign Advisers," James Reston wrote in the *New York Times* that "President Truman's latest statement on Palestine illustrated the influence of domestic politics on United States foreign policy and demonstrated the limitations of the theory that politics stops at the water's edge."[45] Dean Acheson, a frequent critic of the administration's Palestine policy, took exception to these allegations. Truman, he said, "never took or refused to take a step in our foreign relations to benefit his or his party's fortunes. This he would have regarded as false to the great office that he venerated and held in sacred trust."[46]

It is hard to accept that the speech was anything but politically inspired, however, since it came just before the election, and in response to pressure from Democrats concerned that Republican criticism of the administration's Palestine policy would hurt them at the polls. Truman's statement actually said very little and made no commitment, but hinted just enough that he was leaning toward the Zionist position to attract the lobby's support.

Some of the Zionists recognized the ambiguity in Truman's statement and were unenthused. Silver considered it "a far cry" from support for a Jewish state, and wrote to Ben-Gurion that there was now a danger "that having cashed in on whatever good will this statement may have produced among Jews of America, the White House will be content to let the matter drop as it has done time and again in the past after similar maneuvers on the eve of elections."[47] The Zionists would not let the matter drop.

As it turned out, the president's statement did more good for his image with the Zionists than it did for Democratic candidates. The Republicans had plenty of other issues to attack the Democrats on, including the poor state of the economy. Also, the incumbent party typically does poorly in off-year elections. Consequently, the Republicans won large majorities in both houses of Congress for the first time since 1930.

The UN Enters

In the months following the election, the situation in Palestine continued to deteriorate. The British were unable to stop the Jewish paramilitary organizations, and some of the more heinous acts perpetrated by the terrorists had so repulsed the British people that increasing pressure was put on the government to with-draw from Palestine. The British finally succumbed to the pres-sure and decided to bring the problem to the United Nations in February 1947.

The British were not planning to abandon the Mandate, but wanted advice as to how the Mandate could be administered. Their willingness to accept the UN's advice was conditional, how-ever, requiring the UN's solution to be acceptable to *both* Jews and Arabs. This condition assured a stalemate since it was the inability to find such an agreement that had forced the British to go to the UN in the first place. The British expected the UN to be unable to find a solution, and then the problem would be returned to them, and they could then feel free to pursue their imperial interests and crush any remaining Jewish resistance.

The General Assembly decided to set up the United Nations Special Committee on Palestine (UNSCOP) to investigate the cause of conflict in Palestine, and, if possible, devise a solution. Meanwhile, the Americans continued to pressure Britain. In March, the vice-chairman of the ECZA, Emanuel Neuman, suggested to Senator Wagner that U.S. aid to Greece and Turkey be tied to the willingness of the British to yield to American demands re-garding Palestine. Wagner replied that he agreed and had already taken steps in that direction.[48] The following month, Wagner and Senator James Murray sent a telegram reminding Truman that the joint congressional resolution had morally committed the United States to supporting a Jewish state and urging him to support that objective in the UN.[49]

Truman resisted these entreaties, and those contained in thou-sands of similar telegrams sent to the White House from around the country. The president finally conveyed his annoyance to Wise in a letter on 6 August: "I read your telegram of the first with a great deal of interest and appreciate your viewpoint, but there seems to be two sides to this question. I am finding it rather difficult to decide which one is right and a great many other people in the country are beginning to feel just as I do."[50]

Although the UNSCOP had begun its investigation on 26 May, the administration refused to issue any statements despite per-sistent pressure to do so. In a cabinet meeting on 8 August, Truman said that he would not make any statements until the

UNSCOP had announced its findings. "He said he had stuck his neck out on this delicate question once, and he did not propose to do it again."[51] As would be the case throughout the next year, Truman was unwilling to give in to pressure when it was pushing him away from his own beliefs, in this instance a commitment to the UN.

The UNSCOP visited Palestine and found the Jewish community very responsive to its inquiries. The Arab Higher Committee boycotted the commission, but demanded that the UN immediately grant Palestine its independence. Although most of the commission's members acknowledged the need to find a compromise solution, it was difficult to envision one, given Arab intransigence. At a meeting with a group of Arabs in Beirut, the Czechoslovakian member of the commission told his audience: "I have listened to your demands and it seems to me that in your view the compromise is: We want our demands met completely, the rest can be divided among those left."[52] This made the Zionist position look all the more reasonable.

The UN "Solution"

The UNSCOP devised two alternative proposals to replace the mandate. The minority proposal called for the formation of a single federal state in which the Jews would remain a minority. The Jews were to be given certain ambiguous minority rights in the state, but would be under Arab rule. The majority recognized, however, that the question of ownership or right to Palestine was an insoluble antinomy. Rather than try to solve it, they chose the logical alternative of partition in which each nation would be given sovereignty over its own state.

After the UNSCOP report was published on 31 August, Truman again came under pressure to support partition. Governor Dewey, Senator Taft, and House Speaker Joseph Martin were among those who called the majority report "a statesmanlike solution."[53] At the 4 September cabinet meeting, Robert Hannegan urged Truman to issue a new policy statement on Palestine. He did not push for support of partition, only the restatement of the president's position on the immigration of Jews into Palestine. Hannegan said that "very large sums were obtained a year ago from Jewish contributors and that they would be influenced in either giving or withholding by what the president did on Palestine." Forrestal countered that the Yom Kippur speech had actually done nothing to help Democrats in the New York election, and had succeeded only in irritating the British.[54]

The president steadfastly refused to make any statements until the General Assembly met to debate the UNSCOP reports. Even before the United States announced its position, the Arabs had made their views clear. In a telegram to Truman, Uzzuldin Al-naqib, vice-president of the Iraqi Chamber of Deputies, warned that the Arabs "would never accept a Jewish state and that such a move would undermine the peace in the Middle East."[55] The implacability of the Arabs was even more evident, when Jewish Agency representatives made a last-ditch effort to reach a compromise with the Arabs in a meeting with Arab League Secretary Azzam Pasha on 16 September. Pasha told them bluntly:

> The Arab world is not at all in a compromising mood. The proposed plan may be logical, but the fate of nations is not decided by rational reasoning. Nations never give up. You will achieve nothing with talk of compromise or peace. You may perhaps achieve something by force of your arms. We will try to rout you. I am not sure we will succeed, but we will try. We succeeded in expelling the Crusaders, but lost Spain and Persia, and may lose Palestine. But it is too late for a peaceful solution.[56]

On 17 September, Marshall ended the suspense by announcing to the General Assembly that the United States "gives great weight" to the majority proposal, thereby signifying American support for partition. The depth of the commitment to this plan was exposed a few days later when Marshall assured Arab delegates that the United States was keeping "an open mind."[57] Marshall also instructed the American delegation not to make any statements or exert any pressure on other delegations.

At the White House, Hannegan was again trying to persuade Truman to take a public position in favor of partition. At a Cabinet lunch on 6 October, the frustrated president finally told Hannegan that "if they [the Jews] would keep quiet he thought that everything would be all right, but that if they persisted in the endeavor to go beyond the report of the United Nations Com-

mission there was grave danger of wrecking all prospects for set-
tlement."[58] Truman relented, however, and instructed the State
Department to issue a statement in favor of partition. On 11
October, Herschel Johnson of the U.S. delegation announced the
American position to the UN. Two days later, the unthinkable
occurred when the Soviet delegate announced that the Soviet
Union also supported the plan.

It was the American position that caused the most anger in the
Arab world. Lebanon's Camille Chamoun typified the response
when he accused the United States of acting out of a desire to
appease Jewish voters and for the purpose of "political penetration in the Middle East dictated by a pitiless capitalism, with
Zionism in the van."[59]

The Israeli lobby was, of course, grateful for the American
statement, but the Zionists were under no illusions as to the
reasons for the administration's support. The AZEC's Leo Sack
noted that the victory was not a result of the devotion of the U.S.
government to the Zionist cause. "We had won because of the
sheer pressure of political logistics that was applied by the Jewish
leadership in the United States."[60]

Several days later, Truman complained of the Zionist pressure
when he wrote to Claude Pepper: "Had it not been for the unwarranted interference of the Zionists, we would have had the
matter settled a year and a half ago." To give an indication of
the pressure, he said he had received "35,000 pieces of mail and
propaganda from the Jews in this country" but had "put it all in
a pile and struck a match to it."[61] As Grose notes, this does not
sound like a politician who was primarily concerned with satisfying
Jewish voters; nevertheless, the outcome, support for partition,
was consistent with the lobby's interests and contrary to that of
advisers like Loy Henderson, Warren Austin, and James Forrestal, who all feared support for partition would undermine U.S.
security interests.

The Boundary Crisis

The United States was not completely satisfied with the UN-
SCOP majority report because of the way the proposed boundaries of the two states had been drawn. The State Department

preferred to keep the city of Jaffa with its large Arab population, and the Negev desert a part of the Arab state. There were both political and strategic reasons for this position. Politically, the proposal was designed to mollify the Arabs; since the original plan had given the Jewish state a larger territory than the Arabs, it was hoped that by transferring the two areas to the Arab state their opposition might be muted. This would also allow the creation of a land bridge between the Arabs of North Africa and those of the Near East through Jordan. Marshall also foresaw the strategic possibilities, in particular, the opportunity to build a pipeline directly to the Mediterranean through Jaffa.

The UN approved the proposal to exclude Jaffa from the Jewish state over the objections of the Jewish Agency, but the move to also exclude the Negev met with greater resistance. The Zionists immediately protested and persuaded Eddie Jacobson to discuss the boundary issue with Truman. In addition, Jacobson helped set up a meeting between Chaim Weizmann and the president. Truman knew of Weizmann and had a great deal of respect for him, a feeling that grew after each meeting. The president recognized that Weizmann was engaged in politics, but that he was not a politician. He also understood the depth of feeling that Weizmann held for the Jewish people. After Weizmann's death, Truman wrote to Jacobson that he "felt as though he had lost a personal friend."[62] On 19 November 1947, the two met and discussed the fate of the Negev.

Weizmann told Truman that the Negev had tremendous potential that could only be realized if it was under Jewish control. The Arabs, he implied, were incapable of the intensive farming techniques necessary to make the desert bloom. Weizmann described the progress already being made in raising crops where there had not even been a blade of grass for thousands of years. The Zionist leader explained that only the Jews could build a port at Aqaba, and that he could foresee the day when a canal would be built from the Red Sea to the Mediterranean. "I pleaded further with the President," Weizmann wrote, "that if the Egyptians choose to be hostile to the Jewish State, which I hope will not be the case, they can close navigation to us through the Suez Canal when this becomes their property, as it will in a few years. The Iraqis, too, can make it difficult for us to pass through the

Persian Gulf. Thus we might be cut off entirely from the Orient. We could meet such an eventuality by building our own canal from Haifa or Tel Aviv to Aqaba."[63]

Weizmann's optimistic vision, and Truman's own idealistic visions of the Middle East persuaded him to support the inclusion of the Negev in the Jewish state against the policy recommendations of his advisers.[64] He explained in his memoirs that he had long been interested in the region and knew that it had once been the seat of great world powers, but that it had declined over the years and the Arabs had never been able to restore the area to its past glory.

On the other hand, he believed a development program could be established under the Jews to exploit the productive potential of the region for the mutual benefit of Jews and Arabs. "The whole region waits to be developed, and if it were handled the way we developed the Tennessee River basin, it could support from 20 to 30 million people more. To open the door to this kind of future would indeed be the constructive and humanitarian thing to do, and it would also redeem the pledges that were given at the time of World War I."[65] Once again, the significance Truman placed on humanitarianism and keeping promises is evident.

The Partition Vote

As the United Nations vote approached, the Zionists were concerned that the United States would not give its full support to the partition resolution and that its passivity would result in many nations voting against the plan. The Latin American nations, which at the time composed over a third of the UN, were of particular concern, because they were under great pressure from the Vatican to oppose partition. On 22 October, Moshe Shertok warned Loy Henderson that American pressure would be needed to secure the Latin American votes. Henderson replied that the United States had decided not to use "arm-twisting" tactics to influence the outcome.[66]

With 62,850 post cards, 1,100 letters, and 1,400 telegrams streaming in during the third quarter of 1947 alone,[67] the White House was under increasing pressure to exert its influence in the UN. The vast majority of these entreaties were from Jews calling on the president to support partition, but the general public was also favorably disposed to the Zionist position. An AIPO poll (19 November 1947) found that 65 percent of the respondents favored a Jewish state while only 10 percent were opposed.[68] A Gallup poll ten days earlier showed that 65 percent favored partition although only 3 percent were willing to send U.S. troops to keep the peace if war broke out. A large majority, 65 percent, did support the idea of a UN peacekeeping force which might include American troops. In terms of sympathies for the parties, twice as many people (25 percent) sympathized with the Jews than with the Arabs, while more than a third (38 percent) sympathized with neither.[69]

The humanitarian, moral, and realistic reasons for supporting partition were augmented by political factors. On 19 November, Clifford sent a memo to the president reminding him that the Jewish vote is important only in New York, but that Woodrow Wilson (in 1916), was the only president since 1876 able to win an election after losing New York. While acknowledging that the Palestine issue is very important to Jewish voters, he also noted that the Jews were divided over the UNSCOP report. Consequently, his advice was unexpected yet still politically motivated. "It will be extremely difficult to decide some of the vexing questions which will arise in the months to come on the basis of political expediency," Clifford wrote. "In the long run," he advised, "there is likely to be greater gain if the Palestine problem is approached on the basis of reaching decisions founded upon intrinsic merit."[70] Of course, Clifford believed that the merits of the Zionist case warranted support for partition; therefore, he may have simply been trying to persuade Truman, who hated to make overtly political foreign policy decisions anyway, that he was acting in accordance with lofty objectives.

As was the case throughout the debate, Forrestal was particularly annoyed by the political arguments used to try to sway the president. In a meeting with Democratic National Committee chairman Senator J. Howard McGrath on 6 November, Forrestal asserted that "no group in this country should be permitted to influence our policy to the point where it could endanger our national security." McGrath reiterated the importance of the Jewish vote to the election, to which Forrestal responded: "I would rather lose those states in a national election than run the risks which I feel might develop in our handling of the Palestine question." Three days before the partition vote the two men met again with McGrath emphasizing the substantial proportion of campaign contributions made by Jews and their dissatisfaction with the United States' lack of effort to secure support for the UN partition resolution. Forrestal told the Senator that the State Department was consciously avoiding "proselytizing for votes" in the hope of preventing further alienation of the Arabs.[71] It was the view of almost all the Near East specialists in the State Department, according to a secret letter from Henderson to Marshall, that partition was contrary to U.S. national interests; consequently, it was not surprising that the diplomatic corps was giving little support to the pro-partition forces at the UN.[72]

In the days preceding the UN vote, the pressure intensified. Truman explained:

> I do not think I ever had as much pressure and propaganda aimed at the White House as I had in this instance. The persistence of a few of the extreme Zionist leaders—actuated by political motives and engaging in political threats—disturbed and annoyed me. Some were even suggesting that we pressure sovereign nations into favorable votes in the General Assembly. I have never approved of the practice of the strong imposing their will on the weak, whether among men or among nations. We had aided Greece. We had, in fact, fathered the independence of the Philippines. But that did not make satellites of these nations or compel them to vote with us on the partitioning of Palestine or any other matter. . . . The kind of "direct approach" some of my correspondents had been making could never gain my approval.[73]

Truman's account in his memoirs probably reflects his honest inclinations; however, there are a lot of conflicting opinions as to what actually occurred. Early in October, Marshall had instructed the UN delegation not to persuade members of the General Assembly to support partition. Later in the month, however, he told General John Hilldring that the United States should "*line up the vote*" to support the American proposals for modification and implementation of the majority plan. But he apparently did not say whether the United States should do the same on the principle of partition, although Marshall later explained to the

Syrian legation that the United States had not hesitated to explain and defend its support for partition to Latin American states. On 24 November, Truman told Lovett that the United States should not "use threats or improper pressure of any kind on other Delegations."[74] These records suggest that the administration had not adopted a strategy of pressuring delegations; nevertheless, the United States' defense of its support for partition could very well have been construed as pressure.

On 26 November, Representative Celler sent Truman a telegram explaining that he was worried that the partition resolution would fail by one or two votes and "thus all your excellent efforts will be frustrated at the eleventh hour." He called on Truman to call off the restraints placed on the American delegation.[75] That same day, Hilldring persuaded his delegation to delay the vote until after Thanksgiving, thereby giving the pro-partition forces another two days to mobilize support.[76] Grose does not explain whether Hilldring acted on his own, or on instruction from the White House. If the former, then it is clear that Niles' intercession with Truman to appoint the pro-Zionist general to the delegation to balance out the anti-Zionists had an impact on the outcome.

According to some accounts, those extra two days proved decisive, because Truman finally told Niles that he was willing to use American influence. "America's line of action had swung in a new direction," according to the Jewish Agency's David Horowitz. "As a result of instructions from the President, the State Department now embarked on a helpful course of great importance to our own interest."[77] In fact, two weeks earlier, the cabinet had discussed how the United States might pressure wavering delegations.[78] There is evidence that pressure *was* exerted on various delegations; however, it was ex-officials and members of the Zionist lobby who were involved. None of the documents cite a specific case of a member of the U.S. delegation or the administration threatening another country.

Most of the lobbying efforts were focused on small nations, although there were a few exceptions. For example, Cardinal Spellman of New York helped line up votes in Cuba and Latin America.[79] Weizmann telegrammed former French premier, Leon Blum, and persuaded him to lobby his government. Bernard Baruch, who on another occasion had denounced Zionist pressure, warned the French UN delegate that a French vote against partition would mean the end of all U.S. aid to France.[80] Again, it is not clear what, if any, authorization Baruch had to make such a threat. Nevertheless, none of these efforts would have had any chance of succeeding if the nations being pressured did not believe the United States supported them.

The Firestone Tire and Rubber Company informed the State Department that it had been asked by the Zionists to use its influence as a major company in the country to pressure Liberia. According to Grose, Robert Nathan called the Liberian delegate and warned him that if he did not vote for partition former Secretary of State Stettinius would call Harry Firestone, Jr. Grose does not say whether Stettinius placed that call, but he does say that the former Secretary called the Liberian president. Liberia switched its vote in favor of partition.[81]

There was also pressure exerted on the Philippines, whose delegate had bitterly attacked partition during the debates. After his speech, the delegate, General Romulo, left New York and gave his deputy instructions to vote against partition. In the meantime, an American civil servant, Julius Edelstein, called his personal friend, the president of the Philippines, and urged him to vote for partition. The Philippines' ambassador to the United States also called the president of the Philippines, and informed him of the pressure to vote for partition and pointed out that it would be foolish to do otherwise. Justices Felix Frankfurter and Frank Murphy also placed calls to Philippine officials on behalf of the Zionists. A joint telegram from twenty-six pro-Zionist senators was sent to encourage the Philippines to vote for partition and "since seven bills were pending in Congress which would affect the Philippines," Stevens notes, "it seemed wise not to resist."[82] Romulo was contacted in Europe but remained adamantly against partition and said that only the president could reverse his position. The president did.[83]

The Senate telegram was sent to twelve countries, four changed their votes to "yes," seven abstained, and one voted "no." One of the other nations that switched its vote was Haiti. A former governor and assistant secretary of state, Adolph Berle, reportedly called the Haitian government and offered U.S. economic aid to secure their vote for partition.[84] Haiti, Liberia, and the

Philippines also received calls from the director of the National Association for the Advancement of Colored People (NAACP), Walter White, who despite reservations about the Zionist enterprise, responded to the Israeli lobby's requests and lobbied on behalf of partition.[85]

One country that did not give in to U.S. pressure was Greece. According to Snetsinger, Niles asked a Greek-American businessman to lobby the Greek government. "Had the White House been interested in pressuring Greece into supporting the plan," Snetsinger concludes, "a more direct and effective manner would have been employed."[86] The failure of the American delegation to offer any concrete guarantees of economic aid, combined with the assurances that were given by Islamic nations if Greece opposed partition, were also factors in the Greek vote. The leverage of economic aid appeared to be relatively useless, as American dependents Cuba and Greece voted against partition, and El Salvador and Honduras abstained.[87]

On 29 November 1947, the General Assembly voted to recommend the partition of Palestine into a Jewish and an Arab state by a vote of thirty-three to thirteen with ten abstentions. The Jewish Agency's David Horowitz explained the Zionist efforts on behalf of the resolution:

> The telephones rang madly. Cablegrams sped to all parts of the world. People were dragged from their beds at midnight and sent on peculiar errands. And, wonder of it all, not an influential Jew, Zionist or non-Zionist, refused to give us his assistance at any time. Everyone pulled his weight, little or great, in the despairing effort to balance the scales to our favor.[88]

The extent of the pressure was revealed in the frequently repeated quote of Lovett who said that "he had never in his life been subject to as much pressure as he had in the three days" preceding the vote.[89] Horowitz credits Truman's intervention with turning the tide: "The United States exerted the weight of its influence almost at the last hour, and the way the final vote turned out must be ascribed to this fact. Its intervention sidetracked the manipulation of the 'fringe votes' against us."[90]

This view was seconded by the executive director of the AZEC, Henry Shapiro, who wrote to Senator Wagner that the activity of the American delegation "unquestionably was the major factor in this historic decision."[91] The *Wall Street Journal* concurred: "It was the Truman administration that took the lead in securing United Nations approval of partition pushing through the partition against considerable opposition."[92] Sumner Welles was even more explicit: "By direct order of the White House every form of pressure, direct and indirect was brought to bear by American officials upon countries outside the Moslem world that were known to be either uncertain or opposed to partition."[93]

On the other hand, there is no evidence of direct administration involvement in pressuring delegations, or any recorded statements of the president giving his approval for such action. Of course, many presidential discussions with top officials are not recorded, so that alone does not disprove the statements above. When Bevin told Marshall that the Arabs accused the United States of pressuring the Latin American countries, the Secretary said that "the Arabs *also* had been bringing pressure to bear everywhere." Marshall added that he had tried to stop this, and had refused to give the Latin American countries advice even after they had asked for it.[94] Another document provides stronger evidence that Truman had not been involved. In response to a memorandum from Lovett explaining the pressure that the Senate had put on the Philippines, and the U.S. Consul had exerted against the president of Haiti, Truman stated that he had refused to make statements to any country about the vote and that he believed pressure groups would put the UN "out of business" if they were permitted to carry on the way they had during the partition debate.[95]

Paradoxically, Truman's resistance to lobby pressure demonstrated lobby influence and undermined the leadership model. The lobby's only interest was in seeing the partition plan approved, and pressured the administration because Truman's support was seen as the best guarantee of success. Although the United States did support partition, Truman's refusal to pressure other countries was, in effect, a decision to oppose the lobby. Despite this opposition, the lobby was able to use its resources to pressure the delegations itself and to persuade third parties to lobby on its behalf and, therefore, was responsible for the favorable outcome. To a large extent, Truman's position was irrelevant because the other delegations *believed* the failure to support partition was liable to have adverse consequences for their relations with the United States. Usually the threat was implied, but sometimes, as in the case of the U.S. Consul in Haiti, it was explicit though unauthorized.

Notes

1. Francis O. Wilcox, *Congress, the Executive, and Foreign Policy* (NY: Harper and Row, 1971), 138.
2. John Snetsinger, *Truman, the Jewish Vote and the Creation of Israel* (CA: Hoover Institution Press, 1974), 36–8; Steven L. Spiegel, *The Other Arab-Israeli Conflict* (IL: University of Chicago Press, 1985), 18.
3. Margaret Truman, *Harry S Truman* (NY: Quill, 1972), 387.
4. Ian J. Bickerton, "President Truman's Recognition of Israel," *American Jewish Historical Quarterly* (1968 December), 206–7.
5. Peter Grose, *Israel in the Mind of America* (NY: Alfred A. Knopf, 1983), 213.
6. Spiegel, *The Other Arab-Israeli Conflict*, 18; Doreen Bierbrier, "The American Zionist Emergency Council: An Analysis of a Pressure Group," *American Jewish Historical Quarterly* (1970 September), 100; Evan Wilson, *Decision On Palestine* (CA: Hoover Institution Press, 1979), 152.
7. Harry S. Truman, *Years of Trial and Hope*, vol. 2 (NY: Doubleday, 1956), 162.
8. George Kent, "Congress and American Middle East Policy," in Willard A. Beling, ed., *The Middle East Quest For an American Policy* (NY: State University of New York Press, 1973), 287.
9. Bierbrier, "The American Zionist," 91; Earl D. Huff, "Zionist Influences Upon U.S. Foreign Policy: A Study of American Policy Toward the Middle East From the Time of the Struggle for Israel to the Sinai Conflict," (University of Idaho, Ph.D. Diss., 1971), 120; Leon I. Feuer, "The Birth of the Israeli Lobby: A Reminiscence," *American Jewish Archives* (1976 November), 117.
10. Bickerton, "Truman's Recognition of Israel," 188; Herbert Druks, *The U.S. and Israel, 1945–1973* (NY: Robert Speller & Sons, Inc., 1979), 6.
11. H. Truman, *Years of Trial and Hope*, 2:135–6; Druks, *U.S. and Israel*, 6.
12. Grose, *Israel in the Mind of America*, 199–200.
13. Ibid., 200–201.
14. Druks, *U.S. and Israel*, 2–3.
15. Ibid., 2.
16. H. Truman, *Years of Trial and Hope*, 132.
17. Ibid., 132.

18. Snetsinger, *Truman, the Jewish Vote*, 18.
19. Bickerton, "Truman's Recognition of Israel," 191.
20. Snetsinger, *Truman, the Jewish Vote*, 25.
21. Grose, *Israel in the Mind of America*, 185.
22. Ibid., 188–9; Bickerton, "Truman's Recognition of Israel," 188.
23. Ibid., 189; Snetsinger, *Truman, the Jewish Vote*, 15.
24. Druks, *U.S. and Israel*, 1–2; Bickerton says the letter was sent to the ZOA, 189. See also Grose, *Israel in the Mind of America*, 189 and Snetsinger, *Truman, the Jewish Vote*, 15.
25. H. Truman, *Years of Trial and Hope*, 133.
26. Ibid.
27. Bickerton, "Truman's Recognition of Israel," 180–1; H. Truman, *Years of Trial and Hope*, 133.
28. Snetsinger, *Truman, the Jewish Vote*, 20–1.
29. Ibid. 38–9; Bickerton, "Truman's Recognition of Israel," 196.
30. *Foreign Relations of the United States* (DC: Government Printing Office, 1947), 708–17 [henceforth FRUS]; Bickerton, "Truman's Recognition of Israel," 200–1.
31. Druks, *U.S. and Israel*, 9–10; Michael J. Cohen, "Truman, the Holocaust, and the Establishment of the State of Israel," *Jerusalem Quarterly* (Spring 1982), 85–6. The Truman-McDonald exchange took place at a meeting on 28 July 1946.
32. Grose, *Israel in the Mind of America*, 217.
33. Snetsinger, *Truman, the Jewish Vote*, 39–40.
34. Letter dated 2 August 1946, Bickerton, "Truman's Recognition of Israel," 194–5.
35. Snetsinger, *Truman, the Jewish Vote*, 28, 152.
36. Richard P. Stevens, *American Zionism and U.S. Foreign Policy 1942–1947* (NY: Pageant Press, 1962), 153–4.
37. Spiegel, *The Other Arab-Israeli Conflict*, 23–4.
38. FRUS 1947, 682.
39. Conference of Presidents 5 September 1946, Bickerton, "Truman's Recognition of Israel," 197.
40. Snetsinger, *Truman, the Jewish Vote*, 41–2.
41. Ibid., 41.
42. Bickerton, "Truman's Recognition of Israel," 198; Stevens, *American Zionism*, 155; Dean Acheson, *Present at the Creation* (NY: W.W. Norton and Co., 1969), 176.
43. Snetsinger, *Truman, the Jewish Vote*, 5, 9–10, 143n, 144n; *American Jewish Yearbook, 1946–1947*, 244; *Gallup Poll Index 1945–1948*.
44. Hannegan to Truman, 17 October 1946, Snetsinger, *Truman, the Jewish Vote*, 42; Bickerton, "Truman's Recognition of Israel," 198.
45. *New York Times* (7 October 1946).
46. Acheson, *Present at the Creation*, 176.
47. Silver to Ben Gurion, 9 October, 1946, M. Cohen, "Truman, the Holocaust," 88.

48. Stevens, *American Zionism*, 163–4.
49. Bickerton, "Truman's Recognition of Israel," 203.
50. Ibid.
51. Walter Mills, ed. *The Forrestal Diaries* (NY: Viking Press, 1951), 304. [Henceforth Forrestal].
52. Aharon Cohen, *Israel and the Arab World* (NY: Funk and Wagnalls, 1970), 376.
53. Robert Silverberg, *If I Forget Thee O Jerusalem: American Jews and the State of Israel* (NY: William Morrow and Co., Inc., 1970), 344; Huff, "Zionist Influences," 88–9.
54. Forrestal, 309–10.
55. 4 September 1947, Bickerton,"Truman's Recognition of Israel," 212.
56. A. Cohen, *Israel and the Arab World*, 381.
57. Silverberg, *If I Forget Thee*, 351.
58. Forrestal, 323.
59. Silverberg, *If I Forget Thee*, 352.
60. M. Cohen, "Truman, the Holocaust," 93.
61. Grose, *Israel in the Mind of America*, 217; M. Cohen, "Truman, the Holocaust," 85.
62. Druks, *U.S. and Israel*, 34n.
63. Chaim Weizmann, *Trial and Error* (NY: Schocken Books, 1966), 458–9.
64. For description of how decision was relayed, see Silverberg, *If I Forget Thee*, 359; Weizmann, *Trial and Error*, 459; FRUS 1947, 1271–2.
65. H. Truman, *Years of Trial and Hope*, 156.
66. M. Cohen, "Truman, the Holocaust," 89.
67. Silverberg, *If I Forget Thee*, 344.
68. Snetsinger, *Truman, the Jewish Vote*, 9–10, 144n.
69. David Schoenbaum, "The United States and the Birth of Israel," *The Wiener Library Bulletin* (1978), 96–7.
70. Snetsinger, *Truman, the Jewish Vote*, 96.
71. Forrestal, 344–5; Snetsinger, *Truman, the Jewish Vote*, 360–1.
72. Grose, *Israel in the Mind of America*, 245.
73. H. Truman, *Years of Trial and Hope*, 158–9.
74. FRUS 1947, 1173–4, 1198–9, 1248, 1284.
75. Snetsinger, *Truman, the Jewish Vote*, 69.
76. Grose, *Israel in the Mind of America*, 250–1.
77. Snetsinger, *Truman, the Jewish Vote*, 68; Huff, 104.
78. Grose, *Israel in the Mind of America*, 251.
79. Huff, "Zionist Influences," 101; Wilson, *Decision On Palestine*, 125–7.
80. Grose, *Israel in the Mind of America*, 253; Wilson, *Decision on Palestine*, 125–7.

81. Forrestal, 346; Grose, *Israel in the Mind of America*, 252; Silverberg, *If I Forget Thee*, 360; Wilson, *Decision On Palestine*, 125–7.
82. FRUS 1947, 1305–6; Stevens, *American Zionism*, 180–1.
83. Stevens, *American Zionism* 180–1; Grose, *Israel in the Mind of America*, 252; Silverberg, *If I Forget Thee*, 360.
84. Grose, *Israel in the Mind of America*, 252; Stevens, *American Zionism*, 179; Wilson, *Decision on Palestine*, 125–7.
85. Robert G. Weisbord and Richard Kazarian, Jr. *Israel in the Black American Perspective* (CT: Greenwood Press, 1985), 20.
86. Snetsinger, *Truman, the Jewish Vote*, 70–1.
87. FRUS 1947, 1307; Grose, *Israel in the Mind of America*, 253; Snetsinger, *Truman, the Jewish Vote*, 166–7n.
88. Michael Brecher, "American Jewry's Influence on Israeli-U.S. Relations," *The Wiener Library Bulletin* (1971), 3.
89. Forrestal, 346.
90. Snetsinger, *Truman, the Jewish Vote*, 70.
91. Letter dated 8 December 1947, Snetsinger, *Truman, the Jewish Vote*, 70.
92. *Wall Street Journal* (26 February 1948) in Bickerton, 210.
93. Bickerton, "Truman's Recognition of Israel," 210.
94. FRUS 1947, 1313.
95. Ibid., 1309.

6

Truman, Israel, and the Jewish Vote Revisited II

The State and Defense Departments were convinced that the UN partition decision and the United States' role in securing its passage would have severe negative implications for American foreign policy.[1] George Kennan, then head of the Policy Planning Staff said: "U.S. prestige in the Moslem world has suffered a severe blow, and U.S. strategic interests in the Mediterranean and Near East have been seriously prejudiced." Moreover, he added, "our vital interests in those areas will continue to be adversely affected to the extent that we continue to support partition."[2]

Defense Secretary Forrestal remained perhaps the most outspoken critic, however, complaining that "it was a most disastrous and regrettable fact that the foreign policy of this country was determined by the contributions a particular bloc of special interests might make to the party funds."[3] Forrestal was particularly worried about American oil supplies, and told a cabinet meeting in early January that without Middle Eastern oil, the United States would soon have to convert to 4-cylinder cars.[4] Forrestal's concerns were not completely unfounded; in fact, the Arab League announced the following month that American oil companies would not be allowed to lay pipelines across the territory of any member states as long as the United States continued to support partition. Meanwhile, the Zionists claimed that the entire oil issue was being blown out of proportion by the State Department in an effort to scuttle partition.[5]

The Zionists were far less active after the partition resolution was adopted, leaving opponents to impede progress toward implementation of the UN decision. At an AZEC meeting on 6 January, Israel Goldstein acknowledged that there had been a "letdown," but explained that nothing could be done until instructions were received from the Jewish Agency as to what their needs were. Four messengers from Palestine told the council that the agency was shocked by the silence of American Jewry, and that the highest priority was to "enlist White House support" for lifting the arms embargo that had been placed on the region.[6] Nearly three weeks later, Silver informed the Jewish Agency in Palestine that Truman had been responsible for securing the UN vote, but that the implementation of the policy was now in the hands of an antagonist—Loy Henderson. Unlike some of his colleagues, Silver did not believe that the situation had deteriorated, but that Henderson's opposition had to be broken "as we broke it on the previous occasion"; that is, by exerting pressure on the government.[7]

It was much more difficult in the months following partition for the Zionists to exert pressure, however, because of Truman's increasing irritation. "The Jewish pressure on the White House did not diminish in the days following the partition vote in the UN," he complained. "Individuals and groups asked me, usually in rather quarrelsome and emotional ways, to stop the Arabs, to keep the British from supporting the Arabs, to furnish American soldiers, to do this, that, and the other. I think I can say that I kept my faith in the rightness of my policy in spite of some of the Jews."[8] In a letter to Eddie Jacobson (27 February 1948), Truman complained that the issue had been "a headache" and although he hoped everything would work out, he said he came to the conclusion "that the situation is not solvable as presently set up."[9]

Truman not only shut off most contacts with the Zionists, but also with the members of his party who were intent on lobbying him on Palestine. He told Howard McGrath and Gael Sullivan (executive director of the Democratic National Committee [DNC]) that the National Security Council was responsible for policy-making and that he did not want them to offer "unauthorized encouragement to Zionist leaders."[10]

Truman may have been able to insulate himself from direct

political pressure, but he still felt indirect pressure. For example, the defeat of a pro-Zionist Democrat in a special election in a predominantly Jewish district in New York suggested that Jewish voters were disenchanted with the Truman Palestine policy. James Hagerty concluded the election indicated "Truman had little, if any, chance of winning" New York in the presidential election.[11] The immediate reaction of the party bosses was to urge Truman to take a more pro-Zionist position.

There were other pressures emanating from Palestine as well. Even before the partition vote had been taken, it was clear there would be a war in Palestine. On 9 January, the first large-scale assault took place and the number and intensity of attacks gradually increased. By February, the British said that so many Arabs had infiltrated that they lacked the forces to run them back.[12]

The Joint Chiefs were particularly concerned about the possibility of the Soviets taking advantage of the instability in Palestine and allying with the Arabs. It was largely for this reason that the United States had rejected the creation of an international force to implement the UN decision; that is, the Soviets would insist on participation in such a force if the U.S. did, and would thereby obtain a foothold in the region. The alternative, that the United States would send a force of its own to enforce partition, was practically and politically unpalatable. General Greunther had informed the president in mid-February that it would require anywhere from 80,000 to 160,000 troops to do the job, and that partial mobilization would probably be necessary.[13]

Clifford advised the president that the Jews could defeat the Arabs without U.S. troops, but needed arms. He also recommended that the United States stop appeasing the Arabs, and instead brand them aggressors, and ask the Security Council to declare their actions a threat to peace. He suggested that the United States propose an international peacekeeping force composed of volunteers, thereby avoiding the problem of Soviet and American troop involvement. "The cruel fact is that American morale is collapsing right around us today," he wrote, "because the American people feel that their government is aiding and abetting in the disintegration of the United Nations—the one great hope of the American people for peace." Clifford added that "in order to save the United Nations for our own selfish interests, the United States must promptly and vigorously support the UN actions regarding Palestine. The credibility of the president (whose 'insistence' clinched the adoption of partition in the UN), as well as the credibility of the UN are at stake." In answer to Forrestal's concern over oil supplies, Clifford said the "Arab States must have oil royalties or go broke." Finally, he concluded by arguing that unless the United States remained committed to partition, the Soviets would not see any barrier to their expansion.[14]

After ignoring his pleas to see Weizmann, Eddie Jacobson decided to go to visit the president on 13 March. He was told that Truman did not want to discuss Palestine, but Jacobson insisted. Truman, Jacobson says, "was abrupt in speech and very bitter in the words he was throwing my way. In all the years of our friendship he never talked to me in this manner."[15] Jacobson had come with a particular objective, however, and he was not to be deterred. In a now famous conversation, Jacobson compared his feelings toward Weizmann with Truman's hero worship of Andrew Jackson in an impassioned appeal. Reluctantly, Truman agreed to see the Zionist leader.[16]

The secret meeting between Weizmann and the president took place on 18 March. The two men reached a mutual understanding and Weizmann left confident that Truman remained committed to partition.[17] A day later, however, the pro-partition forces were shocked when Austin announced at the UN that the United States had decided partition was unworkable and proposed an international trusteeship for Palestine instead.

The reaction from the Zionists was incredulity and anger. The opinions of others were mixed. The *New York Times* called the trusteeship proposal "a series of moves which has seldom been matched for ineptness in the handling of any international issue by an American administration."[18] Pro-partition senators called the decision "one of the most shocking retreats in the history of our foreign relations."[19] Another Senator, Carl Hatch, saw the decision as a courageous act by the president: "He has cast aside politics and he doesn't care what happens to him politically. He has told me that he intends to do what he thinks is right without regard to the political consequences."[20]

Truman tried to calm the furor by explaining the vote at a press conference on 25 March. He said that trusteeship was an effort to fill the vacuum soon to be created by the termination of the Mandate on 15 May." The president tried to justify the proposal as a means of insuring a peaceful solution:

> Unless emergency action is taken, there will be no public authority on that date capable of preserving law and order. Violence and bloodshed will descend upon the Holy Land. Large scale fighting among the people of that country will be the inevitable result. Such fighting would infect the entire Middle East and could lead to consequences of the gravest sort involving the peace of this nation and the entire world.

When Truman was asked whether he still supported partition at some future date, however, he replied that he was trying to say just that.[21]

Given that there was already large-scale violence, and that the Jews had already made it clear that they would not accept anything less than a state, it was difficult to see how the trusteeship proposal could succeed. Moreover, given the president's assurances to Weizmann the day before the announcement at the UN, it was unclear how the idea ever got past the president. Weizmann called Jacobson afterwards and told him that he didn't believe the president knew what was going to happen at the UN.[22] Several writers argue that Truman was surprised by what transpired. Margaret Truman and Robert Silverberg both report that the president learned about the speech when he read the morning newspaper the next day. Margaret Truman found a note on her father's calender that said the State Department had unexpectedly pulled the rug out from under him and reversed his Palestine policy. "The first I know about it is what I read in the papers!" He lamented that he had been put in the position of "a liar and a double-crosser."[23]

After reading the paper, Silverberg relates, Truman called in Clifford who found the president "as disturbed as I have ever seen him." Clifford called Marshall in San Francisco and Lovett in Florida, and was told by both that they were equally amazed by the trusteeship proposal. Clifford discovered, according to this version, that Marshall had initialled a State Department memorandum that called for trusteeship if partition proved unworkable.

While Marshall was in California, a State Department official, opposed to partition, sent Austin instructions to give the speech. This deception, Silverberg concludes, so infuriated Truman that he became a staunch Zionist for the first time, and insured that he would no longer listen to "the appeasers of the Arabs, the worriers over oil, the frenetic anti-Communists, and the subtle anti-Semites in the Departments of State and Defense."[24]

Marshall apparently was not only aware of the proposal, but had approved it. Robert McClintock, a special assistant to Dean Rusk, wrote the following in brackets on a draft of the Austin speech: "It is undeniable, however, that the establishment of internal order in Palestine by the Security Council in pursuance of its duty to maintain international peace might establish conditions under which the Palestine Commission could succeed in carrying out its mandate according to the terms of the resolution of 29 November 1947." According to McClintock, this phraseology meant the United States supported partition; omitting the sentence, he said, "would knock the plan for partition on its head."[25] In the final draft of the speech, Marshall deleted the sentence.

On 21 February, Truman received a working draft of a speech Austin was to give on the 24th, with a cover letter explaining that Marshall had not yet approved the draft or discussed it with Forrestal. In a separate paragraph, the letter said that if the partition resolution could not be carried out, it would be necessary to refer the issue back to the General Assembly to consider some form of UN trusteeship. Marshall wanted the president to "consider and approve" this alternative "in relation to further development of the problem." On 22 February, Truman approved the draft with the following proviso: "*I want to make it clear, however, that nothing should be presented to the Security Council that could be interpreted as a recession on our part from the position we took in the General Assembly.*" The following day, Marshall gave the final draft to the president with a message attached saying the speech "does not represent recession in any way from the position taken by us in General Assembly. In fact, it is stronger with regard to threats to the peace which have developed since Assembly discussion." This was true of the speech Austin gave on the 24th, but Marshall apparently did not point out the change in the 19

March speech, which included the trusteeship proposal. This suggests that either Marshall did not see McClintock's comment, or that he did and deceived the president. It is not clear, however, whether Truman read the final draft of the 19 March speech, and misunderstood it, or simply accepted Marshall's interpretation.[26]

Three other studies present an entirely different picture suggesting that Truman was not deceived by the State Department, but knew all along about the trusteeship proposal and personally approved it. According to Ganin, it was Marshall who notified Austin on 8 March that the president had approved the draft statement calling for trusteeship. The president had not discussed the draft with either Clifford or Niles, and apparently signed it without realizing it signified a reversal of his position. The State Department then avoided discussing the issue to insure that neither Clifford nor Niles would find out.[27] The idea that the president would sign something like that without realizing what he was doing appears a bit farfetched and, in fact, Cohen presents evidence that the president did not act carelessly.

Cohen relies on a memorandum that provides Lovett's version of the events surrounding the trusteeship proposal. According to Lovett, Clifford was shown the draft of Austin's speech on 6 March and Lovett discussed it himself with Truman on 8 March. Lovett explained that he did not believe partition was viable and that it was necessary to have an alternative. The president's response, according to Lovett, was that "we were to go through and attempt to get the approval of implementation of the General Assembly resolution, but if we did not get it we could take the alternative step. That was perfectly clear. He said it to General Marshall and me." Truman later told Marshall that he would have taken steps to avoid the political heat had he known when Austin would make his speech. On the other hand, Cohen argues that Marshall might not have given Austin approval to give the speech when he did, if Truman had told him about the meeting with Weizmann. Loy Henderson's explanation of the fiasco "was that more than a week had passed between Truman's authorization and the speech itself, and Truman might have presumed by then that the situation did not in fact call for a change in policy." Truman also may have assumed, Henderson suggested, that he would be consulted before the speech was made.[28]

Clifford's strongly worded memorandum on 8 March cited above makes it clear that he was not in favor of any policy that could be interpreted as a retreat from partition. This followed a memorandum sent by Marshall to the president and the cabinet that said it appeared partition would not be possible, and the Palestine problem would have to be returned to the General Assembly for fresh consideration. Marshall then sent Austin "an approved" text for a statement on the Palestine problem, which included the trusteeship proposal on 5 March, the same day he informed the president that partition was unworkable. Over a week later, Marshall told Austin the president had approved the statement on 5 March for use "when and if necessary."[29] The approval, then, came before Lovett's reported meeting with the president. It also conflicts with Spiegel's version, which claims that Truman gave oral approval for the trusteeship plan to Marshall and Lovett on 8 March.

Austin issued the statement after a majority of the Security Council had expressed opposition to the implementation of partition, so he no doubt believed that he was acting in concert with Truman's instructions. It does not appear, however, that Truman knew that it had indeed become necessary to retreat from partition, at least temporarily for the sake of peace, and that State Department officials intent on scuttling partition had taken advantage of the president's faith in Marshall, and his acceptance of the Secretary's interpretation that trusteeship did not represent a "recession" from prior United States policy.

According to Spiegel, the pro-partition forces were outmaneuvered because Truman was preoccupied with other foreign policy issues; the president was still irritated by Zionist pressure; Secretary Marshall had become personally involved; Niles was out of the office with a heart ailment during most of the period preceding the trusteeship proposal; and the president had approved trusteeship as an alternative to partition.[30]

The evidence, then, is contradictory. The Zionists had some warning of the possibility that a policy reversal was on the horizon, but did not maintain sufficient pressure on the White House to prevent Truman from approving at least the possibility of a change. On the other hand, Weizmann did meet with the president and secured a commitment to partition the day before the Austin speech. The most reasonable explanation would appear to be that Truman did approve the trusteeship proposal as a contingency, but not because he had changed his mind about partition. Given his humanitarian interest in the problem, he was probably responding to the deteriorating situation in Palestine by accepting an alternative that was said to be a peaceful solution.

It also appears that Truman did not expect the proposal to be advanced without first consulting him and, given his intense feelings about loyalty and honesty, it is unlikely he would have approved Austin's speech after speaking to Weizmann. Of course, it would be naive to believe that by this time Truman did not know that trusteeship would be opposed by the Zionists and their supporters, suggesting that his willingness to consider it under any circumstances was, as Senator Hatch claimed, based on non-political grounds. Thus, the decision can best be explained by the fact that the deteriorating security situation in Palestine reinforced the realist arguments of Truman's advisers, which the president became more willing to accept, because the threats to peace had become real and imminent, and therefore coincided with his own beliefs. The Zionists' arguments for support of partition became less persuasive as it became clearer that bloodshed could not be averted.

The Decision To Recognize Israel

The apparent American retreat from partition encouraged Arab intransigence. Confident of a military victory as long as the United States maintained its arms embargo and unwillingness to intervene militarily, the Arabs rejected American efforts, spearheaded by the head of UN affairs, Dean Rusk, to negotiate a truce and acceptance of trusteeship.[31] Meanwhile, the Security Council adopted two new resolutions Ambassador Austin had introduced on 30 March calling for a truce and a special session to consider further the future of Palestine. On 16 April, the U.S. delegation proposed a new *draft* trusteeship plan to the special session that once again raised questions as to American intentions.

The president's basic attitude had remained unchanged throughout the period following the UN resolution; he still was irritated by Zionist pressure tactics and the actions of Jews in

Palestine, but was sympathetic to their position. His primary concern was to prevent bloodshed, but domestic politics constrained his policy choices for doing so. He told Rusk to remind the Arabs "that we have *a difficult political situation* within this country. *Our main purpose in the present situation is to prevent a war*" (emphasis added).[32]

The Zionists were suspicious despite the government's official support for partition. As early as March, the Jewish Agency's representatives in Washington had told Ben-Gurion "the only way to bring the half-century of Zionist efforts to a successful outcome would be for the Palestine Jews themselves to take unilateral action as the British pulled out. They should declare a provisional government."[33] The Jews in Palestine reached the same conclusion, and had made it clear that they planned to declare their independence the day the British withdrew. The Zionists knew the State Department opposed the plan, but they were not sure of the president's view until the end of April.

On the eve of Passover, 23 April, Judge Samuel Rosenman, a close friend of Truman's, called Weizmann's New York hotel room and informed him that he had just spoken to the president who told him: "I have Dr. Weizmann on my conscience." Rosenman said the president was trying to repair the damage caused by the trusteeship proposal and, if he succeeded, he would recognize the new Jewish state as soon as it came into being. Truman cautioned, however, that this promise had to remain secret.[34]

As was the case in the trusteeship fiasco, the president apparently did not inform the State Department of his intentions, because it was working feverishly to prevent the Jews from declaring their independence. According to Guatemala's representative to the UNSCOP, Jorge Garcia Granados, the United States "exerted the strongest possible pressure on Jewish leaders in an effort to persuade them not to proclaim a state. Veiled threats of possible American disfavor, even severe economic sanctions, were expressed." A member of Israel's first government, Zeev Sharef, relates in his book *Thirteen Days* that the Americans threatened to impose an embargo on dollars, oil, and continue the one on weapons. In addition, the State Department threatened to expose Zionist activities in the United States pertaining to illegal immigration and arms purchases to damage their public image.[35] The department still hoped to arrange a truce in Palestine and Rusk proposed this on 3 May along with an extension of the Mandate for ten days, but this was rejected by the Jewish Agency. Five days later Marshall and Lovett told Moshe Shertok that they were interested in preventing the situation in Palestine from endangering world peace. According to Shertok, they issued no threats, only a warning that "if the Jews persisted in their course, they must not seek the help of the United States in the event of an invasion."[36]

On 11 May, a day before the meeting to discuss whether to recognize the Jewish State, Rusk told two members of the UN delegation that the department was trying to prevent recognition, but he already knew that the effort was futile: "I don't think the boss [Truman] will ever put himself in a position of opposing that effort when it might be that the U.S. opposition will be the only thing that could possibly prevent it from succeeding."[37] The next day, Marshall, Lovett, and Clifford met with Truman at Blair House to make a decision that Truman apparently had already made three weeks earlier. Clifford made the case for recognition, drawing this objection from Marshall: "Mr. President, this is not a matter to be determined on the basis of politics. Unless politics were involved, Mr. Clifford would not even be at this conference. This is a serious matter of foreign policy determination and the question of politics and political opinion does not enter into it."[38] Marshall was so upset that he said that "if the President were to follow Mr. Clifford's advice . . . [he] would vote against the President" in the upcoming election. Lovett was equally vociferous in his opposition to recognition, complaining that Palestine was filled with "Jews and communist agents from the Black Sea area."[39]

The president did hear another side that day in another meeting with Representative Sol Bloom, the ranking Democrat on the House Committee on Foreign Affairs. Bloom told the president that the United States should go on record as the first nation to recognize the Jewish State. Other Democratic leaders expressed similar sentiments, and once again warned Truman that his vacillation on Palestine would provide the Republicans with ammunition to use against them in the election.[40]

On 14 May, eleven minutes after the declaration of independence, the United States announced de facto recognition of the state of Israel. At that moment, the Zionist lobby had reached the objective of a Jewish state that it had laid out in the Biltmore Program six years earlier. The decision was applauded by most Americans, although it came as a shock to diplomats at the UN who were once again confounded by yet another American policy reversal.

Why did Truman agree to recognize Israel? Well, on the one hand, there was no reason not to, after it became clear that the Jews were going to proclaim their independence regardless of American wishes. Truman knew the Soviet Union would recognize the new state (as it did on 17 May), and did not want the United States to give the Soviets the initiative. Moreover, the decision was consistent with the president's own beliefs and ideology.

Truman's primary concerns were that the suffering of Jewish refugees be relieved and that the promise of the Balfour Declaration be kept. In recognizing the state of Israel, Truman was fulfilling the promise to support a Jewish state; moreover, he recognized nothing more could be done to prevent the partition of Palestine once the Jews had begun to achieve military success (as they had) against the Arabs. The decision to recognize Israel was also a way to ratify the partition decision and, thereby, reinforce the UN's authority. Since Truman was committed to the success of the United Nations, this was a logical step.

Truman had also expressed throughout the years of debate a commitment to resolving the Palestine issue peacefully, and recognition offered the prospect of furthering the cause of peace. "My sole objective in the Palestine procedure," Truman wrote on 18 May, "has been to prevent bloodshed."[41] A few months later, he wrote to Weizmann: "I hope that peace will come to Palestine . . . and that we will eventually be able to work out proper location of all those Jews who suffered so much during the war." Note here the concern for the Jewish refugees. This deep personal concern was reinforced by the political pressure, which made it clear that recognition would provide large political benefits and no costs, while opposition would impose heavy costs and no benefits, and by simple pragmatism:

I had often talked with my advisers about the course of action we would take once partition came about and *it was always* understood that eventually we would recognize any responsible government the Jews might set up. Partition was not taking place in exactly the peaceful manner I had hoped, to be sure, but the fact was that the Jews were controlling the area in which their people lived and that they were ready to administer and to defend it (emphasis added).[42]

In retrospect, it was naive to believe partition would result in peace, since the Arab states had made it clear they intended to oppose partition by military force from the outset and had begun to fight against the Jews as early as January. In addition, the refusal of the United Nations to take action to implement partition, combined with British obstruction, provided evidence to the Arabs that their efforts would not be opposed.

Truman and Israel

Truman's first decision after recognizing the new state was to appoint an ambassador. This decision reflected the weight of influence exerted by Clifford over the president's foreign policy advisers. The State Department wanted the president to appoint a career man to the post, but Clifford convinced Truman of the need to have an independent source of information from Palestine, and that James McDonald would be the best man to provide it. McDonald was dismissed by those at State as "a pro-Zionist," which disqualified him in their minds for the post. Truman did not discuss the appointment, however, with Marshall, Lovett or Henderson. Truman made the decision himself and then McDonald, who disliked Lovett and Henderson, reported either directly to the President or to Clifford.[43]

Not even the appointment of the pro-Zionist McDonald was sufficient to change American policy regarding arms transfers to the region. Ironically, the United States had originally proposed a resolution in October 1947 to establish "a special constabulary or police force" to implement the partition plan and such a force could be expected to require arms. Henderson, Lovett, and Marshall opposed the export of arms, however, "so long as the tension continues." "Otherwise," Lovett argued, "the Arabs might use arms of U.S. origin against Jews, or Jews might use them against

Arabs." The result, he said, would be that the United States "would be subject to bitter recrimination."[44] Consequently, on 5 December the State Department prohibited the shipment of all weapons to the Middle East. According to Slonim, the decision was made without Truman's authorization or consultation.[45] The embargo was subsequently written into UN truce resolutions so that Truman was unable to shift policy without appearing to undermine the UN efforts to bring the Palestine fighting under control, an objective that Truman placed a high priority on.

Lovett warned Marshall almost immediately after the embargo was announced that the Zionists would attempt to obtain weapons from the United States, and that they should be told that all arms requests should be made to the British authorities while the Mandate was in effect, and then after the end of the Mandate to the UN Commission. Since it was the British who were primarily responsible for the Jews' inability to obtain arms in the first place, this was clearly unsatisfactory.

Weizmann wrote to Truman on 9 December urging him to provide arms to the Jews in Palestine, in yet another effort to bypass the State Department.[46] Other Israeli and American Jewish leaders continued to pressure the White House and the State Department and, as was usually the case, they were backed by their sympathizers in Congress.[47] On 28 January, for example, Eleanor Roosevelt, then a UN delegate, pleaded with Marshall to "remove the embargo and see that the Jews and any UN police force are equipped with modern armaments, which is the only thing which will hold the Arabs in check. . . . "[48] In Clifford's 8 March memorandum discussed earlier, he called on the president to immediately lift the embargo and "create and arm the Arab and Jewish militias provided for in the General Assembly resolution. . . . "[49]

Why was Truman willing to resist the pressure to end the embargo, when it was being exerted by the very same people who were able to convince him to support partition and recognize Israel? The answer, again, is most likely to be found in Truman's objectives in Palestine; that is, to end the bloodshed. In the case of the embargo decision, he followed the advice of his foreign policy advisers, not because he had limited the access of pro-Zionists, but because his own views were more compatible with those of Marshall and the others who supported the policy in this instance. Unfortunately, there is not much evidence to support this interpretation, since Truman does not explain his position on the issue, but the aforementioned views regarding his desire to avert bloodshed seem to mesh well with those of Marshall, who expressed similar sentiments in his reply to Mrs. Roosevelt's plea: "A decision by the United States . . . to permit American arms to go to Palestine and neighboring states would facilitate acts of violence and the further shedding of blood and thus render still more difficult the task of maintaining law and order. We are continuing, therefore, to refuse to license the shipment of arms to that area."[50]

There is little doubt that many in the State Department, as well as Forrestal, saw the embargo as yet another means of obstructing partition, but this did not invalidate the argument that the provision of arms to the combatants would only make the situation worse. The problem with this argument, as the Zionists were quick to point out, was that the embargo was effectively one-sided; that is, the Palestinian Arabs had no difficulty obtaining arms from the surrounding Arab countries.

In fact, the British were actively supplying the Arabs, as well as commanding the most potent Arab force—the Jordanian Arab Legion. On 26 January, Lovett urged the British Ambassador to issue a statement saying Britain would suspend all shipments of arms to the Arab states.[51] As perhaps the best example of the British effort to undermine partition, not only did London refuse to issue the requested statement, the government did just the opposite; that is, it signed a treaty with Transjordan to provide *additional* arms to the Arabs. The inequality of the situation infuriated the Zionists, but the British justified their actions as necessary "to prevent internal disorders caused by communist subversives."[52]

Apparently, the president was prepared to lift the embargo at a 24 March White House meeting, but Marshall's views took precedence over Clifford's. The Secretary of State argued that efforts were under way to negotiate a truce in Palestine and that ending the embargo would jeopardize those efforts. It was understood that the department would be given two weeks to finalize the truce otherwise the embargo would be rescinded.[53] This ver-

sion would support the view that Truman was willing to take the
political heat for the embargo so long as he thought it would
contribute to a peaceful resolution of the crisis. Two weeks later,
however, the department had succeeded only in drafting a truce
resolution. Weizmann, meanwhile, tried once again to intervene:

> The practical question now is whether your Administration will pro-
> ceed to leave our people unarmed in the face of an attack which it
> apparently feels it is unable to stop; and whether it can allow us to
> come directly or indirectly under Arab dominion which is sworn to
> our destruction. The choice for our people, Mr. President, is between
> Statehood and extermination. History and providence have placed
> this issue in your hands, and I am confident that you will yet decide
> it in the spirit of the moral law.[54]

Despite Weizmann's persuasiveness, Truman did not change his
mind on the embargo and the State Department resolution was
adopted in the Security Council on 17 April. It called for a political
as well as a military truce, and asked member states to prevent
the entry into Palestine of "armed bands and fighting personnel,
groups and individuals, weapons and war materials." "From a
self-denying ordinance of the State Department alone," Slonim
concludes, "the embargo had become the fiat of the United Nations. The entire truce resolution was, in effect, the logical sequel
to Austin's 19 March speech announcing withdrawal from partition."[55]

Any hope of a policy reversal after recognition was quickly
smothered by Marshall, who told Truman three days later that
the United States had to be very careful about its position on the
embargo to avoid giving "a final kick to the UN." The British
also warned Truman that lifting the embargo would be dangerous.
A message conveyed to the president from Bevin on 21 May
warned that the British would lift "their own embargo" if the
United States changed its policy and "the unfortunate position
will then be reached of one side being largely armed by the Americans and the other by the British."[56] In a memorandum to Marshall that same day, George Kennan cautioned that "the course
of action we are now embarking on threatens not only to place
in jeopardy some of our most vital national interests in the Middle
East and the Mediterranean but also to disrupt the unity of the

western world and to undermine our entire policy toward the
Soviet Union."[57]

Kennan's view was seconded by that of the U.S. ambassador
to Great Britain the next day, who noted a widening "crevasse"
between the United States and Britain, not only in the Middle
East but also in Europe. He pointed out that the British were
angry over the recognition of Israel without having consulted
them, and now warned that ending the embargo would put the
two allies in the ironic position of being on "opposite sides of a
battle line scarcely three years after 8 May 1948."[58]

Thus, the embargo was no longer a means to prevent partition,
but had taken on a greater role. It had become necessary to
maintain American strategic interests in the region and prevent
the erosion of the United States-Great Britain alliance. This argument was not significantly different from that advanced
throughout the debate on Palestine by the State Department. Yet,
on this issue, not even the lobbying of Weizmann and the pressure
of a close election race could sway Truman.

"Dewey Defeats Truman"

In the early summer, after the first truce, the Israeli lobby began
to focus its attention on securing financial aid and de jure recognition. As early as 23 June, Clifford told M.J. Slonim of the
American Jewish Congress: "Rest assured that we have this matter in mind and shall continue to work toward full recognition."[59]
Recognition seemed to be a relatively small gesture that would
yield some political benefits without any perceptible cost; yet,
Truman resisted on principle. He believed that an elected government should be in place first before extending de jure recognition, but made it clear that there would be no hesitation once
that occurred.

Both major parties' political platforms endorsed the idea of
providing economic aid to Israel; however, the Progressive Party
went even further by calling for generous financial assistance without political conditions. Then, on 24 July, the commander of the
New York Jewish War Veterans publicly advocated in a letter to
Truman that the United States loan Israel $100 million, and end

the arms embargo. The loan request subsequently became a campaign issue.[60]

The third issue in the campaign related to Palestine was the American position on the Bernadotte Plan. During the summer, Count Folke Bernadotte was sent to Palestine in an effort to mediate a truce and try to negotiate a settlement. Bernadotte's plan called for the Jewish state to give up the Negev and Jerusalem to Transjordan and receive the western Galilee. This was similar to the boundaries that had been proposed prior to the partition vote, and had been rejected by all sides. Now, the proposal was being offered after the Arabs had gone to war to prevent partition and a Jewish State had been declared. The Jews and Arabs *both* rejected the plan, but Secretary Marshall, apparently without Truman's knowledge, told the UN the proposals "offer a generally fair basis for settlement of the Palestine question." The British added their support for the plan, creating further stress on the president.[61]

With the election less than two months away and polls showing him behind, Truman was faced with tremendous pressure to cater to the Jewish vote. The Democratic candidate for governor in Connecticut, Chester Bowles, wrote to Clifford on 23 September, urging him to persuade Truman to grant de jure recognition to Israel, promise to provide aid, and offer to sponsor Israel as a member of the UN. Bowles suggested that Truman issue a statement announcing these moves on 30 September, the Jewish New Year. He cautioned against waiting until October because "we will get no [Jewish] help as far as registration is concerned and the opposition will charge [Truman] with playing politics with our foreign policy." He was clearly worried about his prospects in Connecticut and suggested that the party's problems might be even more severe in New York.[62]

This sentiment was shared by the chairman of the DNC, Howard McGrath, who also urged Truman to issue a statement on New Year's Day. "Praise and thanksgiving would be echoed from every Jewish home and no Jewish leader could fail to sing the President's praise," one adviser remarked.[63]

Eddie Jacobson also used his influence to try to persuade the president to make his position clear. On the eve of the elections, Jacobson told the president:

Now as on March 19th your State Department has again acted without authority from you—but you are the man taking all the blame. . . . You are out here shaking the branches for a few votes—while you are losing millions of them in N(ew) Y(ork) and Penn(sylvania) by the actions of the State Department who are tied body and soul to the British Foreign Office.[64]

The president resisted the pressure because he did not want to politicize the issue. "It had been my desire all along to keep foreign policy out of the campaign of 1948," he wrote in his memoirs. "I wanted the world to know that, however divided the American people might be on political issues at home, they would stand as one in their relations to other nations."[65]

Although he refused to make a public statement, Truman did take action to "rein in" the State Department. He does not say whether he discussed his views of the Bernadotte Plan with Marshall, but the opinion he expresses in his memoirs was that "it looked to me like a fast reshuffle that gave to the Arabs the Negev area, which still remained to be fully settled."[66] After Marshall's remarks at the UN about the plan, Truman gave orders "that no statement be made or no action taken on the subject of Palestine . . . without specific authority from me and clearing the text of any statement."[67] The president was, it appears, sensitive to the domestic pressure.

Marshall's initial endorsement of the Bernadotte Plan put the Dewey campaign in a difficult position because it provided them with an opening to blast the president and perhaps lure away some of the Democrats' traditional Jewish supporters. Dewey had kept the Palestine issue out of the campaign until he decided to issue a statement on 22 October, calling for full recognition of Israel, pledging economic aid, and suggesting that Truman had negated the Democratic platform. This, according to Truman, violated the tacit agreement between the candidates to keep the issue out of the campaign and, worse yet, had attacked his integrity. Given the importance Truman placed on honesty and integrity, it was not surprising that he would react to Dewey's attack. Of course, the fact that polls two days after Dewey's speech showed the challenger certain to win the election left the president with nothing to lose.[68]

On 28 October, Truman told a cheering Madison Square Garden crowd:

> The subject of Israel . . . must not be resolved as a matter of politics in a political campaign. I have refused consistently to play politics with that question. I have refused, first, because it is my responsibility to see that our policy in Israel fits in with our policy throughout the world; second, it is my desire to help build in Palestine a strong, prosperous, free and independent democratic state. It must be large enough, free enough, and strong enough to make its people self-supporting and secure.

This statement reflected the influence of both the pro- and anti-partition forces. The reference to global policy reflects the State Department view, and the stress the president placed on the building of a free democratic state echoes the opinions of the Zionists. Although vague, the last sentence suggests the arms embargo will eventually be lifted. More specifically, the president said that he remained committed to the Democratic platform and that "when a permanent Government is elected in Israel it will promptly be given de jure recognition." Backing away from any appearance of endorsing the Bernadotte Plan, Truman told the audience that boundary modification "should be made only if fully acceptable to Israel." Finally, the president disposed of the financial issue by announcing that he had instructed the relevant agencies to expedite any applications for loans that might be submitted by Israel.[69]

The president's speech was an almost complete endorsement of Israeli lobby demands. Truman's own statements suggest that he sympathized with them, but he did not want to give in prior to the election. Faced with almost certain defeat, Truman apparently concluded that he had nothing to lose and everything to gain. As it turned out, of course, Truman won the election with only 49.5 percent of the popular vote. Dewey won New York by less than 1 percent of the 6.1 million votes cast. A switch of 29,294 votes in Ohio, California, and Illinois would have made Dewey president. A switch of only 12,487 votes, 0.03 percent, in Ohio and California would have thrown the election into the House of

Representatives. As Snetsinger notes, there were 841,000 Jews of voting age in those three states, implying that Truman's last minute statement could have had an impact on the outcome.[70]

As a postscript, it is worth noting that the United States did not abandon the arms embargo for several years and, in fact, reaffirmed it in the Tripartite Agreement signed with Britain and France on 25 May 1950. Britain, in the meantime, continued to arm Transjordan.

On 19 January 1949, the Export-Import Bank granted Israel a $100 million loan. Two weeks later, on 31 January, shortly after Israel's first elections, the United States extended de jure recognition. Despite the United States' strong support for partition and Israel, only South Africa (of the UN members) withheld this recognition for so long.

Summary

During the three-year period (1945–1948) examined in chapters 5 and 6, Harry Truman made a number of decisions that were of import to the Israeli lobby (and its precursor—the Zionist lobby). In 1946, Truman joined the Zionists in calling on Great Britain to allow large numbers of Jews to immigrate to Palestine. That year he also rejected the Morrison-Grady Plan devised by an Anglo-American committee and announced the decision in a preelection speech on the Jewish New Year.

The following year, Truman also made several decisions favorable to the Zionists. One of the first was to appoint John Hilldring to the American delegation to the UN. The United States then came out in support of the UNSCOP majority report which proposed the partition of Palestine and opposed the effort to modify the plan by excising the Negev from the Jewish State. The United States then supported partition at the UN. Although Truman apparently decided against using American influence to pressure other delegations to support the resolution, the American delegation's defense of partition carried an implied threat. The administration also took one significant step opposed by the Zionists—the imposition of an arms embargo to the Middle East that was maintained throughout the following year.

In 1948, there was an apparent decision to abandon partition that was subsequently reversed by the president. Truman also decided to recognize the new state of Israel immediately after it was declared, and to appoint as ambassador to Israel a man sympathetic to the Zionists. During the remainder of the year preceding the election, Truman made two other decisions that were favorable toward the Israeli lobby: first, he rejected the Bernadotte Plan, and then he offered Israel a generous economic loan and promised de jure recognition.

Over the course of these three years, several policy decisions were opposed by the lobby including the proposal of trusteeship, the imposition of the arms embargo, and the refusal to actively lobby for partition. In addition, the lobby wanted the United States to give de jure recognition to Israel. The U.S. position on trusteeship was later reversed and the lobby's objective, adoption of the partition resolution, was reached without administration pressure. Truman never opposed de jure recognition, but maintained that an elected government should be in place first; once it was, the United States granted de jure recognition.

Since all of these decisions were made in the executive branch, the lobby was at an immediate disadvantage. The president made the ultimate decisions in each case and it was only possible to affect the decision if members of the lobby could obtain access to Truman. Thus, the leadership model would be expected to be more useful in explaining this case, than those found in part I.

The realist perspective dominated the thinking of officials in the Defense and State Departments, who believed that support for the Zionist positions would undermine United States-Arab relations, open the Middle East up to potential Soviet intervention, and threaten American strategic interests. Although there were possible repercussions for U.S. interests by supporting the Zionists, the apocalyptic scenarios presented by Forrestal, Lovett, and others were not generally accepted. The president was very cognizant of the potential Soviet threat, but he did not see it as overriding, except in the case of the use of foreign troops to implement partition. That alternative, however, was not proposed by the lobby. The one decision that appeared to go against the lobby for realist reasons, the arms embargo, was supported by Truman more out of humanitarian concerns than strategic ones.

Although the lobby did not have the same degree of access to the executive branch that it enjoyed in Congress, three important constituents had the president's ear and his respect. Throughout his term, Niles and Clifford were forceful advocates of the lobby position, and usually effective counterweights to Marshall and Forrestal. In addition, Eddie Jacobson intervened at crucial times and was able to convince the president to support the lobby and listen to the persuasive entreaties of Chaim Weizmann.

The fact that the Palestine problem became an important issue on the American foreign policy agenda was largely attributable to the Zionist lobby. By 1947, after the issue had been brought before the UN, the United States would inevitably have been drawn into the dispute with or without the lobby, but the matter had already been on the agenda for years.

As critics of the lobby have contended, elections did play a role in the decision-making process, despite Truman's protests to the contrary. In the election years of 1946 and 1948, congressmen and the president took positions that were most likely to maximize their votes. Since little organized opposition to the Zionist position existed outside the administration, and the general public supported it, there was everything to gain and nothing to lose from supporting the Zionists. Consequently, there are numerous references by congressmen, the president, and his advisers to the political implications of various decisions regarding Palestine.

When Truman deviated from the Zionist position, the lobby provoked an uproar in the trusteeship case; the president responded by letting the proposal die. The decision to maintain the arms embargo throughout 1948 seems to undermine the argument that Truman responded to electoral pressures; however, Truman did make several other decisions, some just before the election, to balance out this one anomaly. In his October 1948 speech, Truman endorsed the Democratic platform, which approved Israel's claims regarding the boundaries set forth in the partition resolution. His endorsement also reaffirmed his rejection of the Bernadotte Plan, which had initially been received favorably by Marshall and stimulated criticism of the administration. His statement also defused the issues of providing economic aid and de jure recognition to Israel by promising both.

In 1946, and even more so in 1948, when Truman appeared on the verge of an election defeat, the Republicans' outspoken endorsement of the Zionist program forced Truman's hand. This

was particularly evident in Truman's decision to announce the
United States' rejection of the Morrison-Grady Plan on Yom
Kippur in 1946, just prior to the congressional elections. If the
election year is considered from November 1947 to November
1948, then the partition decision would also be seen as influenced
by electoral politics.

Truman was under a great deal of pressure to preempt Republican exploitation of the Zionist program because of the elections and the strength of the Republican party in Congress. In
1946, the Republicans recaptured control of the Congress for the
first time since 1930 and were looking forward to winning the
White House in 1948. Thus, despite Senator Vandenberg's incli-
nation toward bipartisanship in foreign policy, the Palestine issue
was politicized even by him. With a six seat minority in the Senate
and a fifty-eight seat minority in the House, Truman would not
be expected to be able to pursue an independent policy, and his
policies conformed fairly closely to the dictates of Congress.

The lobby's success during Truman's term can be best explained
by examining the ideology of the president. Since Truman was
faced with conflicting opinions from advisers who supported the
Zionists' aims—Clifford and Niles—and those who opposed them—
virtually all of the State Department and Forrestal—we need
some means of explaining why he reached the decisions that he
did. Ordinarily, Truman would have been expected to side with
his Secretaries of State and Defense, but in most of the examples
cited in this chapter, he followed the contrary advice offered by
Clifford and Niles. I would expect the lobby's supporters to be
particularly influential because of the reasons mentioned above;
that is, the lobby's balance of lobbying power advantage and the
domestic political context in which the decisions were made. The
president did not always agree with the lobby, however, so the
pluralist model alone cannot explain the outcomes.

The president's willingness to support the lobby was determined
largely by Truman's own beliefs. One of the problems he faced,
and that may explain why domestic politics influenced him to the
extent that they did, was that he did not have a set policy toward
Palestine. Truman's interest in the Palestine issue was basically
in accordance with the Zionist program, but was far more ambiguous; that is, he was interested in doing something for Jewish

refugees, redeeming past promises for a homeland, and bringing peace to the region, but he did not have a clear view of how best to accomplish these objectives. As he explained in his memoirs:

> My purpose was then and later to help bring about the redemption of the *pledge* of the Balfour Declaration and the rescue of at least some of the victims of Nazism. I was not committed to any particular formula of statehood in Palestine or to any particular time schedule for its accomplishment. The American policy was designed to bring about, *by peaceful means*, the establishment of the *promised* Jewish homeland and easy access to it for the *displaced Jews* of Europe (emphasis added).[71]

Notice the emphasis on making good on promises and the humanitarian concern for peace and relieving the plight of the refugees. He reaffirmed these commitments while denying that any particular decision was pro-Arab or pro-Zionist: "[U.S. policy] was American because it aimed at the *peaceful solution of a world trouble spot*. It was American because it was based on the desire to see *promises kept and human misery relieved*" (emphasis added).[72]

Finally, in reference to his support of the 1948 Democratic platform, Truman wrote that: "the statement represented by deep conviction that not only the general *promise* of the Balfour Declaration be kept but also the specific *promise* of the UN resolution. I had *assured* Dr. Weizmann that these promises would be kept" (emphasis added).[73]

All of these statements support the hypothesis that decisions made in the executive branch will be governed by the interests (stemming from ideology) of the president. Since he had no specific program in mind, Truman responded to pressure from the Israeli lobby or his immediate advisers that seemed most compatible with his own predisposition toward the issues. It is therefore easy to explain the seemingly anomalous cases of the trusteeship proposal and the arms embargo. Both were presented to him by his advisers as means of securing the president's goal of a peaceful resolution of the Arab-Jewish conflict. In the case of the trusteeship proposal, the absence of international support and the opposition of the parties, combined with the extent of fighting in Palestine, led Truman to agree with those who argued that trusteeship could not satisfy his objectives. Not surprisingly, he backed away from the plan. Although an argument can be made, and was made by the Israeli lobby, that the embargo was equally useless, given the access the Arabs had to weapons, Truman remained convinced, as were his main foreign policy advisers, that U.S. weapons would further undermine the stability of the region and hinder the prospects for peace.

Similarly, all the decisions that were consistent with the Israeli lobby's interests also coincided with the president's ideology and objectives. Thus, the Zionists' demand for increased immigration and the offer of an economic development loan meshed with the president's humanitarian concerns. The rejection of the Morrison-Grady and Bernadotte plans, support for partition (with the Negev), and recognition all fit Truman's commitment to the redemption of promises and his general honesty and loyalty.

Notes

1. Shlomo Slonim, "President Truman and the Bureaucracy: The Palestine Question as a Case Study," in Allen Weinstein and Moshe Ma'Oz, eds., *Truman and the American Commitment to Israel* (Jerusalem: The Magnes Press, 1981).
2. *Foreign Relations of the United States* (DC: Government Printing Office, 1948), [henceforth FRUS]; 546–54; Peter Grose, *Israel in the Mind of America* (NY: Alfred A. Knopf, 1983), 258.
3. Meeting on 3 December 1947; Walter Mills, ed. *The Forrestal Diaries* (NY: Viking Press, 1951), 304. [Henceforth Forrestal] 358–9.
4. Forrestal, 347.
5. Robert Silverberg, *If I Forget Thee O Jerusalem: American Jews and the State of Israel* (NY: William Morrow and Co., Inc., 1970), 384; Grose, *Israel in the Mind of America*, 267.
6. Zvi Ganin, "The Limits of American Jewish Political Power: America's Retreat From Partition, November 1947–March 1949," *Jewish Social Studies* (Winter-Spring, 1977), 25.
7. Ibid., 27.
8. Harry S. Truman, *Years of Trial and Hope*, vol. 2, (NY: Doubleday and Co., Inc., 1956), 160.
9. Michael Cohen, "Truman, the Holocaust, and the Establishment of the State of Israel," *Jerusalem Quarterly* (Spring 1982), 171.
10. Joseph and Stewart Alsop, *New York Tribune* (11 February 1948) quoted in Ian J. Bickerton, "President Truman's Recognition of Israel," *American Jewish Historical Quarterly* (December 1968), 222.

11. John Snetsinger, *Truman, the Jewish Vote and the Creation of Israel* (CA: Hoover Institution Press, 1974), 80–1.
12. FRUS 1947, 1322; FRUS 1948, 606; Mitchell Bard, "How the Palestinian Arabs Became Refugees," *Discovery* (Spring 1981), 34–5.
13. Meeting on February 18, 1948, Forrestal, 376.
14. FRUS 1948, 687–96.
15. Herbert Druks, *The U.S. and Israel, 1945–1973* (NY: Robert Speller & Sons, Inc., 1979) 19.
16. Druks, *The U.S. and Israel*, 19.
17. H. Truman, *Years of Trial and Hope*, 2:161; Chaim Weizmann, *Trial and Error* (NY: Schocken Books, 1966), 472.
18. *New York Times* (21 March 1948).
19. Silverberg, *If I Forget Thee*, 393.
20. *New York Times* (24 March 1948), Bickerton, "President Truman's Recognitions," 219.
21. Bickerton, "President Truman's Recognition of Israel," 220 and 220n; Silverberg, *If I Forget Thee*, 393.
22. Weizmann call to Jacobson, 22 March 1948, Bickerton, "President Truman's Recognition of Israel," 218.
23. Margart Truman, *Harry S. Truman* (NY: Quill, 1972), 388.
24. Silverberg, *If I Forget Thee*, 392–4.
25. FRUS 1948, 648n.
26. Ibid., 637–40, 645, 649, Slonim, "President Truman and the Bureaucracy," 142–50.
27. FRUS 1948, 651; Ganin, "Limits of American Jewish Political Power," 21–3.
28. FRUS 1948, 749–50, 750n; Michael V. Cohen, "Truman and the State Department: The Palestine Trusteeship Proposal," *Jewish Social Studies* (Spring 1981), 171–5.
29. FRUS 1948, 678–81, 728–9.
30. Ibid., 728–9; Steven L. Spiegel, *The Other Arab-Israeli Conflict* (IL: University of Chicago Press, 1985), 31–4.
31. FRUS 1948, 747; Shlomo Slonim, "The 1948 American Embargo on Arms to Palestine," *Political Science Quarterly* (Fall 1979), 514; Spiegel, *The Other Arab-Israeli Conflict*, 35–6.
32. FRUS 1948, 879.
33. JAAA to Ben Gurion, 6 March 1948, Grose, *Israel in the Mind of America*, 267.
34. Silverberg, *If I Forget Thee*, 399; Druks, *The U.S. and Israel*, 27.
35. FRUS 1948, 917–23; Silverberg, *If I Forget Thee*, 400–1.
36. Silverberg, *If I Forget Thee*, 401.
37. Spiegel, *The Other Arab-Israeli Conflict*, 36.
38. Bickerton, "President Truman's Recognition," 225.
39. FRUS 1948, 972–7; Druks, *The U.S. and Israel*, 30–1.
40. Snetsinger, *Truman, the Jewish Vote*, 104–5.

41. Truman to Weizmann, 15 May 1948 and September 1948, Grose, *Israel in the Mind of America*, 294.
42. H. Truman, *Years of Trial and Hope*, 2:164.
43. Alan R. Balboni, "A Study of the Efforts of the American Zionists to Influence the Formulation and Conduct of United States Foreign Policy During the Roosevelt, Truman and Eisenhower Administrations," (Brown University, Ph.D. Diss., June 1972), 163; David Schoenbaum, "The United States and the Birth of Israel," *The Wiener Library Bulletin* (1978), 93; Bernard Reich, *Quest for Peace* (NJ: Transaction Books, Inc., 1977), p. 21; Spiegel, *The Other Arab-Israeli Conflict*, 48; Snetsinger, *Truman, the Jewish Vote*, 118.
44. FRUS 1947, 1249.
45. Slonim, "The 1948 American Embargo," 1979, 497–8.
46. Ibid., 498–9.
47. FRUS 1948, 537–9; Silverberg, *If I Forget Thee*, 366, 370; Earl D. Huff, "Zionist Influences Upon U.S. Foreign Policy: A Study of American Policy Toward the Middle East From the Time of the Struggle for Israel to the Sinai Conflict," (University of Idaho, Ph.D. Diss., 1971), 43.
48. Slonim, "The 1948 American Embargo," 1979, 500.
49. Ibid., 500–6.
50. FRUS 1948, 629.
51. Ibid., 562–3.
52. Druks, *The U.S. and Israel*, 30.
53. FRUS 1948, 755.
54. Ibid., 807–9.
55. Ibid., 827.
56. Ibid., 1019.
57. Ibid., 1020–21.
58. Ibid., 1031.
59. Snetsinger, *Truman, the Jewish Vote*, 122.
60. Huff, "Zionist Influences Upon U.S. Foreign Policy," 126–7.
61. Silverberg, *If I Forget Thee*, 435–7.
62. Snetsinger, *Truman, the Jewish Vote*, 123.
63. M. Truman, *Harry S. Truman*, 390.
64. M. Cohen, "Truman and the State Department," 175.
65. H. Truman, *Years of Trial and Hope*, 2:167.
66. Ibid., 2:166.
67. Ibid., 2:167.
68. Spiegel, *The Other Arab-Israeli Conflict*, 43; H. Truman, *Years of Trial and Hope*, 2:167–8; Huff, "Zionist Influences Upon U.S. Foreign Policy," 127–8.
69. H. Truman, *Years of Trial and Hope*, 2:168; Huff, "Zionist Influ-

ences Upon U.S. Foreign Policy," 127–8; Silverberg, *If I Forget Thee*, 439.
70. Snetsinger, *Truman, the Jewish Vote*, 134–5.
71. H. Truman, *Years of Trial and Hope*, 2:157.
72. Ibid., 2:157.
73. Ibid., 2:166.

7

The Sale of Phantom Jets to Israel

Although much has been written about President Truman's role in the creation of Israel, much less attention has been devoted to another decision he made, which undermined his support of the UN partition plan, and that was the embargo of arms to the Middle East. That decision put the Jews of Palestine at a disadvantage because the Arabs had access to arms from a number of countries other than the United States, and Israel was able to buy only a limited amount of arms from one country—Czechoslovakia.

The U.S. embargo was, in effect, maintained after the war, as a result of the signing of the Tripartite Declaration in 1950. Throughout the remainder of the decade, Israel and her supporters persistently sought U.S. arms but were consistently rebuffed.

The reasons for denying Israel American arms were:

1. The country was strong enough to defend itself without U.S. arms, a belief reinforced by Israel's success during the Suez campaign.
2. Israel had access to arms from other sources.
3. The United States did not want to start an arms race in the Middle East.
4. The belief that sales to Israel would lead the Arabs to ask the Soviets and Chinese for arms.
5. The fear of a U.S.-U.S.S.R. confrontation in the Middle East.
6. The fear that U.S. military aid to Israel would alienate the Arabs.

It was not until John Kennedy's election, coincidentally with the backing of over 80 percent of Jewish voters, that Israel first received a major weapons system. That sale, in 1962, of HAWK anti-aircraft missiles, was opposed by the State Department, but Kennedy ordered the sale after failing to dissuade Egyptian President Gamal Abdel Nasser from escalating the arms race, and after the Soviet Union had supplied Nasser with long-range bombers that had never been sent outside the Communist bloc or Indonesia. The HAWK sale was significant not only because it was the first major direct arms transfer to Israel, but also because that system required extensive training of Israeli soldiers in the United States, and a supply of spare parts which made Israel increasingly dependent on U.S. arms.

Throughout the period following Truman's instigation of the arms embargo until the HAWK sale, the Israeli lobby was, for the most part, unaware of U.S. military aid to Israel. There was nothing unusual about this, since virtually all U.S. aid to the Middle East was secret.

In 1956, Israeli ambassador to the United States Abba Eban told the president of the American Jewish Committee, Irving Engel, that with the possible exception of jet fighters, Israel was receiving arms in fair amounts.[1] The main source of these weapons was France. In fact, it was U.S. encouragement of third parties that had been largely responsible for Israel's ability to meet its defense needs. In addition, the United States directly supplied small amounts of weapons to Israel, apparently without the knowledge of the Israeli lobby.[2]

Johnson Assumes Command

When Lyndon Johnson became president, the Israeli lobby was encouraged by the fact that he had pledged to carry on the work of John Kennedy and because of his own record of support for Israel, dating back to his leadership in the Senate during the Eisenhower administration. During the Suez War and its aftermath, in particular, Johnson proved to be a friend of Israel by first, denouncing Nasser's nationalization of the Suez Canal, and then opposing Eisenhower's efforts to force Israel's withdrawal from the territories it conquered. In February 1957, Johnson wrote to John Foster Dulles opposing the imposition of any UN economic sanctions against Israel. Johnson also supported the Douglas-Keating "freedom of the seas" amendment and efforts to end the discriminatory practices of the Arab boycott, although he was unwilling, as president, to prohibit compliance with the boycott.

Like most U.S. presidents, Johnson's support for Israel was based on a combination of realism, romanticism, and cold political calculations. In realist terms, Israel was a relatively powerful, pro-Western democratic nation, in a region of strategic importance where communism and Pan-Arabism were seen as serious threats to U.S. interests. Although Israel was not yet perceived as a strategic ally, Johnson recognized that a strong Israel was a deterrent to the forces of radicalism.

The more idealistic view of Israel was that of the nation of pioneers who had turned malarial swamps into a land of "milk and honey." In a letter to one Jewish leader, written shortly after becoming president, Johnson revealed his image of Israel:

> The Marshall Plan, the Point Four program, the Alliance for Progress, and the Peace Corps are certainly among the most noble and important works ever undertaken on this earth. When some wonder and question the value of such efforts, I think we need only to answer with the example of what has been done in creating out of a wilderness the living state of Israel. We live by the faith that what has been wrought there someday will be achieved in all the lands where men aspire to live in freedom, under peace, enjoying justice as a right and prosperity as a result of their labors.[3]

Five years later, under pressure to sell Israel Phantom jets, Johnson told a B'nai B'rith meeting about his biblical connection to Israel. "Most, if not all of you," he said, "have very deep ties with the land and with the people of Israel, as I do, for my Christian faith sprang from yours." The president explained that "the Bible stories are woven into my childhood memories as the gallant struggle of modern Jews to be free of persecution is also woven into our souls."[4] Thus, it is not surprising that when Soviet Premier Aleksei Kosygin asked Johnson why the United States supports Israel when there are 80 million Arabs and only 3 million Israelis, the president replied simply: "Because it is right."[5]

Finally, there was Johnson, the consummate politician, recognizing the fact that Jews are a political force in this country.

As a leader of the Democratic party, he had developed close associations with a number of influential Jewish leaders, several of whom (e.g., Abe Fortas, Abe Feinberg, and Arthur Krim) were among his closest friends.

Even before becoming president, Johnson wrote to Israeli Prime Minister Levi Eshkol to assure him that the United States was prepared to safeguard Israel. He translated this promise into specifics when Eshkol visited him in June the following year, telling him the United States supported the Johnston Plan to allocate water to Israel, Jordan, and Syria according to an agreed formula, would help Israel get tanks and was concerned with Israel's security, and would assist with the development of a desalting plant as much as possible. After the meeting, Eshkol told Felix Frankfurter: "I go back to Israel confident and cheered by the knowledge that the man in the White House is a friend of our cause." [6]

Johnson's dependability was tested immediately when the Israelis began to pressure the administration to sell them tanks and planes. As early as January 1964, Deputy Secretary of State Robert Komer was complaining that Myer Feldman was badgering him about supplying Israel with tanks.[7] Feldman, the holder of the "Jewish portfolio" as an aide in the administration, meanwhile wrote to the president in May that he had "rarely been exposed to as much pressure as I have had recently on the question of tanks for Israel." In the same memorandum, however, Feldman reveals how the White House successfully exerted its own pressure: "It has only been after considerable effort that members of Congress have been restrained against making speeches on the question, the Anglo-Jewish press has killed several articles and responsible leaders of the Jewish community have demonstrated their confidence in the Administration by keeping silent." [8]

The administration had, in fact, begun to consider a tank sale to Israel in January, but the Joint Chiefs of Staff reported that Israel did not need any tanks and that the United States' highest priority should be on restraining the flow of arms to the Middle East. If the administration decided to sell tanks to Israel anyway, then the Joint Chief recommended they be sold only replacements for obsolete tanks, and that those be provided discreetly.[9]

In accordance with the Joint Chiefs' recommendation, the administration pursued a policy of seeking an arms limitation agreement. This was to be a continuing theme of the Johnson years and, in August 1964, one of Johnson's civilian advisers, John McCloy, agreed to probe Nasser's willingness to abide by such an agreement. Earlier efforts to deal with the recalcitrant Egyptian leader had been successful in securing a pledge from Nasser not to acquire nuclear weapons. Secretary of State Rusk was, therefore, optimistic that Nasser could be persuaded to exercise restraint in the acquisition of missiles, if he was told the United States could convince Israel to exercise similar nuclear and missile self-denial.[10] At this time, Egypt remained hostile to American interests, but Johnson, like Kennedy and Eisenhower before him, hoped that by maintaining a "balanced" Middle East policy, and providing Egypt with economic aid, Nasser might be weaned away from the Soviet Union. Perhaps the most positive and surprising outcome of this effort was Nasser's agreement to "freeze" the Palestinian dispute and take no provocative action against Israel, despite the U.S.-U.A.R. disagreement on the issue.[11]

The United States' balancing act fell apart in early 1965, however, when it was revealed that the United States had been indirectly supplying arms to Israel through West Germany since 1962, under the terms of a secret 1960 agreement. The Arabs responded to this revelation by threatening to recognize East Germany and pressuring the West German government to halt the sales. The United States then stepped in and fulfilled the remainder of the $80 million arms agreement.[12] Before the United States agreed to sell Israel tanks, however, relations with yet another country became a consideration.

To maintain an evenhanded policy in the Middle East, Johnson wanted to balance the sale of tanks to Israel with a similar sale to Jordan. In an effort to forestall the opposition of the Israeli lobby, Johnson sent Undersecretary of State for Political Affairs, Averell Harriman, and Robert Komer from the National Security Council to Israel to investigate the Israelis' reaction to a simultaneous sale. The Americans made the usual argument that if the United States did not sell Jordan arms the Soviet Union would. Although it is unlikely the Israelis believed this, they did express a willingness not to oppose the sale.

The administration wanted more than just Israeli acquiescence, however, it wanted the Israelis to make a concerted effort to restrain their American supporters. "Sometimes the Jewish community in the United States tended to run away with the bit in its teeth," Harriman apparently told Eshkol. "We knew the GOI [Government of Israel] could not control all elements of the community, but it was most important to the President that the Prime Minister put these matters into proper perspective for the key leaders of the community." Harriman said the United States still preferred that Israel buy arms from other Western sources, but that the United States was willing to make direct sales "at an appropriate time and with appropriate coordination of the publicity problem." Eshkol responded that Israel could not compete with the Arabs if it had to pay for its arms, and expressed the conviction that if the U.S. interest was to supply arms to Jordan it should simultaneously *and openly* supply them to Israel as well. As for the request that he restrain the Jewish community, the Israeli Prime Minister replied: "How can I as Prime Minister of Israel tell American Jews what they should or should not say in matters concerning citizens of the United States?"[13] Both sides knew, of course, that the message would be relayed.

Although there was substantive agreement, there was no announcement of an arms sale forthcoming. The Israelis grew increasingly impatient and complained about delays in responding to their arms request. They also began to press the administration for Phantom jets in addition to tanks. Once again U.S. officials tried to persuade the Israelis to try Europe and were not moved by Israeli claims that no suitable airplanes were available. Not only did the United States have no plans to sell airplanes to Israel, the State Department threatened the Israelis with an arms suspension if they persisted in trying to solve their dispute with Jordan over water by military means. The Israelis continued to ask for the airplanes and eventually secured a promise to discuss the sale of mutually agreed upon combat airplanes, but not Phantoms.[14]

The administration was receiving pressure from the Israeli lobby as well. Although the American Israel Public Affairs Committee's (AIPAC) Sy Kenen was dismissed by Komer as "a local propagandist," others could be less easily ignored.[15] For example, in a letter to Senator Len Jordan, Peter Solbert, Deputy Assistant

Secretary of Defense, explained that the administration refrained from being a major supplier of arms to either the Arabs or Israel in order to remain impartial. Solbert said the United States was willing to make limited sales to strengthen the ability of nations in the Middle East to defend themselves. *"In no case, however, will the U.S. contribute to providing one state in the area a military advantage against another"* (emphasis added).[16] This statement is highlighted because it reveals a significant difference between U.S. policy prior to the Phantom sale and after; that is, the Phantom sale represented a change from neutrality to a conscious policy of providing and maintaining Israel with a qualitative advantage over its neighbors.

In a further effort to reassure Israel's supporters, the president's National Security Adviser, McGeorge Bundy, arranged a confidential briefing for eleven Jewish House Democrats in August. He told them: "We are Israel's chief supporters, bankers, direct and indirect arms purveyors, and ultimate guarantors." He reminded them that economic aid to Israel actually exceeded that justified by Agency for International Development (AID) criteria, and that the president had overruled some AID positions to insure that Israel received aid. Bundy also told the congressmen that the president was sure Israel's defense needs were being met, either by the United States or other Western sources, and that the Joint Chiefs were confident Israel could defeat the Arabs for the next few years.[17]

Finally, in February 1966, the State Department announced the sale of 200 Patton tanks to Israel and then, in May, announced a new agreement to provide Israel with Skyhawk jet bombers. Militarily, these sales provided Israel with a greater offensive capability. The Skyhawks, with a range of over 2000 miles, would allow Israel's air force to reach beyond the border confrontation states to threaten other intractable enemies such as Iraq and Libya. The sale also had a symbolic impact.

By 1965, the United States had already become Israel's main arms supplier; nevertheless, the tank and plane sales marked a significant shift in U.S. policy. This was the first major sale of offensive weapons to Israel, and the first public acknowledgement that the United States was selling, and willing to sell, the equipment necessary to maintain Israel's defense. Still, the sales represented no more than a willingness to balance Soviet arms supplies to the region; the administration was not yet willing to alter its policy not to provide any nation with a strategic advantage. This was evident when it was learned that secret agreements had been reached about the same time as the decision to sell Israel Skyhawks, to provide F-5 bombers to Morocco and Libya, as well as additional military equipment to Lebanon, Saudi Arabia, and Tunisia.

Nasser, for all his bluster, meanwhile, continued to express a desire to develop good relations with the United States, and therefore was not only willing to accept nuclear safeguards if Israel did, but was also willing to keep the Israel issue "in the icebox." [18] Thus, as long as Nasser was expressing a desire to improve relations, and hinting that it was not inevitable that Egypt would join the Soviet camp, U.S. officials were interested in preserving as much leverage as they could in the region. This, they believed, required that the United States not become too closely allied with Israel.

The Pressure Builds

Israel and her supporters were not satisfied with the agreements reached in 1966; there was still an outstanding request that the Phantoms also be provided. This request took on greater urgency as the rhetoric of Nasser began to push the nations of the Middle East toward war. The Americans remained unconcerned, however, and Eshkol told *U.S. News and World Report* (21 April, 1967) their response was "Don't spend your money. We are here. The Sixth Fleet is here." Eshkol feared that the U.S. fleet might not be available fast enough, so he preferred that Israel be strong enough to defend itself.

Not only did the pressure to provide Phantoms fail to move Johnson, it had the opposite effect. He was particularly irritated because of the lack of support he was receiving for his Vietnam policies from those exerting pressure. He was especially concerned about Israeli lobby opposition, since the support of American Jews was important to his reelection chances.

The generally liberal Jewish community, like most of the nation's liberals, was becoming increasingly disenchanted with the war effort after 1965. As early as March 1966, Hubert Humphrey suggested to Dean Rusk that the United States encourage Vietnam to recognize Israel, in the hope that statements by the two governments might have a salutary effect on the leadership of the American Jewish community. Rusk's response was that Israel was responsible for the current relationship, and that although Vietnam was initially anti-Israel because of its desire to solicit Arab support, the failure to receive that backing had led the Vietnamese to solicit Israeli support.

The United States persuaded Vietnam to recognize Israel and offer diplomatic relations, and encouraged Israel to respond positively to the overture. The president also told Eban during his February 1966 visit that Israel would rightly be the first to be frightened if the United States "cut and ran" in Vietnam. Israel remained cool to the idea, however, because of the potential damage to her relations with Africa and Asia, as well as the lack of support for such a policy within Israel. Meanwhile, Israeli officials did urge American Jewish leaders to try to contain their criticism.[19]

While the United States pursued its diplomatic efforts to recruit Israeli government support for its Vietnam policy, a similar effort was underway at home to tie support for the Israeli lobby's objectives to the lobby's support on Vietnam. On 9 September 1966, for example, the National Commander of Jewish War Veterans, Malcolm Tarlov, paid his annual courtesy call to the president, and was told that "Jews who seek U.S. support for co-religionists in Russia and for Israel should vigorously identify with Administration actions in Vietnam." The president could not understand why the American Jewish community was not supporting his Vietnam policy when he was improving U.S.-Israel relations.[20]

Although administration officials denied that the president had made support for Johnson's Vietnam policy a condition for United States support for Israel, Johnson's obsession with credibility led him to suspect Israeli lobby demands as long as the opposition to Vietnam existed. When it comes to Israel, he told Israeli Minister Ephraim Evron, American Jews are interventionists, but when it comes to Vietnam, they want the United States to be pacifist. Johnson could not understand the contradiction and believed that the Jewish community was too selective. Abba Eban recalled being told by Johnson how a group of rabbis had come to visit him in May 1967, and asked him to put the whole American fleet in the Gulf of Aqaba to show the U.S. flag in the Straits of Tiran. In the meantime, they didn't think he should send a screwdriver to Vietnam.[21]

The Aftermath of June 1967

American policy during the Six Day War is not at issue here, however, the one relevant action was the decision by Johnson to embargo arms to the Middle East. Just as Truman believed that an embargo might avert bloodshed, so apparently did Johnson. Johnson also was disappointed that Israel had ignored his admonition not to go to war; moreover, he remained committed to a policy of evenhandedness, and was anxious not to alienate the Arabs who would surely blame the United States for Israel's "aggression."

Truman's embargo had a one-sided impact, and so did Johnson's, since the Soviet Union continued to supply the Arabs with weapons while Israel's secondary military supplier, France, imposed an embargo of its own. Rusk reiterated the administration arms policy at a press conference on 19 July: "We have ourselves tried not to become a principal supplier. . . . But we are committed to the political independence and territorial integrity of the states of the Middle East. And when imbalance of a major proportion occurred, we felt it was necessary for us to supply some limited military assistance to certain of the Arab countries and to Israel."[22] As it turned out, the American boycott had some holes. The administration did agree to fulfill a 23 May arms request for tank ammunition and a radar complex but only after providing military aid to moderate Arab states.[23]

After the war, the administration once again hoped to persuade the Soviets to join in limiting arms sales to the Middle East but failed to obtain any cooperation. Consequently, Johnson was under increasing pressure to end the embargo and sell planes to Israel. At the beginning of October 1967, Senator Stuart Symington called the White House and said the Israelis were anxious and bitter over United States policy and that he could easily get a bill through Congress supporting military aid to Israel. Walt Rostow, who had replaced Bundy as National Security Adviser, called the situation "political dynamite."

Apparently, Defense Secretary Robert McNamara was not opposed to new sales to Israel so long as the moderate Arabs received arms simultaneously. Rostow said Israel would only object to the sale of arms to Jordan, but McNamara wasn't satisfied, so Rostow wanted the president to convince the Israelis of the necessity of selling arms to the Arabs. He suggested that Johnson use a Jewish leader as a conduit (Rostow says "Abe"—probably Feinberg).[24] Finally, in mid-October, after Egypt sank an Israeli ship (the *Elath*), the news was leaked that the embargo was being lifted. "Some welcomed a coincidence which implied the U.S. government was reacting to the sinking of the warship," the *Near East Report* observed, "but the State Department was worried about Arab reaction."[25]

Soon after the embargo ended, the Israelis requested twenty-seven more Skyhawks and fifty Phantoms. The State Department recommended selling the former, but preferred to put off a decision on the latter until the middle of the following year. The Joint Chiefs, on the other hand, opposed any sale.[26] The State Department opposition to selling Phantoms was based not only on strategic grounds, that is, the Joint Chiefs' analysis that Israel did not need them, but also on the persistent belief that the United States could prevent an escalation of the arms race by refusing to supply Israel more sophisticated weapons, and that arms limitations would make it possible to reach a diplomatic solution to the Arab-Israeli conflict. No decision was reached during the remainder of the year, despite a deluge of letters from congressmen urging the president to sell airplanes to Israel.

Another factor in the president's decision-making calculus had to be the impact of his actions on his reelection chances. Prior to the war, Johnson had received a nineteen-page memorandum titled "1968—American Jewry and Israel," which said the administration enjoyed great support among Jews, but there were three areas of criticism:

1. "over-reaction" by the United States at the Security Council in censuring Israel the previous November (for its retaliatory attack against Jordan);

2. State Department policies calling for the return of the Arab refugees; and
3. arms sales to the Arabs without balance.

The memorandum also noted that despite support from Orthodox and Conservative Jews, Vietnam remained a problem. If Vietnam persists, it warned, "a special effort to hold the Jewish vote will be necessary." [27]

Despite the arms embargo, the Israeli lobby looked favorably at Johnson's handling of the June War and, despite Vietnam, he seemed to be in good shape with Jewish voters. In fact, in a memorandum to the president, Jack Valenti repeated a story he heard from a columnist that Abba Eban had told a group of Jewish leaders at a New York dinner that the president had been very helpful, and that although he never interfered in U.S. elections he believed "you can help Israel by returning LBJ to the White House." The columnist said the remark was off the record but that everyone in New York would still get the message.[28] The Democrats could not take the Jewish vote for granted, however, and the Republicans made the administration's failure to supply Phantom jets to Israel a campaign issue.

The Last Big Push

The pressure to sell the Phantoms mounted at the beginning of January 1968, as the administration prepared for the visit of Prime Minister Levi Eshkol. In anticipation of Eshkol's renewed request for Phantoms, the various agencies prepared their assessments and without exception concluded the sale was not a good idea. The Navy and Air Force were opposed, not only to the sale of Phantoms, but also Skyhawks, fearing that giving up these assets would have "a serious effect on the operational forces" in Vietnam.[29] A briefing book prepared for the visit, on the other hand, expressed the willingness to sell twenty-seven Skyhawks, but to keep that decision secret, to avoid upsetting the peace negotiations then being pursued under the auspices of United Nations mediator Gunnar Jarring. The briefing book also noted, naively, that the sale of Skyhawks would reduce pressure for the Phantoms.[30]

When Johnson met with Eshkol, he said he would keep Israel's military needs under "active and sympathetic examination," but made no commitment to sell Phantom jets. The president did say, however, that he would make a decision during the coming year. Johnson offered to provide thirty Skyhawks and agreed to sell ten more if they were requested. Informally, the president was less tentative about the Phantoms as well. "Awh, Eppie," he is reported to have told the concerned Israeli ambassador, "you know I'm going to give you the Phantoms. . . . "[31] In the meantime, no deal was made, but the speculation and publicity associated with the Eshkol visit helped stimulate further pressure for the sale.

The president apparently was inclined to make the sale after the Eshkol meeting, and was therefore more concerned with the timing of the decision. Johnson asked Secretary of Defense McNamara at what latest date he could make a decision, if the Phantoms were to be delivered by 1 January 1970. The secretary's response was 31 December 1968.[32] So the president did have a target date of delivery and the entire year to make up his mind.

Congress Steps In

Throughout Johnson's term, individual congressmen lobbied on behalf of Israel, but it was not until June 1968, that an effort was made to force military sales to Israel by legislation. The first stage of that effort was initiated by Senator Stuart Symington, who threatened to kill the military sales bill if the president did not deliver the Phantoms. Besides the usual motivation provided by the informal (i.e., pro-Israel voters and public opinion) Israeli lobby, Symington was no doubt interested in the sale because the airplanes were built in his home state.

The administration took the threat seriously and began to discuss possible trade-offs. State Department Near East expert Harold Saunders wrote to Rostow and asked: "What are [the] advantages of holding off on Phantoms longer versus having no military sales bill? Would Phantoms insure passage? If F-4s are going to be sold anyway, might as well go ahead and get credit with Israel and Congress now. In exchange [we] might get [a] commitment to consult before acquiring missiles, [a] commitment to sign NPT, or some limited agreement regarding negotiations with Jordan and the UAR [United Arab Republic]."[33] The president still was unwilling to announce a decision, however, suggesting that the decision had not yet been made.

Back in April 1968, Rep. Bertram Podell had introduced a "sense of the House" resolution calling for the sale of Phantoms. It attracted the support of over 100 members by the time the Foreign Assistance Act of 1968 came to the floor of the House in July. There, unexpectedly, Rep. Lester Wolff offered an amendment to the aid bill calling on the president to sell Israel at least fifty Phantoms as a deterrent to future Arab aggression, and to replace losses suffered by Israel in the 1967 conflict.

Unlike Podell's resolution, which had the backing of AIPAC, Wolff's amendment was opposed because it *ordered* the president to sell Phantom jets and was therefore seen by the administration and AIPAC as intruding on the constitutional prerogatives of the president. Kenen conferred with presidential counsel Ernest Goldstein and agreed to write a more general amendment in the Senate that the president would find acceptable. The substitute, expressing the sense of Congress that the president sell an unspecified number of supersonic planes to provide Israel with a deterrent force, was adopted by the Senate on 31 July and later approved by the House.[34]

The president remained unmoved by the congressional action, but he soon began facing new pressures from both inside and outside the White House. Most administration officials remained opposed to the sale on military grounds, but were becoming increasingly concerned over the political costs of delaying what they believed to be inevitable. On 21 August 1968, Ernest Goldstein wrote a revealing memorandum to the president in which he says he had avoided expressing his views relating to Israel throughout his service as an aide, but the Soviet invasion of Czechoslovakia provided evidence that the Soviets' lack of restraint "might find its counterpart in the Middle East." Therefore, he expressed his hope that Johnson would provide Phantoms to Israel before the election.[35]

Johnson also faced pressure from the two political parties. In August, both national conventions adopted platform planks, suggested by AIPAC, calling for military aid to Israel. In addition, both presidential candidates made strong statements in support of the Phantom sale. At the B'nai B'rith convention in Washington on 8 September, Hubert Humphrey said the "Want of strength whets the appetite for war, for aggression. . . . Israel must have the means to defend itself, including such items as Phantoms." Richard Nixon told the same audience the balance of power must be tipped in Israel's favor to deter Arab aggression; therefore, he said he believed Israel must have "a technological military margin to more than offset her hostile neighbors' numerical superiority. If maintaining that margin should require that [the] U.S. supply Israel with supersonic Phantom F-4 jets—we should supply those Phantom jets." [36]

In his first major Middle East speech since June 1967, the president told the same B'nai B'rith convention that just forty-eight hours earlier had heard the presidential candidates urge support for the Phantom sales, that he had "no intention of allowing the balance of forces in the area to become an incentive for war. . . . We have proposed . . . the urgent need now for an international understanding on arms limitations for the region." [37]

Once again, we see Johnson return to the leitmotif of arms control; meanwhile, he closed a $100 million deal with King Hussein for U.S. HAWK missiles and, two weeks after his speech, the president approved the sale of an additional twelve Skyhawks to Israel.[38] The Skyhawk sale was not expected to eliminate the pressure for Phantoms, but Rostow believed it would demonstrate that the administration was not totally insensitive to Israel's security requirements.[39] In addition, the administration hoped that holding the Phantoms hostage would give the United States leverage to encourage Israeli cooperation with the Jarring peace talks. The Israelis argued, conversely, that they could not negotiate from weakness, and therefore needed the Phantoms before they could engage in serious negotiations.

Johnson had also hoped to arrange a summit meeting with the Soviets to discuss, among other things, a limitation on the sale of arms to the Middle East, but this option was effectively eliminated by the Soviet invasion of Czechoslovakia in August. As the election approached, he was under almost constant pressure from a broad coalition of Israel's American supporters. Johnson also wanted to help Humphrey, who had reiterated his position that Israel should be sold Phantoms after the president's September speech.

The only real opposition to the sale remained within the administration, where the Defense and Intelligence departments still were unconvinced of Israel's need for Phantoms; nevertheless, the Secretary of State concluded after two fruitless days of discussions with the Soviet Foreign Minister that the Phantom deal "is the most we can get away with *in the light of the action of the Congress*" (emphasis added).[40] The next day, 9 October, President Johnson signed the Foreign Assistance Act of 1968 and announced that he had taken note of the section concerning the sale of airplanes to Israel, and was asking the Secretary of State to initiate negotiations with Israel.

The significance of the sale was explained by Assistant Secretary of Defense Paul Warnke in a discussion with Yitzhak Rabin. He said the United States had avoided becoming Israel's arms supplier to reduce the risk of a U.S.-U.S.S.R. confrontation in the Middle East, and would have preferred to continue that policy, but could not because of the refusal of the Europeans, especially the French, to arm Israel. *"We will henceforth become the principal arms supplier to Israel, involving us even more intimately with Israel's security situation and involving more directly the security of the United States"* (emphasis added). He said that it was not just the agreement to provide fifty Phantoms that was significant, it was the sale of the Phantoms *plus* 100 Skyhawks and other equipment requested by Israel that marked a distinct change from past policy.[41]

The sale was finally announced on 27 December, the day after Israel had attacked the Beirut airport in retaliation for terrorist attacks. The agreement called for Israel to receive sixteen Phantoms in late 1969, and another thirty-four in 1970. In response to the sale, the Soviet Union reportedly began delivering 200 MIG-23s to Egypt. The MIGs were capable of carrying nuclear weapons and were more maneuverable than Phantoms.[42] The United States now found itself entwined in the Middle East arms race.

Summary

The sale of arms is directly related to U.S. security; therefore, it is not surprising that realist concerns would have been relevant to this case. The president's reluctance to sell Phantoms to Israel was based largely on the Pentagon's evaluation that Israel did not need supersonic jets, and the fact that other governments, with U.S. backing, were providing the Israelis with sufficient weapons to balance the Arab threat. Since Johnson's military advisers did not see a threat to Israel's security, he could oppose the lobby on strategic grounds. In addition, the sale of Phantoms was likely to harm America's relations with the Arabs, particularly Nasser, who the United States was still trying to cultivate. Johnson was also intent on reaching an agreement with the Soviet Union to limit arms sales to the Middle East. For all these reasons, Johnson could argue the national interest would not be served by the sale of Phantoms to Israel. Since the locus of decision was the executive branch, the president's position stood.

Of course the Israeli lobby and its supporters in Congress saw the national interest differently. The lobby was less sanguine about Israel's strength vís-a-vís the Arabs, partly because its members were not aware of the amount of arms Israel was receiving from European countries and the United States, but primarily because the lobby did not consider the possibility that Israel might not need the arms it requested. Moreover, the lobby asserted that U.S.-Arab relations would not be hurt by the sale since the Arabs already considered U.S. policy unbalanced, and repeated efforts to bring Nasser into the Western camp had failed. Finally, the idea that Israel should not get Phantoms because it would undermine efforts to limit arms sales to the region, was rejected as hypocritical because the Soviets were pouring weapons into the Arab states and the United States was also continuing to sell arms to the Arabs.

Johnson agreed to the sale after it became clear the Israeli lobby was correct. Nasser continued to defy the West, and then provoked the Six Day War; the Soviets refused to limit their shipments to the region; and third countries the United States has relied upon to arm Israel—France and West Germany—stopped supplying weapons to the Jewish State. Thus, the national interest in supporting Israel took precedence over the other American interests in the region. Moreover, a new interest evolved whereby the United States would no longer try to maintain a balance of power in the region, but would seek to insure that Israel enjoyed qualitative superiority.

In this case, it was the state of Israel, rather than the Israeli lobby that set the agenda, but it was persistent lobby pressure that helped overcome Johnson's reluctance to make the sale. According to Pollock, domestic political considerations affected the timing but not the substance of the sale. He says the announcement of the negotiations in October was related to the election, but since the sale was not formally concluded until after the election, the campaign had played no role in the decision. "The 18 preceding months of caution and delay on arms supplies, with but little domestic political outcry, support this interpretation."[43] This analysis seems to be at odds with the evidence presented here.

It is implausible to accept that the election affected only the timing of the decision but not the decision itself. If that were true, there was no reason for the agreement to be signed later; after all, Johnson could easily have said the negotiations were continuing and then left office with Nixon holding the bag. One of the reasons for not doing this, however, was that the informal lobby had helped induce Nixon to support the sale so that he was very likely to not only approve it, but take credit for the shipment as well. Democratic congressmen did not want this to happen and helped pressure Johnson to eschew Clifford's efforts to place conditions on the sale. Pollock is wrong when he says there was no domestic outcry. Individual congressmen had been pressuring Johnson for nearly a year to sell Israel Phantoms, and the Congress had passed a resolution specifically calling on the president to meet Israel's security needs.

A more accurate explanation is that domestic politics were responsible for the substance and the timing of the decision. As Spiegel notes, "Johnson was too much of a politician to ignore the assistance the sale announcement could give Humphrey." Thus, the election played a role in the timing of the decision.[44] The fact that the lobby was unwilling to abandon its campaign after Johnson agreed to sell Skyhawks to Israel suggests the substance was also affected.

The leadership model also provides insight into the decision although, as was the case in chapter 6, the president acted against the advice of his principal advisers. While the members of the cabinet opposed the sale to Israel, others whose opinions the president valued, notably Abe Feinberg and Arthur Krim, pushed him to make the sale. As was the case in the Truman administration, the Israeli lobby obtained access to executive decisions via individual members of the lobby. Given these conflicting opinions, Johnson chose the position that was closest to his own ideology and that, initially, was the view of his cabinet that Israel should not get the weapons.

Johnson opposed the arms race in principle (although his willingness to sell other weapons seemed to belie this), and was determined to secure an arms limitation agreement with the Soviet Union. It was only after the Russian invasion of Czechoslovakia, and Rusk's talks with Gromyko, that he recognized his efforts were futile and made the decision to go ahead with the Phantom sale. This alone does not explain the outcome, however, because domestic politics did play a greater role.

Johnson told Lucius Battle, then the Assistant Secretary of State for Near Eastern Affairs, that "never in all his years of political life did he have such political pressure—Jewish groups and congressional pressures." He said Battle would have to give him a reason not to sell the planes.[45] Johnson was already pro-Israel when he came to office. He had a long record of political service and had been subject to the informal and formal lobby's influence throughout. He also, as noted above, had close friendships with influential Jewish leaders who used their frequent visits to make the case for the Phantom sale. On the other hand, with the exception of some input from the oil industry, and occasional letters from members of the Arab lobby, there was little countervailing interest group pressure. In fact, some of the Arab lobby efforts were so crude that they were dismissed out of hand.[46]

Initially, after taking office, Johnson felt obligated to carry on the policies of John Kennedy who had, the year before, provided Israel with the first significant U.S. weapons system. His personal obsession with credibility, combined with the strategic and political realities created by West Germany's refusal to continue its role as conduit for American tank sales, then forced Johnson to make the United States a direct supplier of weapons to Israel. At this point, however, he still believed in the need for a balanced

Middle East policy and carried that policy out by selling weapons to "moderate" Arab states. Despite consistent pressure, Johnson was able to resist the Israeli lobby's demands for Phantoms until 1968.

One of the reasons Johnson was able to resist the pressure was the strength of his domestic position. He inherited a large congressional majority from Kennedy, which became even larger after the 1964 elections. The Senate Foreign Relations Committee chairman, J. William Fulbright, and the Senate Majority Leader, Mike Mansfield, moreover, were among the most anti-Israel members of the Congress. The sympathetic congressional majority believed the president was responsible for making arms sales decisions and was content to let Johnson handle the issue. In addition, Johnson was extremely popular at the beginning of his term, averaging well over 60 percent approval in 1965.

The situation began to change, however, as the country became more deeply involved in Vietnam. Johnson's popularity plummeted and averaged only 45 percent in 1967. The Israeli lobby's constituents, composed primarily of liberal Jews, became increasingly disenchanted with the president's Vietnam policy. Congress, following the mood of the nation, also became more active, and in 1968 legislation was introduced to pressure Johnson to make the arms sales. In addition, when France embargoed arms sales to Israel, Johnson, as he did when Germany stopped its sales, began to increase the U.S. commitment.

By 1968, Johnson was under siege from Congress, the public, and the Israeli lobby. The pressure, primarily due to Vietnam, led him to withdraw from the election campaign, but it did not relieve him from the demands to provide Israel with Phantom jets.

The Phantom jet sale illustrates how all three models interact when the locus of decision is the executive branch. Since the sale was a security issue, the president was more willing to oppose the lobby so long as he perceived that his position reflected the national interest. That perception changed, however, with a series of events that reinforced the Israeli lobby's arguments. The pluralist model explains how the lobby was able to maintain consistent pressure on the administration, and succeed in persuading individual congressmen, and later Congress, as a whole, to support the sale. Johnson's strong political position prior to 1968 allowed him to resist this pressure, but as his popularity declined and the demands of the presidential election campaign increased, his capacity to resist was weakened. There was also no counter-vailing pressure outside the administration against the sale. Finally, the leadership model illustrates how the president dominates executive decision-making, and how his own preferences are shaped by how closely the positions of those people who are advising and/or pressuring him are to his own ideology.

Notes

1. Etta Z. Bick, "Ethnic Linkages and Foreign Policy: A Study of the Linkage Role of American Jews in Relations Between the United States and Israel. 1956–1968," (Ph.D. Diss., City University of New York, 1983), 95.
2. *Near East Report* (25 September 1962), 77.
3. Letter, LBJ to Louis Segal, 28 December 1963, LBJ Library.
4. Speech on 10 September 1968, cited in Bernard Reich, *Quest For Peace* (NJ: Transaction Books, Inc., 1977), 423n; Steven L. Spiegel, "Religious Components of U.S. Middle East Policy," *Journal of International Affairs* (Fall/Winter 1982–1983), 241–42.
5. "American Jews and Israel," *Time* (10 March 1975), 18.
6. Letter, Felix Frankfurter to LBJ, 24 June 1964; also unsigned memorandum, 19 May 1966, LBJ Library.
7. Memorandum, Robert Komer to McGeorge Bundy, 16 January 1964, LBJ Library.
8. Memorandum, Myer Feldman to LBJ, 11 May 1964, LBJ Library.
9. Memorandum, J. W. Davis, Deputy Director JCS, to Secretary of Defense, 18 January 1964; Memorandum, Earle Wheeler, chairman of JCS, to Secretary of Defense, 12 March 1964, LBJ Library.
10. Memorandum, Dean Rusk to LBJ, 12 August 1964, Country File, UAR, Vol. II., National Security File, Boxes 159 and 161, LBJ Library.
11. Analysis of U.S.-U.A.R. Relationship, 10 August 1964, Country File, UAR, Vol. II., National Security File, Boxes 159 and 161, LBJ Library.
12. Robert H. Trice, Jr., "Domestic Political Interests and American Policy in the Middle East: Pro-Israel, Pro-Arab and Corporate Non-Governmental Actors and the Making of American Foreign Policy, 1966–1971," (Ph.D. Diss. University of Wisconsin-Madison, 1974), 132, 226; Memorandum, David Klein to McGeorge Bundy, 17 February 1965, claims the U.S. was unaware of the German-Israel deal in 1960 but did discuss the sale of U.S. tanks with Germany to Israel

and made clear the U.S. desired the sale. Memorandum, Robert Komer to LBJ, 23 April 1965, reveals that the Germans were grateful the U.S. got them off the hook. There is also a hint that domestic politics play a role in that nation's foreign policy since the German chancellor, according to Komer, believed that recognizing Israel would help him in the fall elections. LBJ Library.

13. Memorandum of conversation regarding Harriman-Eshkol talks, 25 February 1965; Memorandum of conversation between Ambassador Avraham Harman and W. Averill Harriman, Ambassador at-large, 15 March 1965, LBJ Library; Bick, Ethnic Linkages and Foreign Policy, 210; Rehovia U. Yakovee, "Arms for Israel—Oil for Arms: An Analysis of President Carter's 1978 Planes 'Package Deal' Sale to Egypt, Israel and Saudi Arabia," (Ph.D. Diss., Claremont, 1983), 40–41.

14. Memorandum of conversation, Mordechai Gazit, Israel Embassy, and NEA John Jernegan, 3 June 1965; Telegram from State Department to U.S. Embassy Tel Aviv, 5 June 1965; Letter, Avraham Harman to Phillips Talbot, 10 June 1965; Memorandum for Bundy, 14 June 1965; LBJ Library.

15. Memorandum, Robert Komer to McGeorge Bundy, 16 August 1965, LBJ Library.

16. Letter, Peter Solbert to Senator Len Jordan, 2 July 1965, Gen CO 303 Box 75, LBJ Library.

17. Memorandum, Robert Komer to Bill Moyers, 12 August 1965, LBJ Library.

18. Memorandum for the Record, Harold Saunders lunch with Ambassador Kamel, 10 August 1966, Country File, UAR, Vol. IV., National Security File, Boxes 159 and 161.

19. Memorandum, Hubert Humphrey to Dean Rusk, Memorandum, Rusk to Humphrey, Undated; Telegram, State Department to U.S. Embassy Tel Aviv, Undated; Telegram, U.S. Embassy to Secretary of State, 26 April 1966, LBJ Library; New York Times (11 September 1966).

20. Near East Report (20 September 1966), 74.

21. Bick, Ethnic Linkages and Foreign Policy, 208–9.

22. David Pollock, The Politics of Pressure (CT: Greenwood Press, 1982), 33.

23. Memorandum, McGeorge Bundy to LBJ, 11 July 1967, Office Files of Harry McPherson, Box 42, LBJ Library.

24. Memorandum, Walt Rostow to LBJ, 3 October 1963 and 9 October 1967, LBJ Library.

25. Near East Report, (31 October 1967), 86.

26. Memorandum, Harold Saunders to Walt Rostow, 20 November 1967, LBJ Library.

27. Memorandum, unsigned but written by Dave Ginsberg for LBJ,

"1968–American Jewry and Israel," Undated but approximately April 1967, LBJ Library.
28. Memorandum, Jack Valenti to LBJ, 4 November 1967, LBJ Library.
29. Memorandum, Charles Baird to Assistant Secretary of Defense/ISA, 5 January 1968, LBJ Library.
30. Briefing book for Eshkol visit, 3 January 1968, LBJ Library.
31. Steven L. Spiegel, *The Other Arab-Israeli Conflict* (IL: University of Chicago Press, 1985), 160; *Near East Report* (9 January 1968), 1; Marshall A. Hershberg, "Ethnic Interest Groups and Foreign Policy: A Case Study of the Organized Jewish Community in Regard to the 1968 Decision to Sell Phantom Jets to Israel," (Ph.D. Diss., University of Pittsburgh, 1973), 27–8; Trice, "Domestic Political Interests," 231–32.
32. Memorandum, Robert McNamara to LBJ, 6 February 1968, LBJ Library.
33. Memorandum, Harold Saunders to Walt Rostow, 19 June 1968, LBJ Library.
34. I. L. Kenen, *Israel's Defense Line* (NY: Prometheus, 1981), 219. Hershberg, "Ethnic Interest Groups," 28–34.
35. Memorandum, Ernest Goldstein to LBJ, 21 August 1968, LBJ Library.
36. *New York Times* (9 September 1968). Nixon's statement may be the first to call for Israel's military superiority.
37. *Near East Report* (17 September 1968); Hershberg, "Ethnic Interest Groups," 35.
38. Trice, "Domestic Political Interests," 235.
39. Memorandum, Walt Rostow to LBJ, 27 September 1968, LBJ Library.
40. Memorandum, Walt Rostow to LBJ, 8 October 1968, LBJ Library; Trice, "Domestic Political Interests," 238–39.
41. Memoradum of conversation between Yitzhak Rabin et al., and Paul Warnke et al., 4 November 1968, LBJ Library.
42. UPI dispatch, 30 November 1968, Gen CO 304, UAR, Box 75, LBJ Library.
43. Pollock, "*The Politics of Pressure*," 38.
44. Spiegel, "*The Other Arab-Israeli Conflict*," 163.
45. Bick, "*Ethnic Linkages and Foreign Policy*," 165.
46. E.g., telegram from Issa Nakleh, Permanent Representative of the Arab Higher Committee, urging LBJ not to meet with Moshe Dayan because he is an ex-convict among other things. The telegram was so vitriolic that no response was given.

8

The Israeli Lobby and Middle East Peace: The Israel-Egypt Peace Treaty

The preceding cases have all involved essentially American foreign policy decisions; however, the effort to bring about a Middle East peace settlement involved third parties that are immune to U.S. domestic political pressure. In addition, the nature of the negotiations was such that the Israeli lobby would not be expected to have much access to decision-makers; consequently, the lobby has not been attributed with having played a significant role in what is commonly referred to as the Camp David peace process. In his book chronicling that process, former National Security Council member William Quandt has provided substantial evidence that domestic politics did affect the behavior of U.S. officials. When combined with other sources, it becomes clear, the Israeli lobby was able to exert an observable degree of influence on the negotiations by reducing American leverage over Israel.

Carter's Ideology

Jimmy Carter had what national Security Adviser Zbigniew Brzezinski called an "ambivalent" attitude toward Israel.[1] On the one hand, he had a deep spiritual attachment to "the land of the Bible," but, on the other, his almost messianic determination to bring peace to the Middle East led him to view Israel as intransigent when its leaders refused to accept his own formulae.

Carter's own knowledge of Israel came from his exposure to his brother-in-law's Jewish family and a single trip to that nation in May 1973. He summarized his feelings in his memoirs when he said that he "believed very deeply that the Jews who had survived the Holocaust deserved their own nation, and that they had a right to live in peace among their neighbors. I considered this homeland for the Jews to be compatible with the teachings of the Bible, hence ordained by God. These *moral and religious beliefs* made my commitment to the security of Israel unshakable" (emphasis added).[2] Carter admits, at the same time, that he had no strong feelings toward the Arab countries since he had never visited one and knew no Arab leaders. Nevertheless, he sympathized with the Palestinians who he apparently saw as being in a similar situation to American blacks.[3] Since Carter made human rights a focal point of his foreign policy, he found it impossible to ignore the treatment of Palestinians in the West Bank, which he believed was contrary to the moral and ethical principles of both the United States and Israel. Throughout his term, Carter seemed determined to emancipate the Palestinians, and it was this issue, in particular, that was to be most affected by Israeli lobby pressure.

Jimmy Carter's Middle East policy was primarily concerned with persuading Israel to withdraw to roughly its 1967 borders, providing the Palestinians with a homeland, and bringing the Arabs and Israelis together in Geneva to negotiate a final settlement of the Arab-Israeli dispute. The president's top two foreign policy advisers, Secretary of State Cyrus Vance and National Security Adviser Zbigniew Brzezinski, shared Carter's views of the region and were not noted for being particularly sympathetic to the Israeli lobby's goals.

Carter's two highest ranking Jewish aides, Stuart Eizenstat and Robert Lipshutz, were not well-connected to the traditional Jewish-Democratic coalition and were primarily concerned with domestic affairs. The "Jewish portfolio" was held by Mark Siegel, but he had virtually no input and resigned in 1978 after the F-15 sale was announced. His successors were equally uninvolved in policy debates. Vice President Walter Mondale was regarded as pro-Israel, but, like most people in that position, was resigned primarily to going along with the president's policy, although he did become an increasingly vocal opponent of pressuring Israel as the presidential elections approached. Overall, the Carter administration was not composed of officials expected to be particularly sensitive to Israeli lobby concerns.

Quandt asserts that Carter was not concerned about the domestic consequences of his actions at the beginning of his term[4]; nevertheless, his top domestic political adviser, Hamilton Jordan, usually attended the regular Friday foreign policy meetings. Moreover, Brzezinski was particularly cognizant of the political constraints on the administration. "The President had the greatest leverage in his first year of office, less in his second, and so forth," he wrote. It made no sense to challenge the Israeli lobby in the third and fourth years, he admitted, because the "conflict would be adversely reflected in the mass media and in financial support for the Democratic Party."[5] Brzezinski therefore urged the president to act quickly to bring about negotiations in the Middle East before the political cycle intervened.

The First Initiative

Carter took Brzezinski's advice and sent Vance to the Middle East in February 1977. Before Vance left, Carter rejected the Ford administration's recommendation that foreign aid to Israel be cut. By maintaining aid at the fiscal year 1977 level, he hoped to create a positive political climate for Vance's visit to Israel. He also decided, however, that the aid would be linked to the cancellation of Ford's sale of concussion bombs and his approval of the sale of Israeli-built Kfir jets to Ecuador. These decisions were immediately criticized by the Israeli lobby as an abandonment of the U.S. commitment to Israel. Under pressure from Mondale, Eizenstat, and Senator Hubert Humphrey, Carter agreed to make Israel eligible for arms transfers needed for its security, but refused to reverse his decision on the bombs and Kfirs.[6]

The disagreement over arms transfers was only the beginning of the Israeli lobby's disappointment with Carter's Middle East policy. Vance first broached the idea of including the PLO in peace negotiations during his meeting with Foreign Minister Yigal Allon. Vance asked if it would make any difference if the PLO accepted UN Resolution 242, and Allon said that if the PLO accepted UN Resolution 242, it would cease to be the PLO. Vance interpreted this as an invitation to persuade the PLO to accept the resolution, and justified the efforts to do so that followed, which would further antagonize the Israeli lobby.[7]

On 7 March, Prime Minister Yitzhak Rabin came to Washington and was told by Carter that the United States hoped Israel would be willing to accept Palestinian leaders as part of a unified Arab delegation. Carter warned that "it would be a blow to U.S. support for Israel if you refused to participate in the Geneva talks over the technicality of the PLO being in the negotiations," but Rabin reiterated his unwillingness to deal with the PLO. Carter also raised the issue of Israeli settlements in the West Bank, calling them illegal, and then informed the Prime Minister that he believed Israel should only be allowed to keep territory within the 1967 borders with "minor modifications." Finally, Carter emphasized the need to make progress immediately. "If we lose 1977 as an opportunity for peace," he said, in what the Israelis must have understood to be an admission of his political constraints, "it will be hard to mashall such efforts again."[8]

The meeting went very badly and Rabin succeeded in alienating Carter. The Israelis asked the president not to make his views publicly known because they would weaken their bargaining position with the Arabs, but the following day he repeated his conviction that Israel should be willing to accept only "minor adjustments in the 1967 borders" at a press conference.[9] This phrase, in particular, caused an uproar, because it fit the Arab demand for the complete withdrawal of Israel from all the occupied territories more closely than Israel's insistence on maintaining "defensible borders."

The furor over Carter's remark about the borders had barely died down when he said in a speech: "There has to be a homeland provided for the Palestinian refugees who have suffered for many, many years."[10] Carter again inadvertently used code words that set off alarm bells in the Israeli lobby. To the lobby, a Palestinian "homeland" implied a PLO state on the West Bank, an idea that was an anathema. Carter began to "waffle" on the meaning of his statement as soon as he boarded Air Force One to return to Washington, providing an early indication that he could be forced to back down under pressure.[11]

In contrast to the early strains in U.S.-Israel relations, U.S.-Egyptian relations received an unexpected boost after Anwar

Sadat's meeting with the president. The two leaders became friends almost immediately. Substantively, Sadat agreed that he could accept Carter's formulation of an Israeli withdrawal to the 1967 borders with minor adjustments. Carter told Sadat that a strong Israeli-Egyptian relationship would make it possible for the United States to establish economic, military, and political ties with Egypt that would be just as strong as U.S.-Israeli ties.

In the middle of February, Carter decided to send Vance on another trip to the Middle East for a round of talks designed to stimulate enthusiasm for a Geneva conference. Although Vance specifically said the United States should avoid a repetition of the Rogers Plan fiasco, where the United States offered its own peace initiative and had it rejected by all parties, Carter apparently thought he could impose an agreement on them. In his diary he wrote that after Vance returned, they should "put as much pressure as we can bring to bear on the different parties to accept the solution that *we think* is fair" (emphasis added).[12]

The mere hint of an imposed peace stimulated vigorous opposition from the Israeli lobby, such as that expressed by the chairman of the Presidents Conference, Rabbi Alexander Schindler, who complained: "The dim outlines of an American blueprint for an imposed settlement can be seen. They may not be intended as such a blueprint but they are perceived as such. This perturbs American Jews and most of all, it raises the expectations of the Arab world, which, frustrated in the slightest degree, may impede the process toward peace if not plunge all into disaster."[13]

Carter got himself into more trouble with the Israeli lobby after meeting Syrian President Hafez Assad on 9 May. Carter told Assad that he needed to have American Jewish leaders trust him before he could make progress, and apparently thought that eliciting a pledge from Assad that he would try to persuade the PLO to endorse Resolution 242 might secure that trust. Carter found the Syrian President to be "extremely antagonistic" toward Israel and "quite convinced that the Israelis were international outlaws and that all the Arab positions were proper."[14] Despite this, Carter praised Assad afterward as a "strong supporter in the search for peace." Israel's supporters would have found this hard enough to take, but Carter added insult to injury by again calling for a homeland for the Palestinians.[15]

In early June, Carter met with his advisers to prepare a response to what they saw as a campaign against their policy by AIPAC. The president was unhappy that he had carried the burden of explaining his policy and hoped that pro-Israel spokesmen like Mondale, Humphrey, and former UN Ambassador Arthur Goldberg would speak on his behalf to mollify the Israeli lobby's concerns. Carter thought he had made some progress in this direction after meeting with groups of pro-Israel legislators, but instead the word was out, Sol Linowitz told Vance, that if the Jewish community pressured the president he would give in. This news only served to harden the positions of Carter, Vance, and Brzezinski.[16]

Begin Enters The Picture

On 17 May 1977, the Israeli electorate voted to replace the sitting government for the first time in its history. The outcome also set a precedent in putting the Likud Party in power after nearly three decades of domination by the Labor Party. The biggest surprise of all, however, was the man who was elected Prime Minister, Menachem Begin. Although most of his background and beliefs quickly became familiar to the Americans, they never seemed to grasp the strength of either his unwillingness to part with the West Bank or his desire for peace.

The president wanted to size up the prime minister. He approved a number of Israeli arms requests to create a positive atmosphere for their planned meeting and was prepared to approve others during Begin's visit. At the same time, the administration was already discussing strategies for pressuring Begin to make concessions. Brzezinski wanted to try to elicit a reaffirmation of the land-for-peace formula as well as a promise to suspend settlement activity in the West Bank, but he acknowledged that the only way the United States could pressure Begin, *given domestic political constraints*, was to convince the Arabs, especially Sadat, to normalize relations with Israel as part of a peace agreement.[17]

Before Begin came to the United States, a group of fifty Jewish leaders met with Vance, Brzezinski, Mondale, and then Carter in *an Administration effort to lobby* for support of its policy. Carter told the group that he would not draw any boundaries for a settlement and that his call for a Palestinian homeland did not imply the creation of an independent Palestinian state, which he said would be a threat to peace, but he did envision an entity associated with Jordan. He promised the United States would not try to impose a peace and would not withhold arms from Israel.[18]

Begin met Carter on 19 July 1977, and engaged in what diplomats would call a frank exchange of views. Afterward, Carter described Begin in his diary as "quite congenial, dedicated, sincere, [and] deeply religious" and predicted that he would be a stronger leader than Rabin.[19]

Carter's opinion of Begin changed literally overnight when Begin returned home and the Israeli cabinet immediately conferred legal status on three settlements established illegally under the Rabin government. Although the action did not violate any of the agreements Begin had made in Washington, Carter was furious because he had made it clear the United States considered Israel's settlements illegal and an obstacle to peace. He was also embarrassed because he had just approved a $250 million arms package that included credits to enable Israel to build its own tank, the first time such an arrangement had ever been approved.[20]

There was also a great deal of opposition within the ranks of the Israeli lobby to Begin's settlement policy and Carter hoped to mobilize these elements to pressure the Israeli government. He undermined his own effort, however, when he disclosed that his administration would negotiate with the PLO if it accepted *either* Israel's right to exist *or* Resolution 242. This violated the agreement Kissinger had made as part of the Sinai Accords in 1975 that the PLO must meet both conditions. Carter also revealed that the United States was already in contact with the PLO indirectly.[21]

Carter found himself forced to try to put out a fire he had himself set. On 26 August, he met with Rabbi Schindler and Yehuda Hellman of the Presidents Conference and was reminded of the U.S. commitment not to talk to the PLO. Carter replied in a letter, assuring them his position was consistent with the earlier commitments.

The Presidents Conference believed the issue became moot when the PLO Central Committee rejected Resolution 242, con-

demned "all of the United States and Zionist maneuvers," and
called for "increasing our continuous armed struggle against the
Zionist occupation."[22] The administration thought differently,
however, as Carter revealed just three days later when he recorded in his diary: "Assad in an interview in the *New York Times*
proposed that the PLO not participate in the Geneva Conferences, but that the Arab League might substitute for them. We'll
pursue this idea!"[23] Then, a week later, Carter sent an emissary
to meet with Arafat to try to convince him to accept Resolution
242. Arafat was unwilling, however, to take any positive action
unless the United States guaranteed that a Palestinian state would
be the result, something Carter would not do. Subsequently, Carter
gave up on the effort to bring the PLO into the peace process.[24]

The Soviets Enter The Picture

The Carter administration's efforts to coax the Middle East
parties to the negotiating table were based on the expectation
that the talks would take place under the auspices of a Geneva
conference. Since the Soviet Union and the United States were
co-chairmen of the conference, the Soviets would have to be
brought into the peace process eventually. To minimize their
potential for troublemaking, Vance wished to convince the Soviets to sign a joint communiqué outlining the two nations' common views. Vance also hoped the Soviets would be able to pressure their clients—Syria and the PLO—to make the compromises
necessary to participate in the conference and contribute to a final
settlement of the Arab-Israeli dispute.

When the Soviets were queried about their interest in a joint
statement, the Americans found that they were anxious for such
a statement and that their demands were more moderate than
expected. On 1 October 1977, a joint statement was issued. The
most controversial paragraph read:

> The United States and the Soviet Union believe that, within the
> framework of a comprehensive settlement of the Middle East prob-
> lem, all specific questions of the settlement should be resolved, in-
> cluding such key issues as withdrawal of Israeli Armed Forces from
> territories occupied in the 1967 conflict; the resolution of the Pal-
> estinian question, including insuring the legitimate rights of the Pal-

estinian people; termination of the state of war and establishment of sovereignty, territorial integrity, and political independence.[25]

The PLO hailed the statement as did Sadat who called it a "brilliant maneuver" presumably because he saw it as an effort to pressure the Syrians.[26] Sadat's reaction was still surprising, however, given that his emissary had told Moshe Dayan in Morocco only a short time earlier that he wanted no part of Geneva or the Russians.[27]

The Israeli lobby was outraged by the statement; the *Near East Report*, AIPAC's newsletter, called it "the latest blunder by the Carter administration in its ill-conceived efforts to reconvene the Geneva peace conference before the end of the year at apparently any price." The editorial said the statement represented "a major shift in U.S. policy and a victory for the Soviet Union and the PLO."[28] Israel's supporters in Congress also denounced the statement. House Minority Leader John Rhodes, for example, said: "The President succeeded in bringing our foremost adversary back into a position of influence in the Middle East at the same time rousing deep unease about the stability of America's commitment to the only democracy in the Middle East."[29]

It was not only the inclusion of the Soviets that upset the Israeli lobby, it was also the phrase recognizing the "legitimate rights" of the Palestinian people, which went beyond past American recognition of their "legitimate interests." Rabbi Schindler sent a telegram to Vance complaining that the statement "appeared to be a shocking about-face of the president's public pledges of support for the principles of a negotiated settlement within the framework of UN Resolutions 242 and 338." Schindler said that rather than a prescription for peace, the statement was "a formula for reducing Israel . . . into a vassal state dependent in part for its physical protection and thus its very survival on the Soviet Union."[30]

It is hard to understand why the administration did not anticipate the reaction the joint communiqué received. Brzezinski apparently thought it might pressure the Israelis, but admitted in his memoirs that he had made a mistake. The gravest error, however, was the failure to consult the domestic political advisers about the possible repercussions of the statement. This was then compounded by the fact that the administration had made no effort to brief the press, Congress, or Jewish leaders before it was issued.[31]

Brzezinski's reflections reveal a far greater sensitivity to domestic politics than he demonstrated in office. This was typified by his statement that "the United States has a legitimate right to exercise its own leverage, peaceful and constructive to obtain a settlement."[32] Coming on the heels of the U.S.-Soviet statement, this remark only reinforced Israeli lobby fears that the superpowers were preparing to impose a peace settlement. In an effort to dispel these fears, Carter reiterated the need for binding peace treaties negotiated on the basis of UN Resolutions 242 and 338 during a speech to the United Nations on 4 October. He also reaffirmed America's unshakable commitment to Israel's security and explained that the Palestinians' "legitimate rights"would have to be defined by the parties during negotiations and would not be dictated by the United States.[33]

The domestic political pressure forced Carter to minimize the significance of the joint communiqué. In a meeting with Moshe Dayan after his UN speech, Carter explained that his position had been made difficult by the criticism of his policy from American Jews and Congress and felt he was vulnerable because he could not counterattack. He said that it was important to show the world that the United States and Israel were cooperating in the effort to stimulate peace talks. Rather than sympathize with Carter's vulnerability, Dayan skillfully exploited it, explaining that an agreement was possible if Carter reaffirmed all past commitments to Israel and promised there would be no imposed peace or cuts in aid to pressure Israel. Dayan also wanted the United States to acknowledge Israel's right to oppose a Palestinian state and to say that Israel did not have to withdraw to the 1967 boundaries or accept the U.S.-Soviet statement. In return, Dayan said he would tell Israel's supporters that Israel was satisfied with the arrangement reached with the United States. If Carter did not accept these conditions, Dayan warned, there would be a confrontation. Carter said that such a confrontation would not be in either nation's interest and agreed to a joint U.S.-Israel statement.[34]

The joint U.S.-Israel statement was issued on 5 October. That declaration said Resolutions 242 and 338 remained the basis for the resumption of the Geneva Peace Conference and the acceptance of the Joint U.S.-U.S.S.R. statement would not be a prerequisite for the reconvening of the conference.[35] This statement reinforced the perception that the Israeli lobby could force the president to back down if he was confronted with sufficient pressure.

Carter apparently did little to eradicate this perception when he admitted privately to Arab leaders that he had to take American Jewish opinion into account. While the president no doubt saw such admissions as candid appraisals his audience would emphathize with, they were more frequently seen as expressions of weakness. Egyptian sources told Quandt, for example, that Carter's submission to pressure after the U.S.-Soviet statement influenced Sadat in his eventual decision to reduce his reliance on the Americans to break the impasse inhibiting movement toward peace talks.[36]

The administration moved closer to the Israeli lobby position in October when Carter told the Democratic National Committee (DNC) that the "key element" in America's Middle East policy is support for Israel. That 22 October 1977, speech to the DNC in Los Angeles, in fact, sounded as if it could have been written by AIPAC:

> A few days ago in a conversation with about 30 members of the House of Representatives, I said that I would rather commit suicide than hurt Israel. (Applause) I think many of them realize the two concepts are not incompatible. (Laughter) If I should ever hurt Israel, which I won't, I think political suicide would almost automatically result because it is not only our Jewish citizens who have this deep commitment to Israel, but there is an overwhelming support throughout the nation, because there is a common bond of commitment to the same principles of openness and freedom and democracy and strength and courage that ties us together in an irrevocable way. (Applause)[37]

The Israeli lobby did not reduce the pressure on the administration despite these apparent efforts to mollify its concerns. In fact, the same day Carter was addressing the DNC, eighty Jewish leaders were meeting with Vance to complain about the administration's endeavors to bring the PLO into the peace process. Although the administration had all but given up the hope of making the PLO palatable to Israel, the lobby remained on guard for any sign of a concession to the PLO.[38]

Sadat Changes History

The Carter administration circulated a working paper to Egypt, Syria, and Jordan, but it was clear from the responses that its efforts to reconvene the Geneva Conference had reached an impasse. Apparently determined to take some bold step to stimulate the peace process, Sadat told the Egyptian National Assembly on 11 November that he was prepared to go anywhere for peace, even the Knesset in Jerusalem. In response, Begin invited Sadat to address the Knesset. Sadat's subsequent speech to the Israeli Parliament on 20 December was dramatic, but offered nothing new in the way of proposals; nevertheless, the psychological impact of his visit was decisive in overcoming Israeli doubts about Sadat's sincerity in wanting peace.

The Israeli lobby was unreserved in its praise for Sadat, but was concerned by the condemnation that was being directed at him by the rest of the Arab world. The Arab lobby objected to the administration's support for the initiative. In the only reference to the Arab lobby contained in any of the memoirs of the Carter administration, Carter wrote that he was under pressure from the leaders of the American Arab community and its friends. "They [Arab-Americans] have given all the staff, Brzezinski, Warren Christopher, and others, a hard time," Carter recorded.[39]

If Carter's advisers thought he might be able to take credit for the breakthrough, they were mistaken. The *New Republic's* Morton Kondracke, for example, said that it was Carter's unwitting, "freshman-year ineptitude that scared Sadat into dramatic independent action." Tad Szulc wrote in the *New York Times Magazine* that the stalemate had been broken "in spite of, not because of American diplomacy." He said the nation was now witnessing "an embarrassed Carter administration trying to play catch-up ball, propagating theories and rationalizations geared to events as they unfold."[40]

The president was also frustrated by having been pushed to the sidelines after having invested so much time and effort into the Middle East. "One could sense a tinge of jealousy within the administration," Quandt wrote, "that Sadat had thought of a dramatic move that cut across the American plans for Geneva."[41]

Begin Reciprocates

After Sadat's journey to Jerusalem, Begin was under pressure to make an equally bold gesture to demonstrate Israeli sincerity. The response Begin decided upon was the formulation of an autonomy plan for the West Bank, but instead of presenting it directly to Sadat, he chose to take it to show Carter. Spiegel calls this decision "bizarre." After insisting on direct negotiations for thirty years, Begin rushed to Washington for approval rather than take advantage of the long-sought opportunity. "Begin demonstrated by this action that America so dominated Arab-Israeli peacemaking that he dared not make a major proposal without American support. Begin's belief that American backing would strengthen his hand in dealing with the Egyptian leader was also clear."[42]

Zion and Dan see Begin's decision differently. They suggest that Begin saw this as an opportunity to overcome his past image as a terrorist and take his proper place on the world stage. He could also now claim to be a respected man in the American Jewish community. "He had accomplished what none of his predecessors had come close to, and he would be meeting with the President not as a vassal but as a partner, the proud head of the Jewish Nation." Begin also recognized that Carter was having domestic political problems and believed that he "would make Carter into a President" by giving him a peacemaking role. Pride and politics notwithstanding, Dayan urged Begin to go to the United States on the pragmatic grounds suggested by Spiegel; he had learned from David Ben-Gurion that Israel could not make a move without the United States.[43]

When Begin arrived, Carter found that he was very forthcoming in his willingness to return the Sinai from Sharm al-Sheikh up to Eilat and withdraw Israeli troops if Sadat agreed to demilitarize the Sinai east of the Gidi and Mitla passes. He also presented his autonomy plan for the West Bank, which offered the Palestinian Arabs authority over domestic affairs but little else. Carter found the proposal unacceptable but diplomatically labeled it "constructive" in public. Exploiting the support of the Israeli lobby, Begin then read the president a long list of prominent Americans who he said supported his proposals and quoted Henry Jackson as saying the American public would also support them. The Senate would also support his position, Begin said confidently. "This comment came very close to Israeli meddling in U.S. domestic politics and was not much appreciated by the White House," Quandt says. "But," he adds, "since such behavior had long been part of the U.S.-Israeli relationship, no one objected."[44]

When Vance met with Begin, the prime minister apparently played the familiar Israeli game of hinting at concessions in response to increases in U.S. aid. Vance told Begin that it would be hard to justify such increases unless Israel was more forthcoming.[45]

In his notes on the Begin meetings, Brzezinski wrote that the administration believed there was a good chance to bring Hussein into the peace process, but two paragraphs later he says that the Begin and Sadat initiatives marked a turning point in U.S. strategy. From then on, he says, the United States was committed to promoting an Egyptian-Israeli settlement while holding onto the hope of eventually reaching a comprehensive settlement.[46]

Quieter Diplomacy

Menachem Begin had an almost uncanny talent for angering Jimmy Carter and he succeeded in starting the new year by exercising that ability. On 4 January 1978, the Israelis began work on four new settlements in the Sinai after Dayan had reportedly promised Carter no new settlements would be established. Begin had not actually agreed to the president's demand that no new settlements be established during the negotiations, but, with the exception of those Sinai settlements, he did suspend settlement activity for the remainder of the year. The administration was convinced, however, that Begin was unreliable and decided to plan a strategy whereby the United States would work with Egypt to pressure Israel. The plan fell through, however, when it became clear Sadat was even more unpredictable than Begin, and coordination with him impossible.[47]

In February 1978, Sadat came to Washington. Carter tried to

implement the U.S. negotiating strategy, but found the Egyptian president was primarily interested in obtaining the F-5 planes that were to be a part of the F-15 package for Saudi Arabia that the administration sent to Congress. Carter and his advisers did not seem to consider the impact the arms sale fight would have on the peace process, yet it was clear they were concerned with domestic politics. For example, Carter told Sadat about the difficulties he was having with the Panama Canal and SALT negotiations. He explained that the votes on the Canal treaties were coming up the following week and that he did not yet have the votes for their ratification. Some of the key senators in that debate were also friends of Israel so, he explained, a breakdown in the peace process would cause him serious political problems. Sadat understood the president's dilemma; in fact, he told Carter that one of the reasons he had gone to Jerusalem was because "he had felt the weight of the Zionist lobby in the United States and had wanted to ease that burden on Carter by some bold action."[48] At the end of the meeting, Sadat agreed he would continue to negotiate.

The settlement issue had brought the peace process to a virtual halt, however, so the administration looked forward to Begin's March visit in the hope that he might be persuaded to modify his position. In the interim, on 11 March, a PLO attack on the Israeli coast killed thirty-six people and was followed three days later by Israel's invasion of Lebanon, which Carter considered an "overreaction."[49] These events did not create an atmosphere conducive to compromise.

When Begin arrived, Carter found that the prime minister's position on settlements had hardened. Carter was convinced Begin was not willing to make the sacrifices necessary for peace and made no secret of his displeasure. After the meeting with Begin, he said "the obstacle to peace is Israel's desire to perpetuate its political domination of the West Bank and Gaza."[50] Carter also briefed Senate leaders on the talks and conveyed his negative reaction. Mary McGrory observed that the administration had "done everything but write on the sidewalk outside the White House: Jimmy Carter doesn't like Menachem Begin."[51]

By this time, U.S.-Israel relations had sunk to the lowest point since Sadat's trip to Jerusalem. The administration might have succeeded in mobilizing American public opinion, including that of the Israeli lobby, against Israel, had Carter not insisted on selling F-15s to Saudi Arabia. At least one prominent Democratic party leader with close ties to the Israeli lobby asked the administration to delay sending the arms package to Congress, and throw its weight instead behind the negotiation of a bilateral Egyptian-Israeli agreement. That leader said the administration could then count on the support of members of Congress and the Israeli lobby to pressure Israel. He warned, however, that a debate over the arms package could cause an "irreparable breach" between Israel's supporters and the administration.[52] Carter ignored the advice; consequently, most of April and May were taken up by the debate over the airplane package, no progress was made toward peace talks, and the president's political capital was squandered.

The lack of progress during the summer seemed to indicate that the situation was hopeless. Proposals were bandied back and forth without any modification of the main sticking point: Israel's refusal to withdraw its settlements from the occupied territories and Egypt's unwillingness to settle for anything less. With the congressional elections approaching, domestic politics became increasingly a subject of discussion. Mondale, who had been willing to confront his friends in the Israeli lobby for the first eighteen months, now began to urge the president to back off and try to rebuild his credibility with the lobby. Hamilton Jordan disagreed; he believed it was too late to win the lobby back by retreating, the only way to restore confidence in the president was for him to succeed in bringing about a peace settlement.[53]

The president had little leverage after the arms sale. The Senate made it clear its support for the president on the F-15 sale would not carry over to the peace process, when it unanimously adopted an amendment that called support for a "a strong and secure Israel" a "fundamental tenet of United States policy." The amendment also included such standard Israeli lobby formulae as the call for the "establishment of secure, recognized and defensible borders between Israel and its neighbors" and responsiveness to Israel's military and economic aid requests.[54]

Camp David

By the end of August 1978, the negotiations had reached a stalemate; nevertheless, Carter remained convinced that an agreement was still possible. Despite his reservations about Begin, Carter believed both he and Sadat were sincere in their expressed desires for peace, and that Israel's apparent willingness to compromise on withdrawal from Sinai at least made a bilateral agreement a possibility. Carter's Christian idealism led him to believe all problems could be resolved if men of good will simply sat down together; thus, he decided to bring the parties together at Camp David to try to conclude an agreement.

Although Quandt claimed the administration had abandoned its cooperative strategy with Egypt, Brzezinski said it was believed the meeting would allow them to pursue a variant of that strategy: "joint agreement, to be achieved by a subtle combination of U.S.-Egyptian pressure on Israel to make the necessary concessions with regard to the West Bank in order to achieve that which Israel wanted, a separate accommodation with Egypt." [55] One of the problems with this strategy, however, was the lack of leverage the Americans had over the Israelis as a result of Carter's domestic political problems. Carter's popularity was below 40 percent and the elections were rapidly approaching. The negotiation of a peace agreement was seen as Carter's political savior and he committed himself to that end with suitable religious fervor.

Sadat was also under pressure to each agreement. His dramatic journey to Jerusalem had excited the Egyptian masses, but he had failed to regain a single inch of Egyptian territory, succeeding only in alienating the nation from the rest of the Arab world. The Egyptian people, literally starving for results, were running out of patience with a president who had vision for the future but not the present.

Israel found itself in a rare position of strength entering the negotiations. Thanks largely to the pressure of the Israeli lobby, Begin knew the United States could not impose a peace agreement on Israel. Carter had already promised he would not use economic and military aid as a lever against Israel and he had little else with which to threaten the Israelis. Instead of relying on the stick,

Carter was forced to rely more on carrots, such as offering the Israelis *more* aid and/or a mutual defense agreement. Even these inducements could not guarantee Begin's cooperation, because the prime minister, in contrast to Sadat and Carter, was in a politically strong position at home. Although Israelis were no less desiring of peace than the Egyptians, Begin could easily blame the failure of negotiations on the inflexibility or unreasonable demands of the others.

Once the summit was convened on 5 September, the parties were isolated and no one, including members of the press or the Israeli lobby had access to them.[56] After ten days, the talks were on the verge of breaking up over the same issues that had brought the negotiations to a halt prior to the summit: Israel agreed to withdraw from the Sinai, but not to dismantle its settlements there as Sadat demanded, and no agreement could be reached on the future of the West Bank and Gaza. At this point, domestic political considerations entered the picture. With the possibility of the summit failing, Carter was faced with the question of whether he should hold out for a resolution of both contentious issues, at the risk of achieving no agreement at all, or try to compromise in the hope of getting something. To settle both issues he would have had to confront Begin, but this was precluded by his weak political standing and the assured opposition of the Israeli lobby. Thus, his only real choices were to try to put the best face on the summit's failure or to work for a compromise that Begin could accept. Carter decided on the latter. The decision was actually a product of idealism and pragmatism. Carter sincerely wanted to be the one to bring peace to the Middle East, but he also believed, as he told Sadat, that he needed an agreement to guarantee his reelection.[57]

An agreement was finally reached on 17 September. The Camp David Accords actually consisted of two agreements that were ambiguously tied together. The first recognized "the legitimate rights of the Palestinian people" and provided for Palestinian "autonomy" in the West Bank and Gaza. Not later than three years after the establishment of a "self-governing authority" in the territories, there were to be negotiations between Israel, Egypt, Jordan, and the Palestinians to determine the final status of the areas. The second agreement was in essence a bilateral treaty between Egypt and Israel, in which Israel agreed to complete withdrawal from the Sinai, including the dismantling of its settlements, and Egypt agreed to certain security guarantees and normalization of relations.

There is no question that Carter played a key role in achieving the agreements. Sadat and Begin's mutual antipathy virtually insured they would be unable to reach a settlement directly, and both found it easier to give in to the United States than to each other. Despite Carter's rhetoric for a year and a half about his concern for the Palestinians, he was willing to sacrifice their interests to guarantee that Egypt and Israel reached an agreement. He did believe, however, that the Palestinian issue could be resolved later; what he did not realize was that both parties had already obtained what they really wanted and were far less interested than Carter in a broader accord.

The Aftermath

With the signing of the Camp David Accords, it appeared that Carter had succeeded in reversing his political decline; the Israeli lobby applauded the agreement and congratulated the president for his role in bringing it about; Carter's popularity shot up from 39 to 56 percent; Senate Minority Leader Howard Baker said the accords helped to "nullify the bumbler image" of the president; the administration's congressional liaison, Frank More, reported a positive change in the atmosphere on Capitol Hill; and the Senate gave Carter a major legislative victory, by a greater margin than expected, that would allow his long sought energy bill to finally get through the Congress.[58] All was not as bright as it seemed, however, and the optimism of Camp David quickly gave way to fears that the entire agreement would unravel.

One of the major concerns of the administration was the reaction of the Arab world. Sadat had told the president that the backing of Saudi Arabia and Jordan was critical and Carter assured him that he could deliver their support. Almost immediately after the summit ended, however, both countries expressed their opposition to the agreement. Yasir Arafat bluntly called Camp David "a dirty deal,"[59] and the Soviets said Israel had gotten everything in the agreement while the Arabs gained nothing. In the United States, Senator James Abourezk said the Accords tipped the scales overwhelmingly in Israel's favor militarily, disrupted the Arab world, and Sadat had sold the "Palestinians down the river."[60]

All hope of bringing the other Arab nations into the peace process dissipated when the Arab leaders meeting in Baghdad on 5 November condemned the Camp David Accords and announced the Arab league headquarters were going to be moved from Cairo if Egypt signed a peace treaty with Israel. Sadat's answer was that he would not pay any attention to "the hissing of snakes."[61]

While the Arab states sabotaged the administration's grand design for a comprehensive peace from one side, the Begin government seemed to be undermining the existing agreements from the other. The problem stemmed from a misunderstanding over what Begin had agreed to with regard to the West Bank. Carter believed that Begin had agreed to suspend the establishment of settlements in the West Bank and Gaza for the duration of the peace negotiations, but Begin denied making any such agreement. The Israelis insisted that Begin had agreed to a three-month suspension while the final negotiations for an Israeli-Egyptian treaty were completed. Conflicting versions are found in the various memoirs making it impossible to determine the truth. The veracity of the claims is practically irrelevant since Begin carried out the agreement as he understood it. The effect, however, was to generate animosity between U.S. and Israeli officials and, in Carter's opinion, to end any hope of bringing Jordan into the talks.[62]

The Americans were not content to argue with the Israelis over the agreement; they also attempted to pressure them to accept the Carter understanding. The president met with a group of "key Jewish leaders" and asked them to use their influence to restrain Begin, who was acting "irresponsibly."[63] The administration also withheld a letter promising the United States would build two airbases in the Negev to replace the three Israel was dismantling in the Sinai, in an effort to pressure Begin. Finally, Vance told the General Assembly that the United States considered the settlements illegal and that "no peace agreement will be either just or secure if it does not resolve the problem of the Palestinians in the broadest sense."[64]

Despite the flap over settlements, progress was made toward

a bilateral treaty. Israel agreed to accelerate withdrawal to an interim line in the Sinai; Egypt agreed to the establishment of security zones and the exchange of ambassadors; and the United States agreed to finance Israel's withdrawal from Sinai except for the cost of relocating the settlers. After the Israeli cabinet approved the draft treaty, however, Begin announced a plan to "thicken" a number of West Bank settlements. Carter was gratified by the treaty vote but outraged by the settlement decision. "At a time when we are trying to organize negotiations dealing with the West Bank and Gaza, no step by the Israeli government could be more damaging," he said, and threatened that the plan would have "the most serious consequences for our relationship."[65]

What Carter could not seem to grasp, despite the unequivocal statements of the Israeli Prime Minister, was the strength of Begin's conviction that Judea and Samaria were a part of Israel and their sovereignty was not subject to negotiation. This had been Begin's position for all of his political life and he was not about to change it for Jimmy Carter. Moreover, Begin exploited the American political system by delaying the negotiations over the West Bank, knowing that by the end of the year Carter would have to begin worrying about reelection, and would be constrained by the Israeli lobby's opposition to U.S. pressure on Israel. Thus, while the administration hoped to have a peace treaty by Election Day, 1978, Begin no doubt saw his bargaining position as stronger if he dragged out the negotiations until the following year.[66]

After the congressional election, Carter tried to revive the negotiations by sending Vance to the Middle East. The president told him that he was willing to sacrifice reelection because of alienating the Jewish community, but he believed it was necessary to side with Sadat and pressure the Israelis. Vance took a series of "interpretive notes" and "legal opinions" that reflected Egyptian views to Israel, where they were rejected as a retreat from Camp David. On his way back home, a "senior official" aboard the airplane blamed the Israelis for the breakdown of negotiations.

The Israeli lobby then came to Begin's defense, accusing the administration of "siding with Egypt in pressuring Israel to make ever-greater concessions—concessions that could prove fatal to Israel's fragile security." Ted Mann, the chairman of the Presidents Conference, argued that U.S. efforts to link the Israeli-Egyptian treaty to West Bank autonomy and a comprehensive settlement were self-defeating. Reflecting the predominant sentiment of the Israeli lobby, Mann concluded that America's top priority should be a bilateral treaty, which would then serve as an example of the viability of peace with Israel.[67]

Administration efforts to soothe the anxiety of the lobby failed. They were further undermined when Carter decided to establish diplomatic relations with China and abandon Taiwan, bringing into question America's already shaky credibility.

Peace At Last

The year 1979 began with Carter under great political pressure. America's policy toward the Persian Gulf was threatened by the increasing revolutionary fervor in Iran, and the presidential election campaign was already gearing up with Carter facing the prospect of a serious challenge for his party's nomination from Senator Edward Kennedy. Carter knew he did not have much time left to devote to the peace process but remained committed to achieving an agreement.

Early in January, Vance suggested that the United States again try to induce the PLO to join the peace process, but the president was not receptive to the idea. Even Brzezinski, who had made no secret of his willingness to confront the Israeli lobby, saw that the costs of such a strategy outweighed the potential benefits. "I am firmly convinced for the good of the Democratic Party," he wrote in a memorandum to Carter, "we must avoid a situation where we continue agitating the most neuralgic problem with the American Jewish community (the West Bank, the Palestinians, the PLO) without a breakthrough to a solution. I do not believe that in the approaching election year we will be able to convince the Israelis that we have significant leverage over them, particularly on those issues." Brzezinski added: "We have little time left."[68]

The Israeli lobby had effectively narrowed the range of discussion to bilateral issues and the administration was now pre-

pared to accept that reality. In addition, Carter came to the conclusion that Sadat "did not gave a damn about the West Bank"
so there was no reason to press the Arab case more forcefully
than the Egyptian leader was willing to do.[69]

Carter had another opportunity to break the deadlock when
Begin visited him at the beginning of March. Even before the
Prime Minister arrived, the administration seemed convinced that
Begin was determined to hold out for a separate peace and to
undermine the president's chances of reelection. The meetings
reinforced these views as Begin rejected all of the administration's
proposals, and then tried to generate support from the Israeli
lobby for his position at a New York rally on 7 March: "Do what
you can to bring about the quick—as quick as possible—strengthening of Israel. It's in your own interest. When the time comes,
do not hesitate to use your influence."[70]

Sadat sent Carter a message saying he was planning to come
to Washington to denounce Begin's intransigence. This message,
combined with Begin's attitude, stimulated Carter's fighting spirit
and convinced him the only hope of breaking the impasse was
for him to travel to the Middle East to conduct his own version
of shuttle diplomacy. Brzezinski was sent to brief Sadat in advance, and told him that progress toward a peace agreement "was
essential to the President's political fortunes" and that U.S.-Egyp-
tian cooperation was needed to prevent Begin from undermining
the Camp David Accords and bringing down the Carter administration.

When Carter arrived in Cairo, he found that Sadat was willing
to let the American president make whatever concessions he thought
necessary to secure an agreement, and Carter responded to Sadat's faith in him by saying that he would represent Egyptian interests "as if they were my own." These were hardly the words
expected of an honest broker, but they allowed Carter the flexibility he needed to reach an agreement with Begin. On 13 March,
after compromising on the treatment of Palestinians in the territories and receiving assurances regarding oil supplies after Israel
handed over the Sinai, Begin agreed to sign a peace treaty with
Egypt.[71]

The Israeli lobby played no role in the negotiations that took
place in Cairo and Jerusalem, but it had already established the

guidelines within which Carter could work. Consequently, the
treaty Begin signed contained a number of compromises, but *did
not* require him to give up Israeli sovereignty over the West Bank
and Gaza or negotiate with the PLO. Israel did withdraw from
the Sinai and agreed to grant autonomy to the occupied territories,
in exchange for which Egypt agreed to normalize relations and
end the state of belligerency.

The one other aspect of the peace negotiations that was affected
by the Israeli lobby was the promise of aid Carter had made to
both Egypt and Israel. Israel was to receive $3 billion in military
aid to help build new airfields in the Negev, $800 million of which
was to be in the form of grants. Egypt was promised $1.5 billion
in aid over a period of three years. The fact that Carter would
offer such large amounts of aid at a time when the U.S. economy
was in a recession indicates how badly he wanted an agreement.
These promises required congressional approval and this is where
the Israeli lobby was able to help. Despite concerns about the
economy, the Senate (73–11) and House (347–28) both overwhelmingly approved the treaty aid package.

Summary

The realist model was of little use in explaining the decisions
that Jimmy Carter made in the course of peace negotiations.
American officials have always believed the national interest in
Middle East stability could best be served by bringing about a
comprehensive peace agreement, so the model might be said to
explain the objective, but that is not terribly helpful. The disagreements arose over how to bring an agreement about and the
model does not suggest a course of action to pursue in that regard.
Since U.S. security was not directly at stake in the negotiations,
it was possible for the Israeli lobby to find support for its opposition to presidential initiatives that were perceived to be contrary
to the lobby's interests. Thus, for example, there was little support
for Carter's efforts to bring the PLO into the negotiations under
the pretext that the prospects for an agreement could be improved.

The American policy toward peace negotiations was shaped by
the vision of Jimmy Carter. Carter's moral and religious beliefs

led him to support not only Israel but the Palestinians. His faith in face-to-face negotiations and global cooperation led him to believe that he could bring all the parties together at Geneva and hammer out a comprehensive agreement. Even after failing to convene an international conference, his conviction that agreement could be reached by men of good will sitting down together led him to convene the Camp David summit, which did, in fact, bring about an agreement. Although Israel and Egypt did sign a peace treaty, an event of monumental importance, the agreement was very different from that envisioned by Carter. The major reason for this difference was the constraints placed on his bargaining position by domestic politics.

Carter's political aides were involved in most of the discussions regarding Middle East policy, and the entire administration was constantly aware of the domestic constraints they were under; in fact, it was clear there was a time limit on their efforts established by the electoral cycle. Carter did eschew the advice of his political advisers on a few occasions, but the refusal to "play politics" usually hurt rather than helped him. The best example of this was when he insisted on offering the Saudis F-15s at a time when he was trying to mobilize support for his criticism of Begin's settlement policy. Instead, the Israeli lobby closed ranks and increased pressure on the administration not to impose a settlement on Israel. In addition, the arms sale reinforced the lobby's argument that Israel's security had to be insured and that there were limits to the concessions it could make given the Arab threat.

On other occasions, Carter was forced to retreat from positions opposed by the lobby, particularly his support for the "legitimate rights" of the Palestinians and his efforts to solicit PLO participation in negotiations. In several instances, the appearance of giving in to lobby pressure was so obvious that his credibility with the Arab states was undermined. The most notable example was the joint U.S.-Israel statement he agreed to that vitiated a joint U.S.-U.S.S.R. statement made only four days earlier, after the latter aroused a storm of protest from Israel and the lobby.

In fact, the Carter administration was probably the most explicit administration in history in their admissions of the domestic constraints on their foreign policy options. Carter, for example, equated hurting Israel with "political suicide" and told Sadat and other

Arab leaders about how his domestic problems limited his freedom of action.

As first the midterm, and later the presidential elections approached, the administration became increasingly desperate to reach an agreement. The president's political standing deteriorated throughout the negotiations and it became clear failure would almost guarantee he would not be re-elected, perhaps, not even renominated. Thus, even Brzezinski, who relished the opportunity to challenge the Israeli lobby, acknowledged by 1979 that it was better to compromise on the administration's grand design. Carter realized he was in political trouble and had little or no leverage over Israel, because the lobby firmly opposed forcing the Israelis to make concessions; therefore, he was ultimately willing to accept an agreement that did not settle what he considered the major issues.

Although the lobby had little direct access to the decision-makers, it was able to exert influence indirectly. The informal component presented Carter with certain election realities, both in terms of his own re-election and the prospects of Democratic candidates who might be hurt by the association with an "anti-Israel" president. The lobby was not unified behind the policies of Menachem Begin, and Carter might have been able to exploit the divisions had he not insisted on pursuing policies, such as trying to bring the PLO into the negotiations, which the lobby was almost unanimously opposed to. There was no competing interest to lobby for increased pressure on Israel, so it was not surprising the Senate unanimously adopted a resolution supporting the Israeli lobby's position. Once the peace treaty was signed, congressional support for the lobby was also apparent when the foreign aid associated with the treaty was overwhelmingly approved despite the U.S. recession.

Notes

1. Zbigniew Brzezinski, *Power and Principle* (NY: Farrar, Straus, Giroux, 1983), 97.
2. Jimmy Carter, *Keeping Faith* (NY: Bantam Books, 1982), 274.
3. Ibid. 274–5; William B. Quandt, *Camp David* (DC: Brookings, 1986), 31.
4. Quandt, *Camp David*, 62.

5. Brzezinski, *Power and Principle*, 88.
6. Ibid., 92–3.
7. Quandt, *Camp David*, 41–3.
8. Ibid., 45–6; Carter, *Keeping Faith*, 280–1; Brzezinski, *Power and Principle*, 90–1.
9. Public Papers of the President, *Jimmy Carter* (DC: U.S. Government Printing Office, 1977), p. [Henceforth Public Papers]
10. *Near East Report* (23 March 1977), 47.
11. Ibid., 44.
12. Diary entry, 25 April 1977, in Carter, *Keeping Faith*, 285; Quandt, *Camp David*, 54–5.
13. Presidents Conference, *Annual Report* (Year ending 31 March 1978), 3, 7. [Henceforth PC 1978]
14. Carter, *Keeping Faith*, 286; Quandt, *Camp David*, 57.
15. Steven Spiegel, *The Other Arab-Israeli Conflict* (IL: University of Chicago Press, 1985), 332; Bernard Reich, *The United States and Israel* (NY: Praeger, 1984), 48.
16. Carter, *Keeping Faith*, 288–9; Brzezinski, *Power and Principle*, 97–8.
17. Quandt, *Camp David*, 72.
18. PC 1978, 8.
19. Diary entry, 19 July 1977, Carter, *Keeping Faith*, 290.
20. Quandt, *Camp David*, 81–83n; Reich, *United States and Israel*, 51; *Near East Report* (27 July 1977) 123.
21. *Time* (8 August 1977); Spiegel, *The Other Arab-Israeli Conflict*, 335; David Pollock, *The Politics of Pressure* (CT: Greenwood Press, 1982); 232; PC 1978, 10.
22. PC 1978, 11.
23. Diary entry, 29 August 1977, Carter, *Keeping Faith*, 292.
24. Quandt, *Camp David*, 101–2, 111.
25. State Department *Bulletin* (7 November 1977), 639–40; Quandt, *Camp David*, 119–23.
26. Quandt, *Camp David*, 122.
27. Sidney Zion and Uri Dan, "Untold Story of the Mideast Talks," *New York Times Magazine* (21 January 1979), 20.
28. *Near East Report* (5 October 1977), 165.
29. *New York Times* (14 October 1977).
30. PC 1978, 12.
31. Brzezinski, *Power and Principle*, 108–10; Quandt, *Camp David*, 123.
32. *Washington Post* (3 October 1977).
33. Public Papers, 1977, vol. 2, 1720–21.
34. Quandt, *Camp David*, 130–1; Carter quote in Zion and Dan, "Untold Story," 47.
35. Public Papers, 1977, vol. 2, 1728.
36. Quandt, *Camp David*, 131–4.

37. *Near East Report* (26 October 1977), 184.
38. PC 1978, 14.
39. Diary entry, 15 December 1977, Carter, *Keeping Faith*, 299.
40. *Near East Report* (28 December 1977), 228.
41. Quandt, *Camp David*, 147–8.
42. Spiegel, *The Other Arab-Israeli Conflict*, 342.
43. Zion and Dan, "Untold Story," 52.
44. Quandt, *Camp David*, 157; Carter, 299.
45. Quandt, *Camp David*, 154.
46. Brzezinski, *Power and Principle*, 120.
47. Quandt, *Camp David*, 161–75.
48. Ibid., 173–9.
49. *Near East Report* (15 March 1978), 41; Carter, *Keeping Faith*, 310.
50. Reich, *United States and Israel*, 61; Diary entry, 22 March 1978, Carter, *Keeping Faith*, 312.
51. *Washington Star* (24 March 1978); Brzezinski, *Power and Principle*, 246–7; Quandt, *Camp David*, 186; Spiegel, *The Other Arab-Israeli Conflict*, 351.
52. Quandt, *Camp David*, 188.
53. Ibid., 197–8, 204.
54. *Near East Report* (2 August 1978), 139.
55. Quandt, *Camp David*, 204; Brzezinski, *Power and Principle*, 252.
56. For details of what took place at Camp David see Carter, *Keeping Faith*, 319–403; Brzezinski, *Power and Principle*, 252–72; Cyrus Vance, *Hard Choices* (NY: Simon and Schuster, 1983), 218–31; Moshe Dayan, *Breakthrough* (NY: Alfred A. Knopf, 1981), 149–90; Quandt, *Camp David*, 206–58.
57. Quandt, *Camp David*, 239.
58. "Carter's Swift Revival," *Time* (2 October 1978), 9.
59. Ibid., 8.
60. *Near East Report* (20 September 1978), 168.
61. Quandt, *Camp David*, 203, 265, 280; Carter, *Keeping Faith*, 301, 404, 410; Spiegel, *The Other Arab-Israeli Conflict*, 365.
62. For a discussion of the settlements dispute see Carter, *Keeping Faith*, 397; Brzezinski, *Power and Principle*, 270–3; Vance, *Hard Choices*, 228; Dayan, *Breakthrough*, 181–8; Spiegel, *The Other Arab-Israeli Conflict*, 362; and Quandt, *Camp David*, 247–9, 253n, 263.
63. Diary entry, 19 September 1978, Carter, *Keeping Faith*, 405.
64. *Time* (2 October 1978), 11; State Department *Bulletin*, (November 1978), 49.
65. Quandt, *Camp David*, 277.
66. Ibid., 261; Brzezinski, *Power and Principle*, 276.
67. Mann letter dated 22 December 1978 in Presidents Conference *Annual Report* (Year ending 31 March 1979), 17 [Henceforth PC 1979]; Brzezinski, *Power and Principle*, 277–8; Spiegel, *The Other Arab-Israeli Conflict*, 368.

68. Quandt, *Camp David*, 295.
69. Ibid., 296.
70. PC 1979, 19; Brzezinski, *Power and Principle*, 279–80; Quandt, *Camp David*, 298.
71. Brzezinski, *Power and Principle*, 281–4; Carter, *Keeping Faith*, 421–5.

Part III

ISRAELI LOBBY SUCCESS AND ITS DETERMINANTS, 1945–1984

9

The Middle East Policy Data Set

After examining several case studies of the Israeli lobby's role in the formation of U.S. Middle East policy, it became clear that it was impossible to isolate the degree of influence exerted by the lobby or the variables which may have affected the lobby's influence. The only way to surmount this problem was to collect data on a large number of cases and then examine which variables played a statistically significant role in the outcome.

Since there are no data sets that include foreign policies relating to the Middle East, it was necessary to build one. This required the development of a number of decision rules for the inclusion of cases. For the purposes of this study, a "case" is defined as a sentence or group of sentences in a bill, amendment, or official statement or executive action, which affirms, alters, or modifies America's relationship with the nations of the Middle East during the period 1945 to 1984.

The nations that were considered relevant to the study were Syria, Lebanon, Iraq, Jordan, Lebanon, Egypt, Saudi Arabia, and Israel. Israel was chosen for the obvious reason that the Israeli lobby is primarily interested in U.S. policy toward that nation. The Arab nations were chosen because they are the principal countries involved in the Arab-Israeli conflict, and therefore policies affecting them are usually of interest to the Israeli lobby. Several Arab nations, including the Gulf states, Morocco, Tunisia, and Libya, were excluded because they are farther removed from the Arab-Israeli conflict, there were few policies involving those nations during the subject period, and their exclusion reduced the data gathering task somewhat without any expectation that the results of the study would be affected. The most glaring omission is Iran, but that nation was excluded because it was, for the most part, uninvolved in the Arab-Israeli conflict, and is non-Arab and therefore not represented by the Arab lobby.

Most studies of congressional policy simply look at legislative voting records, usually the "key votes" as identified by the *Congressional Quarterly*. There are a number of problems with this procedure. For the purpose of this study, the key votes would have provided too few cases that dealt with Middle East policy. A more serious problem is that the use of "key votes" biases the sample in such a way that the vast majority of relevant cases (i.e., those of interest to the Israeli lobby) are ignored. In addition, by looking only at legislative votes, the investigator misses those cases that do not come to a vote. In this study, for example, if only cases that come to a vote are included, the Israeli lobby wins almost every time. Most of the bills that the lobby supports, however, never come to a vote, and therefore are "losses" for the lobby that would be excluded from the other type of analysis. In addition, this is not a study of Congress but of foreign policy; therefore, it is necessary to include cases that are decided in the White House with little or no input from the legislative branch.

Methodology

To identify the relevant legislative cases, three sources were consulted: the *Congressional Quarterly Almanac*, the *Digest of Public General Bills and Resolutions*, and the *Congressional Record Index*. The *Almanac* was used primarily to double-check for missing data, obtain information about committee deliberations, and to catch amendments to bills not found in the other two indexes. To find cases, the following key words in the *Congressional Record* and *Digest* indexes for the years 1945–1984 were consulted:

AID	Iraq
American Economic Assistance	Israel
American Military Assistance	Jews
Arabs	Jordan
Arms Sales	Lebanon

Economic Aid
Egypt
Executive Branch and Agencies
Foreign Aid
Foreign Affairs
Foreign Economic Assistance Act
Foreign Relations
Foreign Trade
Hebrews
Immigration and Naturalization

Middle East
Mutual Security Act
Near East
Saudi Arabia
State Department
Syria
United Arab Republic
United Nations
United States

The next steps were to look up the digest of each of the bills listed under these key words and then check the legislative history. All relevant bills, resolutions, and amendments were recorded. Since many redundant bills are introduced, only one, usually the first indicated in the index, was included in the universe of cases. Many bills are closely related, although they may not be recorded in the index as being identical, and these were also eliminated. In many cases, the proposal relating to the Middle East was only a provision of a more general bill. In these cases, the bill was included as a case, unless the proposal was offered as a separate amendment on the floor, in which case both the amendment and the bill were included. The reason for including both is that the vote on the amendment reflects congressional sentiment on the particular issue, but that vote becomes irrelevant if the bill is not adopted. In some instances, several different relevant provisions may be part of a single bill; rather than code each separately, however, only the bill itself was included. One of the problems with not coding provisions separately is that a vote on a bill may be primarily based on some provision other than the one related to the Middle East. This was particularly a problem during the Vietnam war when aid bills, for example, were very controversial because of aid to Vietnam and Cambodia; consequently, the Israeli lobby could have lost on an aid vote because of those other appropriations. This rarely happened, however, and when it did, aid to Israel was usually appropriated through some other bill such as a continuing resolution.

Bills that came to a vote were counted only once; that is, not as separate House and Senate cases. Similarly, if a bill was proposed in both the House and Senate, but did not come to a vote in either it was counted only once. If a bill did not come to a vote or pass, but the relevant provisions were included in a continuing resolution, as was the case in several instances involving foreign aid, then the continuing resolution was included.

There are distinctions between the different types of bills; for example, although concurrent resolutions do not have the force of law, all bills were treated equally because, in the case of foreign policy, statements of congressional sentiment often exert pressure on the president to change policy. Similarly, letters to the president or secretary of state expressing a position on Middle East policy were included if signed by a majority of either the House or Senate. By stipulating that the letters be signed by a majority, it is possible to infer that they reflect the sense of Congress. One example of a letter which influenced administration policy was the so-called "letter of 76."

In 1975, Kissinger's shuttle diplomacy broke down and both he and President Ford blamed Israel. As a way of expressing their displeasure, they announced there was going to be a reassessment of U.S. policy in the Middle East. AIPAC's director, Morris Amitay, drafted a letter to Ford urging him "to make clear, as we do, that the United States, acting in its own national interests, stands firmly with Israel in the search of peace in future negotiations, and that this promise is the basis of the current reassessment of U.S. policy in the Middle East." The letter was circulated by Senators Jacob Javits and Birch Bayh and eventually gathered seventy-six Senate co-signers effectively putting an end to "reassessment." Howe and Trott described the pressure to co-sign the letter:

Iowa's John Culver and Louisiana's J. Bennett Johnson, Jr. said they would not sign. Democrat Dan Inouye objected to lobby pressure, besides, he said, there are as many Jews in Hawaii "as there are snowflakes." All signed the letter. Culver told a colleague who reproached him for going back on his word: The pressure was just too great. I caved." He recounted how Jews had been calling him through the night at home. Bennett Johnson said much the same. Inouye bared a row of smiling teeth and said: "It's easier to sign one letter than to answer 5000." "But Dan," his colleague objected, "you said there weren't any Jews in Hawaii." "I don't only get letters from Hawaii," he said.[1]

Similar reasoning suggested that non-binding resolutions adopted by one or both Houses be included even though many may be ignored. No president can afford to completely disregard public opinion, and the opinion behind such resolutions is sometimes (particularly if relating to the Arab-Israeli conflict) "so intense and the threat of action so great that [the President] has been forced to heed them."[2] This has been particularly true in cases where the Congress has called upon the president to sell arms to Israel, as occurred in the 1968 Phantom jet sale described in chapter 7.

The enactment of a bill is a multistage process, but data have only been coded for the floor votes because that is the most important phenomenon to explain; moreover, there usually is no information about bills that do not come to a vote. The two exceptions to this rule are cases involving aid bills, and conference committee decisions that change relevant provisions of a bill adopted on the floor of either House. In the case of aid bills, the reason for including committee actions is that they usually determine the appropriation levels adopted on the floor. The actions included here were those that altered aid levels requested by the administration, including amendments placing conditions on aid. Conference committee actions were included if the changes affected the outcome; for example, if an increase in aid to Israel was eliminated, then the lobby victory on the floor would be offset by the loss in the committee. Floor amendments were counted as separate cases.

Executive Cases

Rather than examine only foreign policy cases that feature legislative involvement, the data set developed for this study also includes those policies that are decided within the executive branch. Since there are literally hundreds of such decisions made within the bureaucracy, the only cases examined here are those that might be regarded as "high policy," that is, affecting the overall policy of the nation and decided at the level of the president or secretary of state. The sources for the cases were:

1. *Near East Report;*
2. *State Department Bulletin;*

3. Steven Spiegel, *The Other Arab-Israeli Conflict;*
4. Allan Dowty, *Middle East Crisis* (for 1958, 1970, and 1973 crises);
5. Ralph Magnus, ed. *Documents on the Middle East;*
6. Miscellaneous secondary sources.

The procedure for identifying executive cases was simply to read all issues of the *Near East Report* to determine policies relevant to the Israeli lobby and positions taken toward relevant issues. The other sources listed above were consulted and any relevant cases were recorded. All statements by the president, secretary of state, or national security adviser, which fall under the definition of a case cited above were recorded. Since officials make a great many speeches in which the same themes are repeated, only one statement expressing a policy position was recorded.

Also falling under the heading of executive decisions are all United Nations Security Council votes. Since General Assembly votes have no force, they were ignored. Two exceptions were made: the vote for partition which, in effect, created Israel, and the vote to admit Israel into the United Nations. Cases where the United States abstained were always counted as losses for the Israeli lobby, because the lobby considers abstentions a reflection of a lack of support.

There is one notable omission from the list of executive cases, and that is secret decisions (e.g., many pre-1973 arms sales to the Arabs). These were excluded for the obvious reason that most remain secret. Also, by definition, the lobby would be denied access to the deliberations preceding these decisions; nevertheless, I would argue that the informal lobby would still influence secret decisions by virtue of the president's concern with re-election. Although there are, no doubt, some secret policies left out, the presumption that secret decisions cannot be made for any length of time in a democracy suggests that few relevant cases have been omitted.[3]

Coding

It is impractical to code all the variables that could conceivably be relevant; therefore, an effort was made to code variables used by other researchers to test their reliability, and also to introduce new variables that would test, not only the pluralist model, but also alternative models.

The dependent variable in the analysis is whether or not the Israeli lobby's policy preference is adopted as U.S. policy. This is consistent with Bertrand Russell's notion of power as "the production of intended consequences." As Salamon and Siegfried have noted, it is difficult, if not impossible, to quantify the political influence process; therefore, the analysis will follow their example and look at policy outcomes rather than process, with the independent variables really being more accurately described as intervening.[4]

The best evidence of influence are those cases where the president or Congress take actions they otherwise would not in the absence of the Israeli lobby.[5] The Jackson-Vanik and antiboycott bill case studies, for example, involve legislation that would not have been proposed if no lobby existed to stimulate congressional action. The ability to place issues of concern to the lobby on the national agenda, then, would demonstrate a degree of influence. But I am less interested in the lobby's ability to set the agenda, than its capacity to have that agenda adopted as U.S. policy; after all, if the lobby raised a lot of issues without ever succeeding in having its desired policies adopted, it would be of little interest. Similarly, if the president and Congress both agree with the lobby, then there is little evidence the lobby has exerted any influence; that is, the outcome may have occurred without the lobby's involvement. On the other hand, if the lobby is able to reach its objectives over the opposition of the president, who the leadership and realist models would expect to dominate foreign policy, then it is possible to demonstrate the lobby has exerted an observable degree of influence on American foreign policy.

To determine whether the Israeli lobby's preference was adopted, it was necessary to identify that preference. This was usually found by looking through the *Near East Report*, AIPAC's newsletter. In many cases, it was not possible to find a specific reference, particularly to bills that did not come to a vote. In those instances, if it was possible to infer the lobby's position, then I coded accordingly. After many years of studying the lobby it was usually not difficult to determine the lobby's expected position, because it has taken consistent stands on most issues relating to the Middle East. Thus, for example, the lobby has typically supported foreign aid, even for Arab states; therefore, most aid bills could be coded without a specific reference. The exceptions, such as the lobby's opposition to aid for Syria in the late 1970s, were cited in the *Near East Report* or elsewhere. Cases that I was unsure of, because they were not similar to policies on which the lobby had expressed a position, were coded as missing.

The universe consisted of 914 cases, but after the missing data were deleted, most statistics were based on a sample of 782 cases or less. Rather than using a random sample, the entire valid universe was used; variation in N occurs, however, due to the difficulty in finding data for certain variables. For example, it was difficult to find the positions of congressional leaders unless the issue came to a roll call vote; consequently, there were far fewer cases for which those variables were coded.

Presidential Preferences

The leadership model holds that the president is the most influential lobbyist and that foreign policy should reflect his will. Similarly, as the ultimate arbiter of the national interest, the president would also be expected by realists to dominate foreign policy decision-making. The pluralist model, by contrast, suggests that the president is subject to domestic political pressures, and that these may lead to policies contrary to his preferences. In the specific case of Middle East policy, the hypothesis might be stated: If the president supports the Israeli lobby, then the lobby should achieve its objective; if he opposes the lobby, it should fail.

The president's position was coded according to whether he supported or opposed the lobby's position. Again, there were numerous instances where the president's position was unclear so unless the issue was similar to one on which the president had a declared position, the case was coded as missing. This was particularly a problem in the case of bills that did not come to a vote, so although the president's opposition may have been a factor in the result it was not coded as such. The distribution of this variable is found in table 9.1, which indicates that presidents supported the lobby's position in a little more than half of the 612 cases on

TABLE 9.1

Distribution of Cases by President's Position

	Percent
President Is:	
For	52
Against	49
Total Number of Cases	612

which the president took a position (percentages in the tables may not equal 100 percent due to rounding).

One of the most controversial coding decisions, I suspect, involved cases where the president was forced to compromise on his initial proposal; for example, deleting bomb racks for F-15s in both 1978 and 1981. In these instances the president's position was coded as though it opposed the Israeli lobby's position. The lobby was coded as being in favor of the compromise. This might be controversial for two reasons. The first is that it is possible to argue that the president supported the compromise he offered, and therefore it is inaccurate to say that it reflected lobby influence. The fact is, however, that most, if not all of these compromises were essentially forced on presidents to enable them to have some chance of having their primary goals met. Consequently, I believe this coding scheme is a fair reflection of the political phenomenon under investigation.

A second objection might be that coding compromises as victories for the lobby is misleading, because the real issue may be decided against its interests, and the compromise was really a minor concession. Again the arms sales provide good examples. Some would argue the F-15 and AWACS sales were unambiguous losses for the lobby, but this coding procedure effectively cancels those defeats out by counting the compromises on basing, fuel tanks, and missiles as victories for the lobby. This, it could be argued, does not take into account that what the lobby *really* cared about was stopping the airplane sales. This is a fair criticism; however, I would suggest that what this study is concerned with is the identification of interest group influence, and the compromises that had to be offered to insure the approval of those sales reflects the influence of the Israeli lobby.

A related criticism may be that presidents should be coded as being for all bills except those they veto. Technically, this would be correct, however, the reality is that presidents sign most bills even though they may oppose some of their content. In those cases where the president did veto the bill, however, the variables were recoded accordingly.

Administration Preferences

The presidential position variable would only provide an indication of the influence of "the presidency." Proponents of the leadership model argue, however, that policies change when the administration changes; that is, the individual rather than the office makes the difference. If this proposition is correct, there should be variation across time, with some presidents opposing the lobby more often than others. Thus, the data were broken down by administration. The distribution of cases by administration is presented in table 9.2. Once again, this table only includes cases for which the president's position was known.

There is a wide variation in the number of cases occurring during each administration according to table 9.2. More than half of the cases in the study occurred in a twelve-year period beginning with Nixon's second term. More than two-thirds of the cases followed the 1967 war. Truman, Eisenhower, and Johnson were preoccupied for most of their terms with other regions of the world (e.g., Asia), and were less involved in Middle East affairs

TABLE 9.2

Distribution of Cases by Administration

	Total Number of Cases	Percent
Truman (1945–52)	41	7
Eisenhower (1953–60)	64	10
Kennedy (1961–63)*	18	3
Johnson (1964–68)	68	11
Nixon (1969–72)	83	14
Nixon-Ford (1973–76)	111	18
Carter (1977–80)	116	19
Reagan (1981–84)	111	18
Total	612	100

* Includes one case decided after Kennedy's assassination.

than their successors. American foreign policy began to focus more heavily on the Middle East, and Israel in particular, beginning with the Six-Day War, and then even more so after 1973.

The activism of the last three administrations also coincides with the period of rapid growth experienced by the formal Israeli lobby—AIPAC. As AIPAC's staff and resources expanded, it became more involved in sponsoring legislation and lobbying for various bills. During the same period, the formal Arab lobby was founded and first began to develop a legislative agenda, although on a far more limited scale than that of AIPAC.

The attitude of different presidents toward the policies preferred by the Israeli lobby has varied across administrations as the leadership model predicts. Table 9.3 presents the distribution of each president's position. Six of the eight administrations supported the lobby a majority of the time. Nixon and Carter *opposed* the lobby in 52 and 64 percent of the cases during their respective administrations. If the Kennedy administration—for which there are only eighteen cases—is excluded, then the other five administrations all support the lobby between 54 and 59 percent of the time.

Party Affiliation

The results in table 9.3 suggest that party identification makes little difference as to whether a president supports the lobby or

TABLE 9.3

Presidential Position by Administration President

	Supports Lobby (%)
Truman (1945–52)	54
Eisenhower (1953–60)	55
Kennedy (1961–63)*	67
Johnson (1964–68)	59
Nixon (1969–72)	48
Nixon-Ford (1973–76)	58
Carter (1977–80)	36
Reagan (1981–84)	54

* Includes one case decided after Kennedy's assassination.

not. Nevertheless, there are reasons to investigate the role of party identification more closely.

Since World War II, American Jews have been very involved in Democratic party politics. A majority of Jewish voters has consistently supported Democratic presidential candidates, raised substantial sums of money, and been active participants in Democratic campaigns. It is not unreasonable, therefore, to expect Democratic presidents to be more sympathetic to Israeli lobby concerns than Republicans, who have traditionally received very little support from the lobby's constituents. On the other hand, it may be that Democrats take the lobby for granted since they know that the generally liberal orientation of the Jewish community discourages it from supporting Republican candidates. In that case, Democrats might actually be less supportive.

From the Republican party's perspective, it may make a difference in the outcome of a presidential election whether the Republican loses the Jewish vote by three-to-one or three-to-two. In addition, many conservatives in the Republican party believe that support for Israel is in the national interest because it is an anticommunist, democratic bastion in a sea of militant Islamic autocracies; therefore, Republicans also have reasons to support the lobby.

Table 9.4 illustrates the distribution of cases by the president's party. Since Republicans have been in office for twelve of the sixteen most active years, it is not surprising that more than 60 percent of the cases occurred during Republican administrations. This table includes all cases, not just those for which the president's position was known.

Political Capital

If the president is the dominant actor in foreign policy decisions then his will should, in effect, be law. This is not always the case;

TABLE 9.4

Distribution of Cases by President's Party

	Percent
Party	
Republican	61
Democrat	39
Total Number of Cases	782

in fact, chapter 10 will show that the Israeli lobby is able to overcome the opposition of the president in more than one-fourth of the cases. The question arises as to why the president ever loses. Neither the leadership nor the realist models answer this question. The pluralist model, on the other hand, holds that domestic political forces enter the decision-making process and are able to affect the president's freedom of action.

Analysts of legislative behavior have suggested that presidential influence is constrained by the president's political capital. Political capital may be defined in different ways; for example, Neustadt thinks of it in terms of presidential prestige and style; presidential staff measure it by the number of votes a president can expect on any given issue; and Light calculates capital using a combination of electoral margin, presidential popularity, and seats in Congress held by members of the president's party.[6] As one Office of Management and Budget (OMB) official told Light:

> Each president enters office facing the same model—the horsepower is generally stable and the gears are all there. What differs is the *fuel*. Different Presidents enter with different fuel . . . Lyndon Johnson entered office with a full tank, while Ford entered on empty.[7]

Spiegel and Bunce assert, however, that a change in leadership, any change, will alter the domestic balance of power between the executive and legislative branches, suggesting that political capital is irrelevant.[8]

Light's measure appears to be the most useful because it provides some indication of public opinion and support for the president, as well as a means of estimating the expected support in Congress. The electoral margin may be somewhat redundant. The margin of victory is supposed to give an indication of whether a president has a mandate to govern, but the presidential popularity score should give an equally good approximation of the public's support for a president's program.[9]

Presidential Popularity

The greater the president's popular support, the more likely it is that his position should prevail. Congressmen are expected to be less willing to oppose a president if the public appears to support his policies. Page and Shapiro provide evidence that popular presidents are also able to increase favorable public opinion toward their policies.[10]

Zeidenstein has conducted two studies of presidential popularity that yielded contradictory results. In the first he found a strong relationship between popularity and presidential success, but nearly half of the strong correlations were inverse; that is, high presidential popularity was associated with *low* legislative success. In a second study, Zeidenstein altered his research design, using the Gallup measure of presidential popularity for the month immediately preceding the relevant vote, rather than the average popularity for the year. He concludes that popularity does not directly affect presidential leadership.[11]

It may be, as Light suggests, that it is not popularity per se that influences outcomes, but the maintenance of some threshold level of approval. He suggests 50 percent may be the level needed to avert the erosion of legislative support. As one Carter aide told Light: "Public opinion can't help you, but it sure as hell can hurt you."[12] Presidents, moreover, *believe* that public opinion matters. Eisenhower, for example was convinced that once he began his second term his influence would be determined by his popularity. "Strength," he said, "can be marshalled on both sides of the aisle only if it is generally believed that I am in a position to go to the people over their heads."[13]

If the president reaches some threshold level of political capital, then his position should prevail. Conversely, if the president's capital falls below that threshold, it may be possible for the Israeli lobby to overcome his opposition. For example, we have already seen how the lobby was able to persuade Congress to adopt the Jackson-Vanik amendment over the objections of Presidents Nixon and Ford. Both suffered from low public approval and faced large, hostile Democratic majorities in Congress.

Congressional composition turned out to have no effect, so I have only included the statistics on presidential popularity here as the measure of political capital. Popularity was coded according to the Gallup Poll surveys of presidential approval the month prior to the decision or vote. Table 9.5 shows the distribution of cases according to presidential popularity.

It may be that members of congress are not impressed by an

TABLE 9.5

Distribution of Cases According to Presidential Popularity

	Percent
Popularity Month Prior to Decision	
Under 50%	52
51–60%	21
61–70%	19
Over 70%	8
Total Number of Cases	754

approval rating of 50 percent. They may not feel the public is sufficiently enthusiastic about the president's policies to punish them for their opposition at such an approval rating; therefore, in addition to testing the effect of the 50 percent threshold, I have also included data for other popularity levels.

The table shows that a majority of the cases occur when the president's popularity is less than 50 percent, and that nearly three-quarters of the cases were decided when the president enjoyed the support of no more than 60 percent of the public. Since there are few instances where presidents have enjoyed the support of more than 70 percent of the public, it is not surprising that only 8 percent of the Middle East Policy Data Set (MEPDS) cases occur during those periods.

There were a few complications involved in the coding process. To code the monthly popularity variable it was necessary to determine the date of decision. In the case of executive decisions this was usually straightforward; however, in the legislative cases I had to choose between the dates of passage, introduction, and signing. In those cases where a bill did not come to a vote, I used the date of introduction. If a bill did come to a vote, I used the date of the Senate vote. This date was chosen because the Israeli lobby considers the Senate far more important than the House, and usually serves as a court of last resort for the lobby's battles. If no Senate vote was conducted, or the date was for some reason indeterminable, the date of the House vote (or introduction) was used.

A second complication arose when Gallup did not take surveys in particular months, or when a decision was reached in the first month of a first term so that no survey was conducted the month before. In the first instance, I ignored election polls, since they do not correspond to the approval surveys, and simply used the last available poll prior to the date of decision. The second problem was solved by using the January (or in rare instances February) poll.

The Electoral Cycle

In the introductory chapter, the informal component of the Israeli lobby was described. The high level of electoral participation of the lobby's members, it was argued, gives it disproportionate influence on the electoral process. Critics of the lobby consistently assert that candidates cater to the Jewish vote, and say that incumbents are reluctant to take any actions that are opposed by the lobby in an election year for fear of being punished on election day. By examining lobby success during election years, it should be possible to test the hypothesis that American Middle East policy is affected by the electoral cycle. The distribution of cases for this variable is presented in table 9.6.

Half the cases occur during non-election years while the other half are almost evenly split between on- and off-year elections.

Policy Type

In chapter 1, I argued that none of the prevailing models fully explain the foreign policy decision-making process. One reason is that the process is different depending on the locus of decision. Since the Israeli lobby has far greater access to the legislative than the executive branch, for example, it should be more successful in the former. Executive decisions are more isolated from

TABLE 9.6

Distribution of Cases According to the Electoral Cycle

	Percent
Election Cycle	
On-Year	25
Non-Election	50
Off-Year	24
Total Number of Cases	782

the pressures of domestic politics; moreover, because the president makes the final decision, his preference should always prevail. Table 9.7 shows the distribution of cases according to the locus of decision.

A majority of the cases were decided in the legislative branch where the lobby is expected to enjoy greater influence.

Policy Content

The locus of decision determines the process by which policy decisions are made, but the realists argue that policy content will also affect the outcome, even in the pluralistic environment of the Congress. Domestic politics, they contend, are ignored when the national interest is at stake; therefore, congressmen will be less likely to disagree with the president on matters of national security. Of course, the president will often try to frame an issue in terms of national security, but the Congress will usually be able to distinguish a security issue from another type that is not directly related to national security. Policy content should not affect outcomes at all if the leadership model is correct, since it is the president's position, regardless of the issue, that is believed to be important. Pluralists would probably agree with realists that security issues are less subject to domestic political pressure, but other policy types, economic issues in particular, would be expected to involve more political considerations.

By coding cases according to whether they involved economic, security, or political issues, using definitions adapted from Brecher et al., it is possible to examine whether there are any differences in the lobby's ability to reach its policy goals across policy types.[14] Security issues are all those which focus on questions pertaining to violence, including weapons sales, and those which are per-

TABLE 9.7

Distribution of Cases by Locus of Decision

	Percent
Locus of Decision	
Executive Branch	45
Legislative Branch	55
Total Number of Cases	782

ceived by decision-makers as posing a threat to national survival. Political issues (primarily UN decisions) involve matters of diplomacy and relations between the United States and foreign governments, but exclude cases dealing with material resources and violence. Economic issues involve the acquisition and allocation of resources (primarily foreign aid cases). The distribution of cases by policy content is found in table 9.8.

The distribution of cases is relatively even, although there are more security cases than economic or political cases. The 331 security cases should also provide an adequate sample to test the realist hypothesis.

The trichotomous coding scheme is not very specific; therefore, I wanted to get a better idea of the lobby's success on particular types of issues. The formal lobby has been primarily interested in foreign aid to Israel and has lobbied intensely on aid bills, so the lobby would be expected to do particularly well in those cases. On the other hand, the lobby would not be expected to succeed as often at the UN, where its interests have been consistently opposed and where it has virtually no access. A third type of issue that is of great concern to the lobby is arms sales. The lobby

TABLE 9.8

Distribution of Cases According to Policy Content

	Percent
Policy Content	
Economic	31
Political	26
Security	43
Total Number of Cases	774

TABLE 9.9

Distribution of Cases According to Specific Policy Content

	Percent
Specific Policy Content	
Aid	36
UN	15
Arms	24
War-Peace	26
Total Number of Cases	537

always supports arms sales to Israel but sometimes opposes similar sales to the Arabs. Finally, the issues that are probably most important to the lobby, because they affect Israel's survival, can be categorized as issues of war and peace (i.e., decisions made during or related to a war or peace negotiations).

Table 9.9 contains the data on the distribution of these content variables and shows that more than one-third of the cases involve foreign aid, roughly one-quarter are either arms sales or issues of war and peace, and only 15 percent are UN decisions.

Summary

1. Data were gathered on legislative and executive decision relating to American Middle East policy and used to construct the Middle East Policy Data Set which contains 782 valid cases.
2. The dependent variable in this study is whether the policy outcome is consistent with that desired by the Israeli lobby as expressed in its literature and testimony.
3. The president is expected to dominate foreign policy decision-making. If he supports the lobby, the lobby's interests should always prevail. The leadership and realist models hold that the president's position will also be adopted when he opposes the lobby. The pluralist model suggests that the lobby will overcome presidential opposition under certain circumstances.
4. The president supports the lobby in 52 percent of the cases.
5. The leadership model asserts that policy changes when the leaders change; therefore, lobby success should vary by administration.
6. Six of eight presidents support the lobby a majority of the time; Nixon and Carter opposed the lobby in 52 and 64 percent of the cases respectively.
7. The Israeli lobby's close association with the Democratic party implies the lobby should be more successful when a Democrat is in the White House. This occurs in 39 percent of the cases.
8. Lobby success should vary inversely with presidential popularity.
9. The lobby should be more successful in election years. Fifty percent of the cases occurred during non-election years, 25 percent in on-years, and 24 percent in off-years.

10. The lobby should win more of the cases decided in the legislative branch (55 percent) than those in the executive branch (45 percent).
11. The lobby will be relatively more successful on economic issues (31 percent) than political (26 percent) or security issues (43 percent).
12. Lobby success will also vary by policy content on specific issues of foreign aid (36 percent), UN resolutions (15 percent), arms sales (24 percent), and issues of war and peace (26 percent).

Given the distribution of the variables and their hypothesized effects, it remains to be seen what the actual relationship is between these variables and the success of the Israeli lobby. A description and analysis of that relationship follows in chapter 11.

Notes

1. Russell W. Howe and Sarah H. Trott, *The Power Peddlers* (NY: Doubleday, 1977), 272–3.
2. Holbert Carroll, *The House of Representatives and Foreign Affairs* (1966).
3. Ernst Haas, "The Balance of Power as a Guide to Policy-Making," *Journal of Politics* (August 1953), 393.
4. Lester M. Salamon and John J. Siegfried, "Economic Power and Political Influence: The Impact of Industry Structure on Public Policy," *American Political Science Review* (September 1977), 1034.
5. James March, "An Introduction to the Theory and Measurement of Influence," *American Political Science Review* (June 1955).
6. Richard Neustadt, *Presidential Power* (NY: John Wiley and Sons, 1980); Paul Light, *The Presidential Agenda* (MD: Johns Hopkins University Press, 1982).
7. Light, *The Presidential Agenda*, 14.
8. Steven L. Spiegel, *The Other Arab-Israeli Conflict* (IL: University of Chicago Press, 1985); Valerie Bunce, *Do New Leaders Make a Difference?* (NJ: Princeton University Press, 1981).
9. George Edwards III, *Presidential Influence in Congress* (CA: W.H. Freeman and Co., 1980), found little correlation between electoral margin and presidential success.
10. Benjamin Page and Robert Shapiro, "Presidents as Opinion Leaders: Some New Evidence," *Policy Studies Journal* (June 1984), 8–9.
11. Harvey G. Zeidenstein, "Varying Relationships between Presidents' Popularity and Their Legislative Success: A Futile Search for

Patterns," *Presidential Studies Quarterly* (Fall 1983) and "President's Popularity and Their Wins and Losses on Major Issues in Congress: Does One Have Greater Influence Over the Other?" *Presidential Studies Quarterly* (Spring 1985).

12. Light, *The Presidential Agenda*, 28–9.
13. John Rourke, *Congress and the Presidency in U.S. Foreign Policymaking* (CO: Westview Press, 1983), 118.
14. Michael Brecher, et al., "A Framework for Research in Foreign Policy Behavior," *Journal of Conflict Resolution* (March 1969).

10

Israeli Lobby Success and Its Determinants

In all that has been written about the Israeli lobby, no one has been able to say anything definitive about the degree of influence it exerts on American Middle East policy. Critics assert, without evidence, as those in the introduction did, that the lobby "controls" U.S. policy, whereas more serious investigators like Steven Spiegel have concluded that the lobby does not have much influence. The analysis of the Middle East Policy Data Set, however, allows us to say, at the very least, that the lobby "wins"; that is, the outcome coincides with its position, on a majority of cases. The lobby's overall success rate, as it will be referred to throughout this chapter, is 60 percent.

This initial finding suggests that Middle East policy is indeed pro-Israel most of the time. In fact, this result actually underestimates the degree of success the lobby enjoys because, as explained in chapter 9, there were a large number of cases (47 percent of the legislative cases) included that did not come to a vote, many of which were little more than proposals introduced to win a few political points with the lobby, without having a serious chance of being adopted. In the aggregate, then, the lobby is very successful, but this result alone does not prove the lobby's critics are correct when they say it "controls" foreign policy. It may be that the lobby is able to pile up a lot of victories on relatively insignificant issues, or that the lobby's interests simply coincide with those of the United States and, therefore, the lobby's real influence is marginal. The data below will examine these possibilities more closely.

The above finding alone is an advance over previous research, but the result tells us very little about the nature of lobby influence or the constraints on that influence. Although the lobby's rate of success does indicate that the pluralist model is useful in the analysis of foreign policy-making, it is necessary to examine a rank ordering of the different variables to isolate their relative impact on policy outcomes. This has been done by calculating the correlation ratios for the independent variables using Israeli lobby success as the dependent variable. The results appear in table 10.1.

Clearly, as the leadership model suggests, the president's position is the dominant factor in the determination of policy outcomes. If the lobby's success is simply a reflection of the fact that its position coincides with that of the president, then it cannot be said that the lobby has exerted influence, and support for the pluralist model will be undermined. On the other hand, if the lobby's success reflects its ability to have its policies adopted over the president's opposition, then we will have stronger evidence of lobby influence and hence undercut the leadership model.

The other variables, table 10.1 indicates, have negligible effects on lobby success. This is also an important result because it shows that variables such as the electoral cycle, the president's party, and the number of Democrats in Congress, which were expected to have an impact on lobby success, did not. Nevertheless, we

TABLE 10.1

Correlation Ratios for Independent Variables with Israeli Lobby Success as Dependent Variable

Variable	Eta	Eta-Squared
President's Position	.70	.49
Specific Policy Type	.46	.21
Monthly Popularity*	.37	.14
Average Annual Popularity*	.28	.08
Policy Type	.22	.05
Locus of Decision	.17	.03
Administration	.14	.02
House Democratic Composition**	.10	.01
Election Cycle	.08	.01
President's Party	.07	.01
Senate Democratic Composition**	.00	.00

* Interval Level Data.
** 60% Threshold of Democratic representation.

shall see that some of these variables do act as constraints on the lobby's ability to overcome presidential opposition to its desired policies.

Presidential Preferences

In the case studies, we saw how presidential support insured lobby success. When Ford decided to compromise with Senator Jackson, the Jackson-Vanik amendment was approved. In the antiboycott case, the change from the hostile Ford administration to the supportive Carter team led to easy approval of legislation sought by the lobby. In the executive cases, the president made the ultimate decision, so his approval guaranteed success except, perhaps, in the case of the UN partition decision. But even in that case, Truman's support made it very unlikely the lobby would lose. In each of the executive cases, top administration officials opposed various lobby initiatives, but their opposition could never overcome the president's support. These cases implied that the leadership model was correct in asserting that the president's position is the most important determinant of policy outcomes and this is confirmed by the data.

In those cases where the president's position is known (N = 612), the lobby's winning percentage is actually better than for the whole universe of cases—62 percent. Table 10.2 illustrates that the lobby's ability to reach its objective is primarily dependent on whether the president supports its position. When the president *supports* the lobby's position (N = 315), as he does in more than half the cases, the lobby wins almost every time (95 percent). As the most influential lobbyist on foreign policy, it is not surprising that the president's views would dominate the decision-making process.

TABLE 10.2

The Relationship between Presidential Preference and Lobby Success

	Lobby Wins (%)
President's Position	
For	95
Against	27
Number of Cases	612

If the president agrees with the lobby, and the result is favorable, it is difficult to demonstrate that the lobby has exerted any influence. In other words, the president may have arrived at a position consistent with the lobby's, independent of any lobby influence. In the Jackson-Vanik and antiboycott cases, for example, it was shown that Congress was prepared to pass legislation supported by the lobby despite presidential opposition.

The best evidence of lobby influence on policy are those cases where it succeeds despite the opposition of the president. When the president's position *conflicts* with that of the lobby (N = 297), the lobby wins 27 percent of the time. This suggests that the lobby does have influence and that the president is not the sole arbiter of foreign policy. That brings us to the question of what enables the lobby to overcome presidential opposition.

Partisanship and Lobby Success

In the preceding chapters, the process by which the lobby attempts to influence the president, directly through lobbying, and, indirectly, by virtue of its members' involvement in the electoral process, was described. The likelihood a president will support or oppose the lobby may also depend, however, on other domestic variables such as political capital, policy content, and decision arena. It was suggested in chapter 9, for example, that differences in the degree of support the two parties receive from the Israeli lobby's constituents may affect a president's policy preferences.

The results from the case studies were mixed. In the Jackson-Vanik case, Richard Nixon and Gerald Ford were both Republicans, yet Ford compromised and accepted the lobby position. A Republican and a Democrat—Ronald Reagan and Jimmy Carter—both proposed arms sales to Saudi Arabia that were strongly opposed by the lobby. In the executive cases, three different Democratic presidents took various stands, which sometimes supported the lobby and at other times opposed it. Thus, no clear pattern of partisan support for the lobby was evident.

The data in table 10.3 indicate there is a difference in the level of support presidents from different parties give to the lobby. The lobby receives greater support from Republican presidents than Democrats. While Republicans support the lobby more than half

TABLE 10.3

Distribution of Cases by President's Preference and Party

	Number of Cases	President Supports Lobby (%)
President's Party		
Republican	370	54
Democrat	242	48

TABLE 10.4

The Relationship between Lobby Success, the President's Position, and Presidential Partisanship

	Number of Cases President Opposes Lobby	Lobby Wins (%)
President's Party		
Republican	170	28
Democrat	127	26

the time, Democrats actually oppose the lobby in a majority of cases. This finding suggests the lobby's consistent support for Democratic presidential candidates has not been rewarded with support for its positions, and that Democrats may indeed take the "Jewish vote" for granted.

Although Republican candidates have an incentive to reduce the margin of the Jewish vote carried by the Democrats, the lobby still does not play a major role in Republican politics; therefore, the fact that Republican presidents supported the lobby 54 percent of the time reflects more of an identity of interests (for example, stopping the spread of communism) than a willingness to give in to Israeli lobby pressure. Similarly, Democratic presidents appear to be able to resist lobby pressure in most cases.

On the other hand, table 10.4 shows the lobby's success rate under presidents from different parties is almost identical. Since the lobby wins more than 90 percent of the cases when the president supports its position, regardless of his partisan identification, table 10.4 (and those that follow) contains only those cases where the president opposes the lobby.

The finding that the lobby does slightly better with a Republican president might be explained by the claim of Michael Gale, who held the "Jewish portfolio" for a time under Ronald Reagan.

According to Gale, Republican presidents are more sensitive to the concerns of the Israeli lobby, because they lack close ties with its leaders, whereas the Democrats tend to take the lobby for granted since they have had long associations with these leaders.[1] The difference in success rates is so small, however, that it is safer to conclude that the leadership model, which emphasizes individual characteristics such as personality and ideology over party distinctions, provides a better explanation for the result.

Presidential Popularity

The lobby is expected to be more successful when presidents are unpopular; we might also anticipate that unpopular presidents are less likely to risk incurring the lobby's wrath by opposing its positions. An unpopular president might also consider support for the lobby as a means of attracting greater support. On the other hand, popular presidents may feel that they are politically strong enough to take on the lobby.

In the Jackson-Vanik case, the Israeli lobby overcame the opposition of Gerald Ford, whose popularity the month before the decision was less than 50 percent. In the antiboycott case, Congress passed the legislation over Ford's objection when the president's popularity was again below 50 percent. The two arms sales were exceptions, as the lobby lost both votes despite the fact that Carter's popularity was under 50 percent and Reagan's below 60. This does not contradict the data above; however, because, at best, the lobby is only expected to win a little over one-fourth of the cases when the president opposes its position. In the executive cases, Truman was particularly supportive of the lobby in 1948, after his popularity had plunged below 50 percent. Similarly, Johnson relented and agreed to sell Israel Phantoms when his popularity was below 40 percent. Carter also was constrained in his negotiations with Israel and Egypt by the fact that his popularity was below 50 percent.

Table 10.5 provides the distribution of presidential support for the lobby according to presidential popularity. Presidents with over 60 percent approval are more supportive of the lobby. But when approval exceeds 50 percent, presidents support the lobby, on average, only 52 percent of the time, compared to 54 percent

TABLE 10.5

Distribution of Cases by President's Preference and Popularity

	Number of Cases	President Supports Lobby (%)
President's Popularity the Month Prior to Decision		
Under 50%	302	54
51–60%	116	44
61–70%	117	55
Over 70%	51	57

TABLE 10.6

The Relationship between Lobby Success, the President's Position, and Presidential Popularity

	Number of Cases President Opposes Lobby	Lobby Wins (%)
President's Popularity the Month Prior to Decision		
Under 50%	138	32
51–60%	65	29
61–70%	53	17
Over 70%	22	23

when approval is under 50 percent. Thus, presidents support the lobby more when they are relatively unpopular.

The lobby's capacity to overcome presidential opposition is affected rather dramatically by presidential popularity. If the lobby success rate in table 10.6 is averaged for the levels above 60 percent, then we can see that, as expected, there *is* a steep drop in lobby success as presidential popularity increases. When presidential popularity is below 50 percent, the lobby is able to overcome their opposition in 32 percent of the cases, but when presidential popularity is between 50 and 60 percent the lobby's success rate drops to 29 percent, and when presidential popularity exceeds 60 percent the lobby wins only 20 percent of the time.

Lobby Success and the Electoral Cycle

Critics of the Israeli lobby frequently charge that presidential candidates pander to Jewish voters, and an examination of campaign rhetoric and platforms would seem to confirm these allegations; nevertheless, it is important to distinguish rhetoric from action. In the case studies, it appeared that Truman's decisions regarding Palestine/Israel were influenced by the 1948 election, Johnson's willingness to sell Israel Phantoms was affected by the 1968 election, the presidents' willingness to support the Jackson-Vanik and antiboycott legislation was influenced by the 1974 and 1976 elections, and Carter's hesitancy to oppose the lobby on various aspects of the peace negotiations was a product of his concerns about the 1980 election.

Is it true that presidents are more likely to support the lobby in election years to attract a larger proportion of the pro-Israel vote? The data presented in table 10.7 would suggest that this proposition is not correct, at least not for on-year elections.

Presidents not only fail to support the lobby in on-years, they oppose it in a relatively large number of cases—59 percent. This result might be explained in combination with the findings for the other two points in the electoral cycle; that is, presidents know that their actions in a particular year will not determine the lobby's attitude toward their policies, because the lobby will consider the president's policies over the course of his entire term and evaluate the incumbent accordingly. The president's tendency to support the lobby in off-years might be explained by his desire, as the nominal head of his party, to help congressional candidates who are more likely to be affected by the informal Israeli lobby because of the relative size of their constituencies.

There is no statistically significant difference in the lobby's success rate across the electoral cycle when the president's position is controlled for, as can be seen in table 10.8. To the extent that there is a relationship, it is contrary to the conventional

TABLE 10.7

Distribution of Cases by President's Preference and the Electoral Cycle

	Number of Cases	President Supports Lobby (%)
Point In Election Cycle		
On-Year	159	41
Non-Election	303	55
Off-Year	150	55

TABLE 10.8

The Relationship between the Electoral Cycle, the President's Position and Lobby Success

	Number of Cases President Opposes Lobby	Lobby Wins (%)
Point In Election Cycle		
On-Year	94	29
Non-Election	136	24
Off-Year	67	33

wisdom; that is, presidents are *not* more likely to give in to the lobby during on-years, nor is Congress more likely to take the lobby's side against the president.

It would appear that elections do not have a very important impact on the lobby's success. It is more likely, as suggested in the previous chapter, that this is not a meaningful variable in the sense that the informal Israeli lobby exerts influence throughout the election cycle; because the lobby has a notoriously long memory, the lobby will punish or reward politicians regardless of when the decision is made. A good example is the case of the AWACS decision, which was made in 1981, a non-election year. Subsequently, the lobby targeted senators who supported that sale and thereby served notice that future transgressions would be politically costly. If this notion of a lobby memory is accurate, there should not be any difference in lobby success across the election cycle. If the non-presidential years are averaged, then there is no difference in lobby success. The data make it clear, however, that the impact of presidential elections on the case studies was overstated.

Lobby Success and the Locus of Decision

The pluralist model suggests that there will be a difference in the degree of lobby success depending on where the final policy decision is made. Due to the relative isolation of the White House and the broader constituency of the president, the lobby is expected to have less success on executive decisions; that is, those made in the executive branch which do not require congressional involvement, than on legislative decisions where the full force of lobby influence, direct and indirect, can be exerted. On the other hand, if the leadership model is correct, then the lobby's success in the legislative branch should be closely related to the president's position and its ability to overcome the president's opposition should be no greater there than in the executive branch. This would also support the realist model since the president's view of the national interest should carry equal weight in either branch.

The results in table 10.9 conform to expectations. The president is indeed far more likely to support the Israeli lobby's position if the decision is made in the Congress, than if it is made at the White House. When the president opposes the lobby, there is also a great disparity in the lobby's success rate across policy arenas as illustrated by table 10.10.

There is a strong association between the president's position and the policy arena. As expected, the lobby does poorly when the decision is reached in the executive branch. Of the 186 cases in which the president opposes its position, the lobby wins only 11 percent. In the legislative branch, however, the lobby actually wins a majority (55 percent) of the 111 cases *despite* the president's opposition. Twelve cases, or 15 percent of the total (20 percent of the legislative cases) the lobby "won" over the president's

TABLE 10.9

Distribution of Cases by President's Position and Locus of Decision

	President Supports Lobby (%)
Locus of Decision	
Executive Branch	47
Legislative Branch	57
Total Number of Cases	612

TABLE 10.10

The Relationship between the President's Position, the Locus of Decision and Lobby Success

	Number of Cases President Opposes Lobby	Lobby Wins (%)
Locus of Decision		
Executive Branch	186	11
Legislative Branch	111	55

opposition, were letters signed by a majority of the Senate (a majority of the House also signed three of the letters).

Thus, we can see that the lobby is able to exert a significant degree of influence on legislative decisions, thereby providing evidence to support the pluralist model. This is an important result because most studies of foreign policy do not devote a great deal of attention to policy emanating from Congress and, as table 9.7 in chapter 9 illustrated, more than half (55 percent) of all Middle East cases are actually decided within the legislative branch. Even if one wants to argue that decisions reached in the executive branch are in some respects more important, it is impossible to discount over 400 instances where policy is either made, suggested, or ratified in Congress.

Although it is an imperfect measure, some indication of a legislative policy's importance may be gleaned from the distinction of whether it came to a vote or not. As noted earlier, by including cases that did not come to a vote, relatively insignificant policies were included which minimized the overall influence of the lobby, since many of those non-voting cases involve pro-lobby legislation that is introduced primarily to obtain the lobby's attention and favor for the sponsor. Although those cases are coded as losses, the very fact that they were introduced is an indication of the lobby's influence. When a policy does come to a vote, the lobby is extremely successful, winning well over 90 percent of all roll call votes, with the average vote for the lobby's position in the House being 260 and the average Senate vote 61.

Lobby Success and Policy Content

The political process is expected to vary, not only according to the locus of decision, but also by the policy content. The realists argue, for example, that domestic politics are ignored when the national interest is at stake and that Congress is less likely to challenge the president on security-related issues. The leadership model does not allow for distinctions across policy types, therefore, there should not be any difference in lobby success. Pluralists, like realists, would expect to find variation, with those policy types that most directly affect the interest groups' constituents being more subject to their influence than policies that are more remote.

The data in table 10.11 indicate that presidents are more likely to oppose the lobby on security issues than on the other two types. This is consistent with the realist position that the president would be more willing to oppose the lobby on a security matter. Support for the lobby's position on political issues is split evenly, which suggests that the president's position on diplomatic issues is also relatively immune to lobby influence. The president does support the lobby's position in a large majority (61 percent) of economic cases, however, which is not surprising since presidents have, with only a few exceptions, supported aid to Israel and the Arab states. Disagreements between the lobby and the president have occurred occasionally when the lobby has opposed a particular allocation to an Arab state (e.g., Syria in the late 1970s), or in those cases where the Congress has increased the level of aid for Israel above that recommended by the president.

In those cases where the president does oppose the lobby's position, shown in table 10.12, there is a wide variation in the lobby's rate of success, from 54 percent on economic issues to

TABLE 10.11

Distribution of Cases by President's Position and Policy Content

	Number of Cases	President Supports Lobby (%)
Policy Content		
Economic	182	61
Political	141	50
Security	282	46

TABLE 10.12

The Relationship between the President's Position, Policy Content, and Lobby Success

	Number of Cases President Opposes Lobby	Lobby Wins (%)
Policy Content		
Economic	71	54
Political	70	13
Security	152	22

only 13 percent on political issues. Since most economic decisions are made by Congress, the lobby would be expected to be more successful on these issues than on the others. In addition, the lobby has been generally regarded as successful in persuading Congress to increase foreign aid levels to Israel, earmark funds for Israel, and adopt amendments to aid bills that are supported by the Israeli lobby. The vast majority (78 percent) of cases in this category are related to foreign aid. For example, the anti-boycott case study in chapter 4 describes how Congress consistently adopted amendments to the aid bill expressing opposition to the discriminatory practices of the Arab states. Congress did, however, tend to compromise on "anti-Arab" proposals that threatened presidential flexibility, while taking a more confrontational approach on measures directly benefitting Israel. This contradicts the earlier finding of Carroll who asserted that interest groups do not have influence over aid decisions, but is consistent with the conclusions of Irish and Frank and Feuerwerger.[2]

Perhaps a more surprising result was that the lobby was so unsuccessful on political issues. This might be explained, however, by the fact that the majority of the political cases were decided in the executive branch, where the lobby does not have much influence. Moreover, more than a third of these cases were UN decisions, which are even less subject to lobby influence, and which went against the lobby 71 percent of the time regardless of the president's position. Another possible reason for the lobby's poor performance on political issues is the tradition of deference which suggests that Congress will usually respect the president's wishes on matters of diplomacy and not seek to conduct an independent foreign policy.

As noted in the introduction, the realist perspective holds that foreign policy is made on the basis of geostrategic interests, but it is apparent a whole range of issues are not directly related to those concerns. Table 9.8 in chapter 9 showed that security issues comprise only 43 percent of the total cases; nevertheless, this category still reflects the largest percentage of the three types: economic cases make up 31 percent and political cases 26 percent of the total cases. The realist would not expect the lobby to overcome the president's opposition on any matters of national security; yet, the Israeli lobby does just that in 22 percent of the

cases. It does appear, however, that the lobby's ability to overcome presidential opposition is primarily restricted to economic
issues.

Lobby Success and Specific Policies

Given the differences in lobby success across policy types, it is
useful to look at another typology, breaking policy content into
categories reflecting the most important (from the lobby's point
of view) types of cases. More than two-thirds of the cases fall
into the four categories listed in table 10.13.

The president's willingness to support the lobby on particular
types of issues is illustrated in table 10.13. The president supports
the lobby in two-thirds of the foreign aid cases and just under
two-thirds of the issues related to war and peace. By contrast,
the president opposes the lobby on more than 70 percent of both
UN and arms sales decisions. Some of the arms sales decisions
involve requests by Israel for arms and others are administration
proposals to sell weapons to Arab states that are opposed by the
lobby. In both instances, the president argues that the sales involve matters of national security, and places realist concerns
above domestic political pressures.

The lack of support on UN decisions may come as a surprise,
given the fact that the United States is Israel's only consistent
supporter at the United Nations; but the data indicate the president, and therefore the United States, has opposed the Israeli
lobby's preferred position at the UN most of the time (72 percent).

Table 10.14 indicates that if economic cases involving foreign
aid are isolated, the lobby wins 82 percent of the time, even if

TABLE 10.13

Distribution of Cases by President's Position and Specific Policy Content

	Number of Cases	President Supports Lobby (%)
Specific Policy Content		
Aid	136	67
UN	79	28
Arms	119	27
War-Peace	133	62

TABLE 10.14

The Relationship between the President's Position, Specific Policy Content, and Lobby Success

	Number of Cases President Opposes Lobby	Lobby Wins (%)
Specific Policy Content		
Aid	45	82
UN	57	4
Arms	87	28
War-Peace	51	8

the president opposes it. This again fits the pluralist model and the general finding that interest groups are particularly successful in obtaining their objectives on issues that most directly affect their self-interest; that is, economic issues. It is interesting to note, however, that aid for Israel is more indirect than in the usual cases where interest group members derive financial gains from the outcome. The Israeli lobby's members only receive what economists refer to as "psychic income" from the knowledge that Israel's economic and military aid needs are being met. According to Olson, people will only join interest groups if they receive selective benefits, but this result supports the broader interpretation of group benefits suggested by Moe, whereby people, such as members of the Israeli lobby, will join an interest group because of what he calls "purposive incentives"; that is, intangible costs and benefits that are based on suprapersonal values.[3]

As noted in the previous section, the lobby does not do well on cases classified as political, and most of those are UN decisions. Overall, the lobby wins only 29 percent of these cases and can overcome presidential opposition only rarely (4 percent). This result is less a reflection of lobby impotence on American policy than it is an indication of the lack of influence of the United States at the UN. Since cases were coded as defeats if the lobby did not reach its objective; that is, a favorable vote at the UN, many of the lobby's defeats might be claimed to be a function of the large anti-Israel majority that dominates the UN. To minimize this effect, only Security Council votes were included (with two exceptions cited in chapter 9), so the United States could have insured lobby success in many instances by vetoing resolutions.

But it usually chose not to; therefore, the lobby was relatively less influential in those cases.

Table 10.14 also isolates arms sales decisions. The lobby loses more than half of all the arms sales decisions (55 percent), and only is able to overcome presidential opposition in 28 percent of the cases. There is a distinction, however, between the lobby's success on arms sales to the Arab states and those to Israel, as illustrated in table 10.15. Of the 126 arms sales cases, a little more than half (53 percent) involve sales to Israel. In those cases, the lobby actually is successful 57 percent of the time, whereas it loses more than two-thirds of the cases involving sales to the Arab states.

Presidents are much more likely to oppose the lobby on sales to the Arabs than to Israel (88 percent to 62 percent). Nevertheless, the large percentage of cases in each instance suggests that presidents are more than willing to take on the lobby when it comes to arms sales; that is, a specific type of security issue. This result is consistent with the realist model and the case studies of the Phantom sale to Israel discussed in chapter 7, and the two sales to Saudi Arabia analyzed in chapter 2. In addition, table 10.16 shows that there is no difference in the lobby's ability to overcome presidential opposition to sales to either Israel or the Arabs.

TABLE 10.15

Lobby Success and Arms Sales to Israel and the Arab States

	Number of Cases	Lobby Wins (%)
Arms Sale To:		
Arab States	59	32
Israel	67	57

TABLE 10.16

The Relationship between the President's Position, Arms Sales, and Lobby Success

	Number of Cases President Opposes Lobby	Lobby Wins (%)
Arms Sale To:		
Arab States	52	27
Israel	37	27

On issues of war and peace the lobby does surprisingly well, considering the perception among many in the lobby that the United States has not been very supportive of Israel during its wars or in formulating peace proposals, and the fact that the vast majority of these cases are decided within the executive branch. The lobby has actually won 61 percent of the time, although it has fared considerably worse when opposed by the president, winning only 8 percent. In these cases it is difficult to determine whether presidential support was a result of lobby pressure or a perception that U.S. and lobby interests were consistent. The Camp David case study in chapter 8 provides evidence, however, that lobby pressure can indeed influence American policy on matters of peace.

Lobby Success and the Chief Executive

The leadership model holds that it is the idiosyncrasies of the individual and those around him that determine whether decisions will be favorable to the lobby. The data above suggest that other factors play a role, but it is also possible to identify differences across administrations that support the model.

Table 10.17 shows that the lobby won more than half the cases during each administration (for cases where the president's position was known). The lowest level of support was during the Carter administration, which does not come as a surprise given his sympathy for the Palestinian cause, willingness to speak to the PLO, and frequent criticism of Israel. In table 9.3 of chapter 9, we saw that Carter opposed the lobby significantly more often

TABLE 10.17

The Relationship between Lobby Success and Administration

	Number of Cases	Lobby Wins (%)
Truman	41	59
Eisenhower	64	61
Kennedy	18	72
Johnson	68	60
Nixon	83	57
Nixon-Ford	111	69
Carter	116	55
Reagan	111	68

284 The Water's Edge and Beyond

than any other president (64 percent). On the other hand, he did support the antiboycott bill (see chapter 4) and played an important role in the negotiation of the Israeli-Egyptian Peace Treaty (chapter 8), so the lobby would still be expected to have had success during his term.

Besides Carter, the other president who has not generally been thought of as being particularly pro-Israel was Eisenhower, but table 10.18 indicates the lobby won 61 percent of the cases during his two terms. One of the reasons for this somewhat surprising result is that more than one-fourth of the cases during his administration involved foreign aid. The Israeli lobby supported the annual aid bills, but the level of aid during this period was low compared to the amounts provided to Israel after 1973. Of course, the lobby did not seek large amounts of aid at this time either; nevertheless, the large number of aid bills tend to distort the overall success rate. Since the cases are not distinguished by their relative importance, moreover, it is impossible to factor in the impact of Eisenhower's opposition to the lobby on probably the most important issue of the 1950s—Israel's Sinai campaign. The lobby also failed to obtain support for direct U.S. arms sales to Israel, but did succeed in obtaining the approval for third party sales. This is not to say the finding has no meaning, however, since the lobby was still successful on a wide variety of issues affecting American Middle East policy.

The lobby enjoyed its greatest success under the Nixon-Ford administrations of 1972–76 (Kennedy is excluded because of the small number of cases). This is not surprising given the large number of aid bills (41—exceeded only by the 49 during Carter's term) and issues related to war and peace. In the latter cases, the lobby did well because a number of them involved decisions the United States made to support Israel in the 1973 war and in the subsequent armistice negotiations. As noted above, it was after the 1973 war that aid to Israel began to increase significantly so the lobby was particularly successful; moreover, there were a large number of favorable amendments to those bills. Another factor was the change in the relationship between Congress and the White House as the former became more assertive in exercising its prerogatives to shape foreign policy.

Lobby Influence by Administration

Evidence for both the leadership and pluralism models can be obtained by examining the variation in the lobby's ability to overcome presidential opposition by administration. The data presented in table 10.18 again provides evidence for the pluralist model, because the lobby is able to overcome presidential opposition anywhere from 11 to 34 percent of the time. The variation also supports the leadership model, since there do appear to be differences across administrations although they are, with the exception of Truman and Eisenhower, relatively small.

The lobby was least successful in overcoming the opposition of Truman. This is largely attributable to the UN decisions that were made—particularly relating to cease-fires during 1948—that the lobby had little or no opportunity to overcome. In fact, more than two-thirds of the policy decisions during Truman's term were made in the executive branch, by far the most of any administration; consequently, the result is more easily understood.

The lobby's inability to overcome Eisenhower's opposition comes as no surprise, given his popularity and the fact that he had a Republican majority in Congress for part of his term. In addition, nearly 60 percent of the cases were decided in the executive branch.

By contrast, the Israeli lobby has succeeded in overcoming the opposition of the last three administrations in nearly a third of the cases. This may be partly a result of the fact that a majority of the cases during each of those terms were decided in the leg-

TABLE 10.18

The Relationship between Administration Position and Lobby Success

	Number of Cases President Opposes Lobby	Lobby Wins (%)
Truman	19	11
Eisenhower	29	17
Kennedy	6	33
Johnson	28	21
Nixon	43	23
Nixon-Ford	47	34
Carter	74	31
Reagan	51	33

islative branch and, in the case of the Nixon-Ford administration, they occurred during the period of congressional assertiveness.

Summary of Results

1. The Israeli lobby wins; that is, achieves its policy objective in 60 percent of the 782 total cases.
2. When the president supports the lobby, it wins 95 percent of the time.
3. When the president opposes the lobby, it still wins 27 percent of the cases.
4. Republican presidents support the lobby in 54 percent of the cases compared to 48 percent for Democrats, but there is no difference in lobby success when presidents of either party oppose the lobby's position.
5. Unpopular presidents support the lobby more than popular ones and the lobby is far less successful in overcoming the president's opposition as presidential popularity increases.
6. The president's position is not significantly affected by the electoral cycle, but presidents do oppose the lobby more often in on-years. The electoral cycle does not affect lobby success.
7. Presidents are more likely to support the lobby when the locus of decision is Congress (57 percent) rather than the White House (47 percent). The lobby also overcomes presidential opposition in Congress far more than it does in the executive branch (55 percent to 11 percent).
8. The lobby wins more than 90 percent of roll call votes, receiving an average of 260 votes in the House and 61 in the Senate.
9. Presidents are very supportive on economic issues (61 percent), but *oppose* the lobby on security issues 54 percent of the time, and split their preferences evenly on political issues. Lobby success also varies by policy content. The lobby is very successful in overcoming presidential opposition on economic issues (54 percent), but rarely is able to defeat the president on security (22 percent) and political issues (13 percent).
10. If policy content is broken down into more specific types, the president supports the lobby 67 percent of the time on aid decisions, 28 percent on UN issues, 27 percent on arms sales, and 62 percent on the issues involving war and peace. The lobby is very successful in overcoming presidential opposition

on aid cases (82 percent), less so on arms cases (28 percent), and rarely successful in doing so on UN (4 percent) or war and peace cases (8 percent).

11. More than half (53 percent) of the arms sales cases involve Israel and the lobby wins 57 percent of those, but it *loses* 68 percent of the arms sales cases involving Arab states. Although the president is more likely to oppose the lobby's position on arms sales to the Arabs (88 percent to 62 percent), there is no difference in the lobby's ability to overcome presidential opposition to its position on either type of sale.

12. Lobby success varies by administration, from 55 percent during the Carter administration, to 69 percent during the Nixon-Ford years (72 percent during the comparatively short Kennedy term). The lobby was particularly unsuccessful in overcoming the opposition of Truman (11 percent) and Eisenhower (17 percent), but did manage to win more than 30 percent of the cases in which Kennedy, Nixon-Ford, Carter, and Reagan opposed its position.

Notes

1. Wolf Blitzer, *Between Washington and Jerusalem* (NY: Oxford University Press, 1985), 158.
2. Holbert Carroll, *The House of Representatives and Foreign Affairs* (1966), 125–7; Marian Irish and Elke Frank, *U.S. Foreign Policy* (NY: Harcourt, Brace Janovich, Inc., 1975), 156–7; Marvin Feuerwerger, *Congress and Israel* (CT: Greenwood Press, 1979), 170.
3. Mancur Olson, *The Logic of Collective Action* (MA: Harvard University Press, 1975); Terry Moe, "A Calculus of Group Membership," *American Journal of Political Science* (January, 1980).

11

Conclusion

This study began with a series of quotes from critics of the Israeli lobby who asserted that the lobby essentially controls American Middle East policy, and I have attempted to evaluate the validity of these claims. After examining six case studies and testing a series of hypotheses on the Middle East Policy Data Set, it is now possible to state a few conclusions.

At the most general level it is possible to conclude that, while the lobby may not "control" U.S. policy, it does play a significant role in shaping it by stimulating pro-Israel initiatives that would otherwise not be considered, insuring the adoption of executive and legislative proposals that are perceived to be pro-Israel, and constraining the behavior of foreign policy officials, so that policies seen as hostile to the lobby's interests are either defeated, modified, or prevented from being seriously considered. More specifically, it is possible to discern differences in lobby influence depending on the locus of decision.

The Legislative Branch

Foreign policy studies have generally neglected decisions made in the legislative branch, so the four cases examined in part I provided a much needed insight into an important arena of foreign policy decision-making. In each case, the president argued that his position represented the national interest, but the Israeli lobby and its supporters usually maintained that a different national interest was at stake in each particular case. Even with the disagreements, however, Congress was expected to defer to the president's judgment in matters of national security. In chapter 2, for example, opponents questioned whether the arms sales to Saudi Arabia would serve national security by threatening Israel and placing American technology at risk; nevertheless, the issue was generally acknowledged to involve national security, so it was not surprising that the lobby was unable to overcome the president's opposition to its position.

The Jackson-Vanik and antiboycott cases were different, however, since they involved economic and political interests instead of security interests. The presidents opposed each on the grounds of national security, arguing in the Jackson-Vanik case that detente, and hence world peace, would be threatened by the amendment's passage and, in the antiboycott case, that U.S.-Arab relations and oil supplies would be put at risk. Congress in each case saw "fundamental American principles" to be more clearly at stake, however, than national security. Values like freedom of emigration, trade, and religion were being supported by the two bills and were difficult for members of Congress to oppose. Given these differences in perception of the national interest, and the fact that these two cases were not defined as security issues, there was a greater probability that the president's position would be challenged and his opposition overcome.

Presidents are expected to dominate foreign policy decision-making, but the Jackson-Vanik and antiboycott amendments were adopted *despite* presidential opposition. The Israeli lobby's ability to overcome opposition supports the notion of interest group influence. The leadership model still has some explanatory value. For example, presidential support for the Israeli lobby's position, as occurred in the antiboycott case when Carter was elected, insured a lobby victory. The power of the president was also evident in the arms sales cases, particularly the AWACS case, where Reagan actively lobbied senators and succeeded in persuading the necessary number to switch their positions. These cases were more a result of the power of the institution of the presidency, however, than the individual leaders.

Changing leaders does not necessarily effect policy outcomes, as we saw in chapter 2. There, two presidents who could not have been more different in terms of their parties, ideologies, and foreign policy views maintained a consistent policy of selling arms to Saudi Arabia. In the Jackson-Vanik case, Gerald Ford had expressed support for tying emigration to trade in the past, but adopted Nixon's opposition to the amendment when he became president. The antiboycott case followed the leadership model, however, with the change in leaders from Ford to Carter bringing a change from opposition to support of the bill.

It is also possible to explain the arms sales proposals in terms of ideology; that is, Carter and Reagan arrived at a similar policy by different logic, which was based on their beliefs, but these ex post facto explanations do not allow for reliable predictions of policy outcomes. Ford's opposition to the Jackson-Vanik case can also be explained in terms of the leadership model, because the model suggests that it is not only the president, but his close advisers who determine foreign policy. In the case of the Jackson-Vanik amendment, the president changed, but the Secretary of State did not. In fact, Kissinger made foreign policy throughout Ford's term, so it would not be surprising that Kissinger's opposition would have been accepted by the new president as administration policy. On the other hand, as Senator Jackson said, Ford did bring new momentum to the negotiations, which ultimately resulted in a compromise.

The leadership model can be useful in explaining why presidents support or oppose the Israeli lobby and why there are changes in foreign policy proposals; however, it is not very helpful in predicting whether a president's desired policy will be adopted when it requires congressional approval and is opposed by the lobby. The pluralist model implied the Israeli lobby should influence legislative policies, since the lobby has a high degree of access and enjoys the advantage in the balance of lobbying power. This was in fact the case. The lobby's influence was demonstrated by its capacity to put the issues on the agenda: approval of the two arms sales would have been routine if not for the lobby's opposition, and the Jackson-Vanik and antiboycott amendments would never have been proposed by Congress if it were not for the presence of the lobby.

In the case of the arms sales, the Israeli lobby enjoyed an advantage in the balance of lobbying power, although the Arab lobby, particularly in the AWACS case, exerted a previously unheard of degree of pressure. Despite this advantage, the Israeli lobby still lost. This demonstrates what should have been obvious;

that is, lobby influence is limited. Even in this case, however, the lobby was able to demonstrate its power by forcing the presidents to make compromises opposed by the Saudis. Even then, the sales were barely able to win approval in the Senate.

The informal component of the Israeli lobby was also found to have only limited influence. In the arms sales cases, both presidents took positions that were clearly unpopular with the lobby's voters. The lobby did punish senators who voted for AWACS by actively trying to defeat them in the following election, and the F-15 sale was at least one reason for the desertion of Jewish voters from the Democratic party in 1980. The fact that majorities in the House opposed the sales also provided evidence that the informal lobby has influence. Although senators are relatively remote from the voters, and therefore less subject to that influence, the fact that near majorities (majorities of Democrats) in the Senate did vote against the sales suggests that senators are not totally immune to informal lobby pressure.

The Executive Cases

The United States has several conflicting interests in the Middle East. The choice of which interest to pursue is determined by the president when the locus of decision is the executive branch. In chapters 5 and 6, Truman repeatedly ignored the recommendations of his foreign policy advisers, who argued that support for partition and other Israeli lobby positions would undermine U.S.-Arab relations, threaten American oil supplies, and could lead the nation into war. Even the one security issue, the arms embargo, which was maintained over the lobby's objections, was decided less on the basis of national security than on Truman's beliefs. This was one of the few decisions that Truman made, however, that the lobby opposed but was unable to reverse. This supported the argument that the lobby has a more difficult time overcoming presidential opposition on security matters. Other issues, political ones, such as United States support for redrawing the partition map to exclude the Negev from the Jewish state, were more subject to lobby influence and were reversed or abandoned under pressure.

The realist model was more relevant to Lyndon Johnson's decisions regarding the sale of Phantom jets to Israel, since this was essentially a security issue. The president opposed the lobby, again backed by his advisers, and was able to withstand the pressure until the presidential election year. Changes in the international situation, however, reinforced the lobby's arguments and undermined those of Johnson's advisers; that is, it became clear U.S. security would be enhanced by arming Israel because the Soviets were arming the Arabs.

Jimmy Carter's pursuit of a comprehensive peace settlement in the Middle East was consistent with the national interest in regional stability. There was consensus on the objective, but not on the means of achieving it. Thus, chapter 8 illustrated how the lobby was able to prevent Carter from pursuing policies that appeared to threaten the U.S. commitment to Israel's security. Since the negotiations were more a political, than a security issue for the United States, the president was unable to overcome the lobby's opposition to initiatives it perceived as subverting that commitment.

Pluralist forces were influential in each of the cases in part II. Since the Israeli lobby has relatively little access to the executive branch, it would not be expected to have a great deal of influence on decisions made there; moreover, the Arab lobby, to the extent that it existed, was composed almost entirely of administration officials. Consequently, the balance of lobbying power within the White House was always in favor of the Arab lobby; yet, the Israeli lobby was successful in reaching its objectives on most of the decisions relating to Palestine, on the ultimate decision to sell Phantoms to Israel, and in limiting the scope of the negotiations and final agreement between Israel and Egypt.

One reason the lobby was successful was that it enjoyed the balance of lobbying power outside the White House, and served as a kind of constant background noise which the presidents had to confront. In the cases of Truman and Carter, the desire first, to prevent off-year debacles for Democratic candidates, and later on-year defeats for themselves, were strong incentives for taking positions supported by the lobby. Truman, for example, gave pro-Palestine (Israel) speeches right before the elections in 1946 and 1948 and, in the latter, silenced criticism for his policy by promising aid and de jure recognition to Israel. From the beginning of his term, Carter and his advisers were conscious of the political clock, and realized after failing to reach an agreement in the first year, that they would have less leverage over Israel because of the proximity of the elections. In 1979, with the presidential primary season on the horizon, Carter felt particularly anxious to reach some agreement, and was willing to abandon his vision of a broader agreement that would have contained elements opposed by the lobby.

The elections seemed to clearly affect Truman and Carter's decisions, yet they also pursued policies that were sure to generate enmity from the lobby. In Truman's case, it was his unwillingness to lift the embargo and, in Carter's, it was his persistent courting of the PLO, sale of F-15s to Saudi Arabia, and criticism of the Begin government. Of course, the lobby opposition to these policies might help explain why Truman was narrowly re-elected. It was certainly a factor in Carter's defeat, one in which there was widespread defection of Jewish voters from the Democratic party.

In the Phantom case, Johnson was under electoral pressure to make the sale, and several memorandums cited in chapter 7 made it clear the president's aides were concerned with the Jewish vote. After withdrawing from the race he might have been expected to be relieved of this pressure, but he was not, largely because his vice-president was running in his place and he wanted to support him. Not only did Hubert Humphrey support the sale, but so did Richard Nixon. Thus, the failure to approve the transfer would have reflected badly on the former and, when Nixon was elected, would have allowed the Republican to take all the credit for the proposal. It was therefore not surprising that Johnson agreed to the sale despite the opposition of his advisers.

The Israeli lobby, despite its relative lack of access, was able to maintain constant pressure on all three administrations. Members of the lobby paid numerous visits to the presidents and their advisers, so that there could be no doubt about the lobby's position or the probable consequences of opposing its interests. In addition, the lobby did have spokesmen—particularly in the Truman administration—within the White House to lobby on its behalf. Even in the Truman case, however, it is unlikely that the president would have chosen to follow the recommendations of his political advisers, over that of his Secretaries of State and Defense, if it were not for the lobby's informal component.

In addition, the lobby took advantage of the greater degree of access it enjoyed in Congress to indirectly pressure the administrations. In each case, individual congressmen pressured the presidents to support the lobby position, and warned of the electoral consequences for the presidents' party for failure to do so. Congress also supported the lobby by passing resolutions, usually by overwhelming margins, that called on the presidents to endorse the lobby's objectives. In chapter 5, Congress endorsed the establishment of a Jewish state; in chapter 7, Congress called for the sale of Phantom jets, and the president specifically cited this resolution in his announcement of the sale; and, in chapter 8, Congress passed a resolution stating support for a strong and secure Israel was a fundamental tenet of American policy. In each case, the lobby placed constraints on the presidents' freedom of action; hence, none could be understood without taking into account the pluralist dimension.

In addition, the presidents' ability to overcome lobby opposition was undermined by the deterioration of their political bases. In each case, the president became steadily less popular and could not afford to take positions that threatened to further erode their popularity. Although the decline in popularity was not directly attributable to their Middle East positions, none of the presidents could expect to reverse their slides by opposing the Israeli lobby. In addition, each president faced difficulties in Congress. Truman faced a hostile Republican majority in Congress, and even his own party looked upon him as a lame duck. Johnson and Carter both enjoyed majorities in Congress, but became increasingly unpopular within their own parties as their terms expired. As a result, none of the presidents could turn to Congress for support against the lobby.

In each presidential decision, the president followed the recommendation of the adviser(s) that was most compatible with his own beliefs. If the lobby's position was consistent with the president's views, then he was willing to accept it over the opposition of his advisers. In some cases, such as the Phantoms sale, the president's position changed as circumstances changed to fit more closely with the arguments of the lobby.

In chapters 5 and 6, Truman had no particular policy toward Palestine. His primary interests were in easing the suffering of the refugees, preventing war, and fulfilling past commitments. These interests were based on Truman's humanitarian concerns and his strong feelings about loyalty and honesty. Thus, Truman supported Jewish immigration as a way of helping the refugees, he acquiesced to the trusteeship proposal and embargo because of the prospect that both decisions would reduce the chance of bloodshed, and he supported partition and recognized Israel because the United States had promised to do so.

Johnson was also interested in preventing bloodshed, as well as maintaining a balance of forces in the Middle East without direct American involvement. After 1967, however, it became clear that U.S. policy would not prevent war and that the Soviets were not interested in limiting arms supplies to the region; moreover, the third parties the United States relied upon to supply Israel no longer were willing to do so. As a consequence, Johnson saw that the direct supply of weapons to Israel was now compatible with his beliefs. He still might have refused to sell Phantoms, however, if not for the lobby, whose arguments had become more compatible with Johnson's views.

The policies pursued by Carter were even more clearly related to his ideology, particularly his beliefs in global cooperation and the efficacy of face-to-face negotiations. His almost messianic desire to bring peace to the Middle East led him to try to bring about a comprehensive agreement, without adequately taking into account the obstacles to his design. He also was interested in bringing the PLO into the peace process, and pressuring Israel for territorial concessions on the West Bank, because of what he saw as the necessity to solve the "Palestinian problem" to assure peace. These efforts were opposed by the lobby, but consistent with his ideology, as was the final decision to convene a summit at Camp David after his effort to schedule an international meeting at Geneva failed. By bringing the antagonists together, Carter was sure an agreement could be reached. The lobby's positions were never fully compatible with the president's; therefore, he never accepted them, and was only willing to retreat from his own when forced to do so by lobby pressure in the context of the electoral cycle.

The Middle East Policy Data Set

If this study had followed the precedent of past investigations relying solely on case studies, it would be impossible to go much beyond the preceding level of generality; that is, to say the lobby has some influence some of the time. The development of the Middle East Policy Data Set, however, allows for a greater degree of specificity.

The case studies indicated that the Israeli lobby sometimes achieves its objective and other times fails. From 1945 to 1984, however, the Israeli lobby won; that is, achieved its policy objective in 60 percent of the 782 total cases. When the president supported the lobby, it won 95 percent of the time. The president's position was the most important determinant of lobby success, so it appears, at first glance, that the lobby was successful only because its objectives coincided with those of the president. The lobby's influence was demonstrated, however, by the fact that the lobby won 27 percent of the cases, even when the president opposed its position.

Since the primary constituents of the Israeli lobby, Jews, are predominantly involved in Democratic politics, it was expected that there would be some difference in lobby success depending on the president's party. The relationship was actually the opposite of that anticipated, with Republican presidents supporting the lobby in 54 percent of the cases compared to 48 percent for Democrats. This indicates the latter may take the "Jewish vote" for granted. There was no difference in lobby success, however, when presidents of either party opposed the lobby's position, so it appears that both parties are able to resist the lobby's pressure.

The lobby was expected to be more successful when presidents are unpopular. In addition, unpopular presidents were thought to be less likely to risk upsetting the lobby by taking contrary positions. Conversely, popular presidents were thought to be politically strong enough to challenge the lobby. As it turned out, unpopular presidents supported the lobby more often than popular ones. Moreover, as the case studies suggested, the lobby was far less successful in overcoming the president's opposition as presidential popularity increased.

One of the most surprising results, particularly in light of conventional wisdom and evidence presented in the case studies, was that the president's position was not significantly affected by the electoral cycle. Moreover, contrary to popular belief, presidents opposed the lobby more often in on-years. Although candidates may appear to pander to Jewish voters, the data indicate the electoral cycle does not affect lobby success.

The data show that the president is more likely to support the lobby when the locus of decision was Congress (57 percent), than the White House (47 percent). The lobby also overcame presidential opposition in Congress far more often than in the executive branch (55 percent to 11 percent). Of those legislative cases that came to a vote, the lobby was victorious more than 90 percent of the time, receiving an average of 260 votes in the House and 61 in the Senate. It is also important to note that 55 percent of the cases in the data set were decided in the legislative branch, which suggests that those foreign policy studies that neglect these policies are missing a significant part of the policy-making process. These results support the belief that interest groups do have influence, and that they are most able to exert that power in Congress where their access is greater.

The case studies provided evidence that there is a difference in lobby success depending on the policy content. This supported the realists who assert that domestic politics are ignored when the national interest is at stake, presented a challenge to the advocates of the leadership model who do not allow for distinctions across policy types, and also supported the pluralists who expect interest groups to have the most influence on policy types that most directly affect the groups' constituents.

The results showed that presidents are very supportive on economic issues (61 percent), but *oppose* the lobby on security issues 54 percent of the time, and split their preferences evenly on political issues. These results are consistent with the realist view that presidents will be more willing to oppose the lobby on security matters. The split on political issues provided evidence that the president's position on diplomatic issues is also relatively immune to lobby pressure. The tendency of presidents to support the lobby on economic issues was not surprising because, with only rare exceptions, they have favored foreign aid to Israel and the Arab states.

Lobby success also varied by policy content. The lobby was very successful in overcoming presidential opposition on economic issues (54 percent), but rarely was able to defeat the president on security (22 percent) and political issues (13 percent). The lobby was more successful on economic issues, because most of those were decided in Congress where pro-Israel congressmen frequently fought for increased aid levels for Israel, earmarked funds for Israel, and adopted amendments to aid bills that were endorsed by the Israeli lobby. The lobby's lack of success on political issues was more surprising; however, it was most likely a result of the fact that most of these cases were decided in the executive branch where lobby influence is relatively weak.

The result might also be explained by the tradition of congressional deference to the president on matters of diplomacy. The inability of the lobby to overcome presidential opposition on security issues, again reinforces the realist argument that domestic concerns are secondary to those of national security. The fact that the lobby does overcome presidential opposition on more than one-fifth of the security cases does, however, illustrate that the lobby *is* capable of exerting some influence on security issues.

If policy content is broken down into more specific types, the president supported the lobby 67 percent of the time on aid decisions, which is consistent with the argument presented above that aid is popular with presidents. A more surprising result was that the president supported the lobby only 28 percent of the time on UN issues. This will come as a particular shock to those who believe that the United States has been Israel's protector at the United Nations. It may also come as a surprise to those who believe that the United States has been Israel's protector outside the UN, that the president opposed the lobby on 27 percent of the arms sales cases, although 47 percent of those cases involved sales to Arab states. On issues involving war and peace, presidents were more supportive of the lobby, taking a favorable stand 62 percent of the time.

The lobby was very successful in overcoming presidential opposition on aid cases (82 percent); again, largely because they were decided in the Congress. This is consistent with the conventional wisdom that interest groups are most successful in obtaining their objectives on issues that most directly affect their self-interest; that is, economic issues. In this case, the effect was less direct than in most, because the lobby's interest was in obtaining "psychic income" from the knowledge that Israel's economic and security needs were being met.

The lobby had considerably less success, however, on arms (28 percent), UN (4 percent), or war and peace cases (8 percent). The lobby's apparent lack of success on arms sales is actually deceiving, since it was very successful, winning 57 percent, on sales to Israel. The lobby was rarely able to prevent sales to the Arab states, however, losing 68 percent of the time. Although the president was more likely to oppose the lobby's position on arms sales to the Arabs (88 percent to 62 percent), there was no difference in the lobby's ability to overcome presidential opposition to its position on either type of sale. The lack of success on UN (Security Council) issues is not surprising, given the strong anti-Israel consensus that prevails in the international forum; nevertheless, the United States' willingness to use its veto on only rare occasions indicated that the lobby was not very influential on matters of international diplomacy. The results on issues of war and peace might be an indication that when the issues are particularly important, the lobby's influence is circumscribed, but they are also another reflection of the relative lack of influence the lobby has in the executive branch, where most of those decisions were made.

By examining lobby success by administration, it was possible to find evidence that the idiosyncrasies of presidents and those around them affect policy outcomes. Lobby success varied from 55 percent during the Carter administration, to 69 percent during the Nixon-Ford years (72 percent during the comparatively short Kennedy term). The results of this analysis also demonstrated that the lobby was able to overcome presidential opposition in each administration. The lobby was particularly unsuccessful in overcoming the opposition of Truman (11 percent) and Eisenhower (17 percent), but did manage to win more than 30 percent of the cases in which Kennedy, Nixon-Ford, Carter, and Reagan opposed its position.

Implications

It is now possible to predict the likely outcome of a particular proposal if we know the Israeli lobby and president's positions, the policy type, the locus of decision, and the level of presidential popularity. This is a considerable advancement beyond existing research, which provides no clue as to what the outcome of a particular proposal would be, or the variables that would be most important in determining that outcome.

To make further progress toward explaining U.S. Middle East policy, and U.S. foreign policy in general, it will be necessary to expand the data set to include a broader range of policies and interest groups. The Israeli lobby is generally considered to be the most powerful foreign policy interest group, so I would not expect other interest groups to enjoy the same degree of success in reaching their foreign policy objectives; nevertheless, the pluralist forces described in this study should apply to other foreign policy areas. Thus, other interest groups should win fewer cases, enjoy less success in Congress, and only rarely be able to overcome presidential opposition.

Lobbying and the National Interest

The question of whether support for Israel is in the national interest is an important one; most of the arguments have been touched on throughout the paper, and I believe they present a persuasive case for maintaining the U.S. commitment to Israel. For all intents and purposes, as noted in the introduction, this answer has been taken for granted. The difficulties arise when that interest conflicts with other U.S. interests in the Middle East, such as those relating to the Arab world. One cannot say a priori that all such conflicts should be resolved in favor of one side or the other; therefore, I would prefer to leave the issue to policymakers.

The issue that I would like to address here, is whether the act of lobbying by an ethnic lobby, like the Jews, is in keeping with democratic principles and the pursuit of the national interest, or if the behavior described in the preceding chapters actually undermines U.S. foreign policy, as suggested by the critics in the introduction. Nathan Glazer has framed the issue from the perspective of the Israeli lobby:

> At a time when Jewish leadership is more unified than ever before, when fewer issues of interest, culture, style, and orientation divide it, when it is more united in spirit—if not organization—than ever

before, one central problem . . . rises up more intensely for Jews
than for any other group: how does one defend group interests without affecting—or being seen to affect—adversely the public interest.[1]

The divisiveness of the AWACS battle stimulated the discussion of the proper role for interest groups in the formulation of
policy, but the issue is by no means new. James Madison warned
in *The Federalist* of the dangers of "faction," which he defined
as citizens "who are united and actuated by some common impulse
of passion, or of interest, adverse to the rights of other citizens,
or to the permanent and aggregate interests of the community."[2]
Woodrow Wilson went so far as to label such factions un-Amer-
ican: "America does not consist of groups," he said. "A man who
thinks of himself as belonging to a particular national group in
America has not yet become an American."[3] This outlook spawned
the charge of dual loyalty among American Jews, an allegation
given publicity by the arrest of Jonathan Pollard, an American
Jew convicted of spying for Israel.

What is particularly disturbing to members of the Israeli lobby
and its supporters is the double standard of accusing American
Jews of dual loyalty, but ignoring the lobbying interests of Americans of Polish, Greek, or Irish descent who actively support their
homelands. AIPAC director Dine reacts angrily to charges of
dual loyalty:

> Will a group's views of America's national interest be neglected be-
> cause of the group's size, skin color, religion, or country of origin?
> Can anyone be excluded from the formation of a true national in-
> terest? It is the ethnic interest groups, because of their ties, passions
> and preoccupations, that sensitize the relevant parts of government.
> It is the ethnic interest groups that remind U.S. officials of the moral
> considerations in our foreign policy. Such considerations have always,
> and will always differentiate us from our enemies. It is ethnic interest
> groups that ask the government challenging questions and remind the
> bureaucracy and politicians of past and future commitments. Can less
> than three percent of the population really force its views on the
> remaining 97 percent? Nonsense! Our public actions meet the test of
> public interest.[4]

In an eloquent defense of the Israeli lobby, Hubert Humphrey
argued that concern about the "cultural or physical genocide" of

Jews in the Soviet Union and in the Middle East is as appropriate as the concerns of oil producers, doctors, unions, or any other interest groups. "We have some people in this government," Humphrey said, "who think that if they make a statement, everybody is supposed to agree with them. I thought we had gotten over that nonsense. I say it will be a sad day for this country when citizens stop using the precious guarantees of the first amendment to petition their government."[5]

Public debate, according to this line of thought, is a good thing for democracy. Interest group input prevents foreign policy from becoming the exclusive province of experts. In addition, in the free market of political thought, an "invisible hand" works through the competing interests to produce an outcome beneficial to society. The fact that U.S. policy maintains a pro-Israel tilt is a function of the fact that it holds the balance of lobbying power over the Arab lobby. Even Senator Charles Mathias, in his critique of lobby influence, conceded that the Israeli lobby would not "command the support they do in Congress and with the American people if their case did not have substantial merit."[6]

Although he acknowledges the merit of the Israeli lobby's case, Mathias still subscribes to a more elitist notion of decision-making, which holds that no real competition exists because all decisions are made by "wealthy behind-the-scenes wire-pullers" without regard for the public interest. According to this conception, interest groups do not perform a useful democratic function. As Fuchs explains:

> It may also be argued that minority group propaganda is emotional and narrow, and cannot help to clarify debate. The parochial claims of nationality groups are not likely to elevate public thinking. The best judge of compatibility of minority groups' propaganda and the national interest is not the minority group itself or an informed and uninformed public opinion but the elected and appointed officials responsible for making foreign policy. Foreign policy-making is highly specialized and technical and demands expert and not public direction.[7]

Mathias adds that even if the Israeli and Arab lobbies were equal, "the result would not necessarily be a sound, cohesive foreign policy because the national interest is not simply the sum of our special interests and attachments."⁸ This, of course, is the position of the State Department and has substantial merit. There are undoubtedly matters of foreign policy beyond the understanding of the general public, the best examples are probably issues relating to nuclear deterrence, which should not be decided on the basis of public opinion. It is, moreover, not only politicians' prerogative, but also their obligation to ignore public views that are uninformed. As Edmund Burke suggested, representatives betray rather than serve their constituents if they sacrifice their judgement to public opinion. This does not mean, however, that lobbies cannot make some valuable contribution to foreign policy debates, or that the lobbies are necessarily wrong in their perception of the national interest.

Mathias would like to somehow do away with ethnic lobbies. He wrote that ethnic groups should be preserved to enrich American life and culture, but they should not be allowed to organize to act against the national interest. This, of course, is the remedy foreseen by the man who started the debate. The only available methods for eliminating the "mischiefs of faction," Madison wrote, is by destroying liberty or by giving everybody the same interests and opinions. The first remedy, he said, was far worse than the disease and the second impracticable.⁹ American foreign policy might very well be in some sense better, at least more consistent, if politics stopped at the water's edge, but the democratic system of government that Americans hold dear insures that the domestic determinants of U.S. Middle East policy, at least, stretch to the water's edge and beyond.

Notes

1. Murray Friedman, "AWACS and the Jewish Community," *Commentary* (April 1982), 33.
2. James Madison, *The Federalist Papers* (NY: New American Library, 1961), vol 10, 78.
3. Michael Parenti, "Ethnic Politics and the Persistence of Ethnic Identification," *American Political Science Review* (September 1967), 725.
4. *Near East Report* (14 August 1981).
5. Wolf Blitzer, "The AIPAC Formula," *Moment* (November 1981).

6. Charles Mathias, "Ethnic Groups and Foreign Policy," *Foreign Affairs* (Summer 1981), 997.
7. Lawrence Fuchs, "Minority Groups and Foreign Policy," in Fuchs, ed., *American Ethnic Politics* (NY: Harper and Row, 1968), 161.
8. Mathias, "Ethnic Groups," 981.
9. Madison, *Federalist Papers*, 78.

Index

Abourezk, James, 1, 11, 232
Acheson, Dean, 142
Action Committee on American Arab
  Relations, 14
Aid, foreign, 15, 17, 202, 204, 215, 226,
  228, 236, 238, 246–9, 252, 262, 278–
  81, 284, 287, 298–9
Airborne Warning and Control System
  (AWACS), 5, 11, 15, 18, 23, 35, 46,
  48, 50–60, 253, 275, 290–92, 302
Akhdar, Farouk, 97
Akzin, Benjamin, 131–2
al-Salayim, Suleiman, 97
Albert, Carl, 77
Albright, Joseph, 81
Alireza, Ali. A, 41
Alkhimov, V. S., 68
Allon, Yigal, 95, 215
Amalrik, Andrei, 74
American Arab Affairs Council, 14
American Arab Anti-Discrimination
  Committee (ADC), 11, 14
American Christian Palestine Commit-
  tee, 136
American Educational Trust (AET),
  11–12
American Israel Public Affairs Commit-
  tee (AIPAC), 6, 9, 12–15, 34, 42,
  47, 51, 53, 55–6, 66, 70, 84, 92, 95,
  108, 109, 123, 194, 202, 218, 221,
  223, 248, 251, 255, 275, 302
American Jewish Alternatives to Zion-
  ism, 14
American Jewish Committee, 9, 95,
  107, 190
American Jewish Congress, 70, 95–7,
  100, 107–9, 175

American Lebanese League, 10
American Palestine Committee, 14
American Zionist Committee for Public
  Affairs, 14
American Zionist Emergency Council
  (AZEC), 130–1, 139, 146, 153, 160
Americans for Democratic Action, 74
Americans for Near East Refugee Aid,
  14
Amitay, Morris, 9, 34, 42, 47, 66–7, 75,
  84, 108, 248
Angermueller, Hans, 108
Anti-boycott, 24, 35–6, 92, 95–6, 100–
  6, 108–15, 251, 270, 274, 284, 290–
  1
Anti-Defamation League (ADL), 11,
  95, 97, 100, 106–8, 110
Arab, 8, 10, 11, 15–17, 21, 33, 39–43,
  45, 49, 53, 58, 91–4, 96, 98, 100–3,
  105, 107, 111–12, 129, 137–9, 143–
  50, 154, 160–1, 167–8, 170–4, 176–
  7, 184, 189, 193–5, 197–200, 203,
  205, 214, 216–18, 223–4, 231–2,
  235, 237–8, 245–6, 250, 252, 263,
  278–80, 282, 287, 290, 292–3, 298–
  301
Arab American Institute, 14
Arab-Americans, 8, 14, 42, 123, 224
Arab boycott, 36, 91, 92, 93, 94–102,
  104–5, 107–8, 110–4, 191
Arab Higher Committee, 144
Arab Information Center, 101
Arab League, 91, 94, 100, 112, 145,
  159, 220
Arab Lobby, 7–11, 13–15, 17–18, 40–
  1, 45, 52, 54, 59, 101, 103, 112, 123,
  131, 207, 224, 246, 255, 291, 293,
  303